Psychotherapy and Mental Handicap

D1425646

Psychotherapy and Mental Handicap

SAGE Publications
London · Newbury Park · New Delhi

First published 1992
Reprinted 1993

SAGE Publications Ltd
6 Bonhill Street
London EC2A 4PU

SAGE Publications Inc
2455 Teller Road
Newbury Park, California 91320

SAGE Publications India Pvt Ltd
32, M-Block Market
Greater Kailash – I
New Delhi 110 048

British Library Cataloguing in Publication Data

Conboy-Hill, Suzanne
    Psychotherapy and mental handicap.
    I. Title   II. Waitman, Alexis
    616.89

    ISBN 0–8039–8372–7
    ISBN 0–8039–8373–5 pbk

Library of Congress catalog card number 91-51055

Typeset by The Word Shop, Bury, Lancashire
Printed and bound in Great Britain by
Biddles Ltd, Guildford and King's Lynn

Contents

Foreword

People with intellectual disabilities are just as likely as other people to experience emotional problems; in fact they are more likely to have emotional difficulties given the generally devaluing manner in which they are treated in our society. In recent years, though, the climate has been changing, and people are demanding, and increasingly being given, access to the services and environments which other people take for granted. Access to psychotherapy – however defined – is just one of these new options. A few years ago it came as something of a surprise to me to find that I had some trouble in identifying a psychotherapist to speak at a conference on psychological therapies for people with intellectual disabilities. On looking at the literature it became clear that this is a problem which has persisted during the past few decades. While we have concentrated on personal self-care skills, social skills, challenging behaviours and the like, we have rarely attempted to deal with the emotional needs of clients. Indeed, I have been involved in some experimental work which shows that many people with quite mild levels of intellectual impairments have trouble even recognising all but the simplest of emotional states. There is a real need for help from appropriate professionals, and this book is a welcome attempt to outline how things are changing, and what can be achieved.

Psychotherapy is a broad church. It is not delineated by professional background but by what the therapist actually does relative to the client. One of the many refreshing aspects of this book is the way in which a broad definition is exemplified. The reader will find both a wide variety of styles and a broad coverage of issues. From individual to group therapy; from sexuality to bereavement; from coming to terms with one's identity to the effects of disability on siblings and other family members.

Psychotherapists have generally been at the forefront of 'political' thinking, challenging people to re-examine their values. The contributors to this book are no exception. Not only are we forced to consider the intellectually disabled person as a person, but as someone on the same level and with the same needs and demands, as the friend, the family member and the therapist. For many this is not a comfortable message, but it is an urgent one.

It is refreshing to read the different styles of writing in each of the chapters. Some are pragmatic and down to earth; some contain a good deal of theory; all are informative and readable. The authors do not dash blindly into claiming to be eclectics (or, worse, cognitive-behavioural therapists) but are proud to present and defend their own forms of psychotherapeutic working. This book is a pleasure to read and it should make a significant impact on the field. I hope it will encourage psychotherapists to offer their skills to people who have intellectual disabilities. Some flexibility and new thinking may be needed to deal with clients who are less verbal and articulate, and who may have little experience of dealing with their private events – their emotions, feelings and thoughts. I hope too that this book will encourage carers and others to realise how important – and how necessary – it is to help clients to cope with emotional difficulties, and even to realise that people with quite severe levels of intellectual impairment do have feelings and emotions! Most of all I hope that this book will set the occasion for a new way of thinking about our work with people who have intellectual disabilities.

Chris Cullen
Professor, Learning Difficulties
St Andrews

Preface

The need, to us, for this book was concretised in 1986 at a British Psychological Society conference exhibition of books but the seeds had been sown much earlier. One of us (AW) had come to mental handicap from a social work background with its ethos of worker–client cooperation and sharing. The other (SC-H) arrived via general nursing where again the emphasis upon physical, psychological and informational care was clear even if it was not always done very well.

Both of us then found ourselves involved in the contrasting worlds of profound institutionalisation, community care, normalisation, behaviourism and our own core feelings about what constituted dignity, respect and appropriate treatment.

Thus we helped decant chronically disabled 'patients' from hospital into a brave new world where they would become 'clients'. Despite the efforts of hospital staff and a team of imported trainers from the new service, vestiges of institutional life came with them; low self-esteem, poor physical condition, lack of motivation, few appropriate skills and, eventually, tales of the desolation and degradation associated with living in a large, impersonal, devalued and poorly resourced system.

We worked with an excellent team of nurses, trainers, care staff, psychologists and consultant psychiatrist. The overt model was behavioural–psychiatric with large doses of improved opportunities through the individual planning system, but as people's social relationships developed, this was gradually extended to include techniques such as reality orientation, reminiscence and counselling.

The idea that you could talk to clients or, indeed, listen to them while they talked to you, came as no surprise to the consultant (RB) who had been using psychotherapy for some time. Nor did it to the training department (led by AW) who had been recording the life stories of some ex-residents. Nevertheless, the use of 'talking therapies' developed by mainstream psychological and therapeutic services still seemed rather adventurous and we introduced them cautiously.

Our clients' response to this was embarrassingly prompt and

positive – why had we not tried these ideas before? Had we missed a wealth of research literature in which such techniques and their outcomes were described and evaluated? Apparently not. Most of the published work was either behavioural or medical and did not seem to recognise mentally handicapped people as individuals with feelings and desires of their own. Our search among the new books at the conference drew a blank thus confirming the gap and underlining the need for literature which would bring together the skills of experienced therapists and a client group which could make good use of them.

This book is an attempt to begin the process of validating practitioners' use of their specialist skills with a client group not previously thought capable of benefiting from therapies involving thought, reflection and abstraction.

There is no system to the choice of authors; we simply asked people whom we knew to be working in these ways to describe how they do this. Thus, each chapter is aimed primarily at practitioners with comparable skills whose client population has not yet included people with a mental handicap. For this reason, there is no attempt to teach psychotherapy, counselling, Transactional Analysis and so forth to beginners. The chapters stand as illustrations of therapeutic application by experienced practitioners.

A secondary focus, however, is upon field workers and other professionals for whom the knowledge that these techniques may be applied in this way is likely to be useful. Social workers, general practitioners, care service managers, senior nurses, educators, mental health psychologists and psychiatrists may find that the book contains helpful ideas regarding staff training, client referral and philosophy of care.

Finally, workers in more remote systems, such as general medicine, paediatrics, obstetrics, terminal care, adult education, HIV/AIDS services or family planning, may find particular chapters relevant to their own field.

We asked contributors to write in a narrative style rather than to a fixed formula so that the process and flow of their individual approaches would not be lost, so there is considerable variability in both style and structure throughout the book. However, each chapter contains elements of background information, current status or a practical description of therapeutic application and finally some comments regarding the implications of working in this way. We have learned a lot from these contributors and hope that you will enjoy reading their work.

SC-H/AW

Acknowledgement

Thanks go to the Bromley team without whom this book may not have been possible: Rosalind Bates, Terry Clarke, Colin Lambert, Hedy Ditchfield, Dan Donelly and many others in the nursing, training and care services.

For Donald and Margaret Hill, and for Richard and Charlie Wilson

1

Introduction

Suzanne Conboy-Hill and Alexis Waitman

Terminology

People with a mental handicap have been called many things, often to their detriment. It cannot have been uplifting to be described as subnormal or defective, and some of the more *vox pop* terms such as 'mental' or 'spaz' (spastic) are both hurtful and unhelpful. As a result, many services have gone to considerable trouble to label people meaningfully and non-judgementally and there exists a range of terms in current use. The USA broadly classifies people as *mentally retarded* in line with DSM-III criteria and distinguishes this from *learning disabilities* which is a term currently on the ascendant in the UK, having begun to edge out its predecessor, *learning difficulties*. This latter has been used in preference to *mental handicap* which was thought to carry with it too many of the old institutional connotations. For similar reasons, *client* replaces *patient* and, at the time of writing, *consumer*, *service user* and *tenant* are beginning to replace *client* and *resident*, as terms that represent the status quo.

With the exception of patient, which was felt to maintain the image of healthy expert and sick recipient, contributors have used a variety of categorising labels, sometimes to make a point, sometimes to define clearly the receiving or acting client group.

As editors, we have taken the line that any applied label must be meaningful, helpful and non-stigmatising but we also recognise, along with Szivos and Griffiths (Chapter 5) that stigma may attach to the label via the disability rather than the reverse.

Within this framework, it is difficult to find any label which meets the criteria. 'Learning difficulty' seems to be an oversimplification of the problem, isolating it to the learning mode and implying through the word 'difficulty' that this may be remediable. 'Learning disability' acknowledges the fundamental nature of the problem but still confines it to a particular mode, leaving aside all the issues about developmental and emotional maturation problems. 'Mental handicap' is an older term with some old connotations but it does locate the difficulty within the broad spectrum of mental life and so is arguably more meaningful than the others. The use of 'handicap' rather than 'disability' remains problematic if one takes the view that 'handicap' is socially defined and is thus a function of the attitudes of others towards the primary disability. In the UK, 'mental retardation' carries with it images of institutions and 'retardates' and is little used here, yet it probably has as much (or as little) objective value as 'mental handicap'.

Current fringe terms include 'intellectual disadvantage' and 'cognitive disability', the latter seeming to make an attempt at defining the primary dysfunction while the first arguably embarks upon a reality-dodging mission.

If one accepts that there is a primary disability which is developmental, life long and involves impairment of intellectual and social functioning to varying degrees (see Mental Health Act 1983) and that handicap is a function of society's response to this, then it would appear that the term disability has a place in the definition.

If one then accepts that society's (and carers') own defences may impede clear definition of that disability in order to deny its existence, it becomes self-evident that objectivity will be sacrificed to self-preservation.

There are no solutions to this dilemma here and we ask the reader to examine carefully his or her own motives for rejecting or preferring any particular label.

About the book

The premisses upon which psychotherapy and counselling were based and the possibilities and options available to people with learning disabilities were, and to a great extent still are, in conflict. So long as people were fundamentally 'less than human' there was no need to believe that they were capable of human emotions. Neither was there a need to address the challenges involved in adapting an essentially middle-class technique to fulfil the needs of a less able, less articulate population. There is still little research to show that 'talking therapies' are beneficial to people with mental handicap or, if they are, which clients with what disorders are best offered which technique.

Clearly, talking therapy assumes some sort of language skill although not necessarily expressive, while particular therapies require a level of cognitive ability commensurate with a degree of reflection and abstraction.

However, the basic premiss throughout this book is that empathic human contact at a fundamental emotional level can be made with the vast majority of people and that this in itself may be therapeutic (see Decker, 1988). Thereafter it simply remains to adjust and apply the techniques in which each practitioner is skilled to the problem being presented at the level at which it can usefully be accepted.

The chapters

Many of the following chapters contain illustrations of the application of well established techniques. Others contain discussions of research, philosophies, experiences or methodologies which have a bearing on the lives of mentally handicapped people either directly or through their families or care services.

In Chapter 2, Hedy Ditchfield, a clinical psychologist, National Childbirth Trust tutor and qualified nurse, examines the way in which news about the disability of a child is broken to its parents and the processes of grieving, adaptation, resolution or conflict which then ensue. Models of grieving and their implications for therapy and support of parents are evaluated. A most poignant comment from one mother sets the tone: 'I never got any baby congratulations cards for my little girl with Down's syndrome.' And another: 'The doctor stood by my bed, he just said that my son had Down's syndrome and then he left before I could say anything. . . .'

This chapter has messages for obstetricians, midwives and paediatricians regarding their communication with the parents of mentally handicapped babies and for social workers, health visitors and educators in their support of parents and moulding of public attitudes to disability.

In Chapter 3, Robert Wilkins, a consultant psychiatrist and psychotherapist, discusses family therapy with the siblings of mentally handicapped children. Here the fact of disturbed family relationships in the presence of a disabled member is addressed and shows how family therapy, systemic and strategic, may be used to identify the roles which young siblings take on and some of the techniques which can be used to help children relinquish them. The chapter adds to that of Hedy Ditchfield in its concern for the system into which the mentally handicapped child is born and the reciprocal dynamics which ensue. General practitioners, health visitors and community nurses among others may be interested to know that this kind of therapeutic intervention could be appropriate.

Valerie Sinason and Jon Stokes of the Tavistock Clinic were among the first, along with Neville Symington, to apply psychodynamic psychotherapy to people with mental handicap, although they have been able to point to research going back to the 1930s. In

Chapter 4 they discuss the concepts of secondary and defence mental handicap and illustrate them with accounts of therapy with individuals. Given that this type of therapy has traditionally been seen as perhaps the most dependent upon the recipient being intelligent, articulate and capable of insight, this work is quite remarkable. Valerie and Jon make the point that 'intellectual' and 'emotional' intelligence do not appear to equate and that, as long as the client is capable of establishing an emotional relationship with the therapist, work can take place.

In Chapter 5, Susan Szivos and Eileen Griffiths, both psychologists, present a research-based evaluation of the implications of labelling and label-dodging which appear to have been features of pre- and post-normalisation respectively. They examine the roles of consciousness raising and loss paradigms in dealing with a stigmatised identity, showing, through a description of groupwork, how denial of handicap can inhibit personal growth and, while the individual may not be pleased at the identification with disability, how acceptance may lead to a more productive channelling of energies.

Clearly, disability remains fundamentally undesirable and so it is unreasonable to expect someone to like being disabled, thereby making a positive group identity less realistic. However, it may be reasonable to assume that ownership (or acceptance) of the label permits needs to be identified in a way that denial does not.

In Chapter 6, Rosalind Bates, a consultant psychiatrist working in a community mental handicap team, describes in very pragmatic terms the techniques she has developed to help people for whom she is often the last resort within the district. The simplicity of these techniques arises from a sophisticated understanding of the nature of handicap and a deep concern for the humanity of those it afflicts. Rosalind uses humour in liberal doses to lighten the load of both therapist and client and so gains the cooperation of some highly resistant and difficult people. Her humour extends to her own account of her work and her style cuts through the sometimes alienating mystique of 'professionalism'.

Chapter 7 presents a discussion of the use of Transactional Analysis (TA) by Joanna Beazley-Richards, a qualified Transactional Analyst whose background is in social services and who uses TA both therapeutically with clients and in staff training. Joanna gives an account of the elements of TA and illustrates its use with mentally handicapped people through a description of groupwork. This model has much to offer both clients and staff through helping them to recognise the particular roles into which they place each other. Service systems have a tendency to require gratitude, compliance and dependency in their recipients, thereby effectively confining them to the Child role. This not only sets up an underlying obstacle to any attempt at liberating those recipients – through assertion training, independence skills and so on – but forces carers into the Parental role such that relinquishing control becomes a near impossibility. Non-dependent, assertive clients may be seen by staff as difficult or awkward and so receive messages about not being liked, while helpless, grateful ones are rewarded with kindness and care. This chapter has messages for service systems as well as direct therapists.

Chapter 8 is by Joan Bicknell, Emeritus Professor of the Psychiatry of Mental Handicap, and Suzanne Conboy-Hill, clinical psychologist in mental handicap services, and is based on Joan's development of the concept of the deviancy career. Here Joan and Suzanne describe how negative events in an individual's life will, if that individual has a mental handicap, frequently result in a further negative event presented as a solution to the first. Cycles of distress, deprivation, further distress and eventual isolation are described along with illustrations of cases where a deviancy career was aborted in the nick of time by some creative thinking.

Techniques or methods such as Gentle Teaching and Individual Planning are introduced as ways of interrupting the deviancy spiral and, in one poignant tale, the use of regression in terms of *permission* to regress is described in the rehabilitation of an unloved, unloving, distressed individual. This chapter looks at some of the issues surrounding disability including the motivations of those whose work is to care for such people. In 1957 Tom Main wrote about the dynamics of treating chronic patients who failed to get well despite the carers' best efforts. This chapter makes links between those early observations and current practices in services where no one can 'get better' because they cannot be reborn unhandicapped.

Neville Symington is a psychologist and psychotherapist working in Australia. He was an originator of the mental handicap workshop at the Tavistock Clinic and so facilitated the use of dynamic psychotherapy with this client group. In Chapter 9 Neville looks at the dynamics of therapists' interactions with clients with particular reference to the concept of contempt in which unconscious attitudes to disability are expressed. He describes a variety of behavioural adaptations, allowances or lapses such as meeting mentally handicapped (but no other) clients from the lifts or feeling that a particular old dress 'will do' because 'it's only my mentally handicapped client'.

In disability services we appear to tread a fine line between contempt as described by Neville and a kind of ideological denial which one might argue is also a form of contempt. Normalisation principles have forced carers and practitioners to confront old methods, attitudes and styles of communication in order to open up ordinary life opportunities for clients. Nevertheless, many of us, if we are prepared to look closely, will discover the old prejudices lurking in far less obvious places: offering inappropriate compliments about appearance, providing plastic beakers for clients while staff have china mugs, and so on. One might also add behaviours which come at the more noble end of the range – using sophisticated language which is designed to sound 'normal' but is well beyond the client's comprehension, allowing people choice beyond the limit of their information 'because they are adults', failing to respond to rudeness for what it is.

Sheila Hollins is Professor of Psychiatry and a prime mover, along with Joan Bicknell and the Tavistock team, in the use of psychotherapeutic techniques with this client group. In Chapter 10, Sheila describes the use of group analytic therapy, making the point that such therapy is primarily an affective rather than an intellectual process. Its stated objective is to enable individuals to come to an acceptance of themselves and so improve their social adaptation and acceptance by society. This notion may be a little hard to take: why should clients have to accept themselves in order to become more socially acceptable to others? Why should society not be required to make its own effort towards accepting mentally handicapped people? Well of course society should (and does) make its own efforts but the reality is that it does not need to and no one can make it – the mountain must go to Muhammad.

Psychotherapists would also argue that acceptance of oneself is a necessary prerequisite for healthy psychological development and coping. Discussions in other chapters indicate that it may also be essential to proper identification of needs through acceptance of the reality of disability and to examination of defensive structures in clients, service systems and society which seek to maintain the status quo.

Chapter 11 is written by Suzanne Conboy-Hill, clinical psychologist in mental handicap services. It considers approaches to grief and loss and is aimed primarily at carers whose support of clients going through a bereavement is likely to make the difference between normal and abnormal grieving. The chapter describes research which attempts to understand the meaning of loss for people of varying levels of cognitive development and goes on to elaborate intervention techniques which staff or families can use to help people through a grief reaction. Some case descriptions illustrate the techniques, responses (and some of the pitfalls) in this work and there is the basis of a workshop designed to facilitate an appreciation of clients' special, and not so special, needs at times of loss.

In Chapter 12, Helen Fensome, a clinical psychologist who conducted and wrote up this work as part of her qualifying examination, describes the facilitation of a grief reaction through the use of reminiscence with a group of elderly men. These men, mostly in their 80s, had been discharged from their hospital home of some 60 to 70 years into a 'nice new' hostel in the community. The environment was fully 'normalised' and many earlier residents had blossomed upon encountering the newly available opportunities on offer. These men, however, did not. They were resistant, grumpy and thoroughly uncooperative, much to the dismay of staff who often resorted to telling them how lucky they were to be there.

Helen's approach placed the men's behaviour within the idealisation mode of a grief reaction, reinforced by staff exhortations, and tackled it by allowing them to reminisce about their past lives at the hospital through discussion, photographs and, finally, a visit to the partially closed institution.

The hypothesis underlying the need for this work is about staff defences. In their need to justify and promote their (our) own skills and the value of a new service, they were inadvertently negating a grand total of over 400 years of life experience. This set up resistances in the form of idealisation of the old ways and the two groups began to polarise. Group therapy allowed non-judgemental discussion of the past, removing the need for idealisation and so allowing room for reality.

In Chapter 13, Hilary Brown, a trainer and educator for a Regional Health Authority, discusses the issues surrounding sexuality, directing this towards those caring for or educating mentally handicapped people and those involved in the training of carers. In Western society the discussion of sexuality is almost as taboo as discussion of death: we are able to make jokes and innuendo about both but fall short of open, honest and reasoned appraisal of either. This has resulted in the past in clients being infantalised, maintained in the child role and never accepted as having a sexuality in need of expression, thus obviating the need for education or counselling.

Our more enlightened age claims a better appreciation of the problems and of people's rights but one has to question how far this change in expressed attitude reflects real change when most mentally handicapped adults have no privacy within which to learn or practise their sexual skills.

Where sexuality is acknowledged, this tends to be implicit rather than explicit – female contraception, sterilisation and abortion rather than education and support. Feminists may wish to consider the proposition that all this effort is directed towards women in order to disguise sexuality by avoiding its most obvious manifestation, pregnancy. No one routinely teaches men about the use of condoms or hauls them through the courts in pursuit of vasectomies, but women are regularly subjected to personal invasion and mutilation 'in their best interests'.

This is not, however, simply an issue of ideology and women's rights. Denial of sexuality, expressed in this way, leaves people open to a wide variety of the sequelae of ignorance – exploitation and abuse, sexually transmitted diseases and HIV. Hilary's chapter is essential reading if people are not to suffer ill-health or to die because of our own defences.

Chapter 14 is written by Alexis Waitman whose background in social work led her to establish a training department within a district mental handicap service which placed as much emphasis upon feelings and individuality as it did upon skills acquisition. This chapter considers the motivations for traditional ways of working, uncovering defensive attitudes which determined treatment strategies, philosophies and service systems. She goes on, with François Reynolds, to outline approaches such as Neuro-Linguistic Programming, Educational Kinesiology and Gentle Teaching and their use in facilitating therapeutic relationships with clients through which they might grow in self-knowledge and self-expression.

Alexis' final section is an assault on current attitudes and trends which serve to maintain systems as they are, and the implications of change for those of us who work in these systems.

In writing the introduction to this book, we have felt rather like door-to-door traders assembling a collection of samples to be laid out in front of a prospective customer. We anticipate that some chapters will carry more meaning for some people than others but hope that the sampling process will be enjoyable to any customer who chooses to open the door.

References

Decker, R.J. (1988) *Effective Psychotherapy: The Silent Dialogue*. New York and London: Hemisphere Publishing Corporation.

Main, T. (1957) 'The ailment', in T. Main, *The Ailment and other Psychoanalytic Essays*. London: Free Association Books (2nd edn 1989).

2

The Birth of a Child with a Mental Handicap: Coping with Loss?

Hedy Ditchfield

> Everyone creates a dream child when pregnant: none of our children fulfil all of our dreams but for most the dream recedes and reality takes over. For us the dream was broken in one sentence.

During pregnancy nearly all parents admit to speculations and fantasies about their unborn child, about its sex, temperament and experiences in the years to come. Most acknowledge that the chance of these dreams reaching fruition do not (and should not!) lie within parental control and that once the baby is born it is quickly accepted as an individual in its own right.

Throughout all this, however, the expectation is of an essentially 'normal' baby, one that will (barring illness or accidents) develop in accordance with expected milestones and who will, eventually, achieve full independence as an adult. Perhaps one of the hardest experiences to accept, at least initially, is the birth of a child who has a marked learning disability (mental handicap). For these families the challenges posed by any baby are both heightened and increased, and may last for months or years (Gath, 1972, 1977; Hanson et al., 1989).

How such parents adjust to their circumstances has been much debated in recent years and the processes involved are still uncertain. Some are devastated and appear to remain so for many years, while others appear to 'get on and cope' remarkably quickly. An understanding of these processes could, therefore, have more than theoretical importance. It could facilitate a clearer identification of the needs of an individual family, as well as leading to the provision of better, more effective services.

Early views and current values

In fact there is remarkably little reported in the literature on the subject prior to the late 1950s, presumably on the grounds that parents either 'got on and coped' as best they could or because they followed the advice of involved professionals and placed their child in an institution (Aldrich, 1947). The last 25 years have seen a change in emphasis from institutional to community care, so that now the assumption is that the child will be brought up in a family home: either with his or her natural parents or, failing that, with foster or adoptive parents. Wikler (1986) suggests that the amount of attention now devoted to observing and assessing the way in which parents (and families) adjust to the birth of a handicapped child is a direct result of the process of normalisation. If, by avoiding institutional care, the main placement, especially for young children, is the family, then it is self-evident that the family has to be able to cope. Little will be gained if the family is so stressed that their functioning is impaired to the extent that they can no longer function. We are reminded that one of the original purposes of institutional care for children with a mental handicap was to lift the 'burden of care' from the family on the grounds that 'they are happiest when allowed to grow up in situations where they can compete with their peers – in institutions' (Aldrich, 1947).

The few, early papers in the field derived much of their content from psychoanalytic thought and had, as such, a tendency to view parental reactions as being frequently neurotic and thus in need of therapy. Nearly all parents were assumed to experience guilt to a greater or lesser degree and were effectively placed in a 'no win' situation. Whatever outward reaction they displayed could be interpreted as evidence of underlying hostility, rejection or, at best, ambivalence to their child to some degree. It was at this time that Solnit and Stark (1961) used the term 'chronic mourning' to describe parental reaction to the loss of the perfect baby that had been expected. As a consequence some parents were offered psychodynamically orientated counselling but practical help and support was still limited: the prevailing view was one of pessimism towards the development of the child and institutional care was still the main 'treatment' available (Aldrich, 1947; Menolascino, 1977).

One of the most obvious limitations of this approach is that it fails to acknowledge the very real difficulties surrounding having a child with a mental handicap. To have a child who differs markedly in any way from his or her peer group is hard but this is especially so if this difference is a result of a mental handicap, which still carries particularly strong negative values.

How then do parents adjust to the news that their child has a learning disability? Is there a useful model of the processes involved which means that the parents receive appropriate support, or is the help offered still a serendipitous mixture of the good, the bad and the indifferent?

Coping with loss?

One of the most influential models of conceptualising the reaction and subsequent adjustment to the birth of a child with a learning disability is derived from studies of reactions to bereavement. The hypothesis is that throughout pregnancy the parents have expected and planned for a normal, healthy baby and that these hopes are dramatically dashed by the birth of a baby which is less than perfect. It is, therefore, suggested that before the parents can begin to accept and care for the child they now have, they need to mourn the loss of the child that 'might have been' in a way not dissimilar to that experienced when a person dies (Solnit and Stark, 1961; Kew, 1975).

There is no doubt that it is an attractive theory, as superficially the two situations do have much in common and many parents, especially those for whom the disability is confirmed at or very soon after birth, spontaneously use the analogy:

> We did a lot of crying (almost like mourning the child we might have had), a lot of talking about the future, had a lot of highs and lows as N. had good days and bad days . . . and gradually a fair amount of anger at the attitude of the consultant. . . .

However, another was less sure, commenting: 'It's all very well saying you go through a process of mourning after the birth of a handicapped baby but you must be given some idea what you are mourning.'

Attempts have been made to categorise this process, many of which tend to be based on Kubler-Ross' (1970) stages of death and dying and which can be summarised thus:

1 *Shock, disbelief, denial*: many parents cannot believe the news and may reject the baby.
2 *Anger*: at the staff for any real or imagined difficulties with the birth; at God; or at themselves. Some parents blame themselves or their partner for some event during pregnancy, however irrational this may be.
3 *Bargaining or searching*: an attempt to go back in time to re-create the pregnancy with a different outcome, search for a 'cure'.
4 *Depression and withdrawal*, which gradually give way to acceptance and resolution.

However, while nearly all parents appear to identify with the feelings of loss, shock and disbelief, subsequent adjustment is much less predictable and many question the concept of acceptance and resolution, commenting that there is often a mix of feelings: 'I love my child for himself but still wish that he didn't have Down's syndrome'; 'I would never reject my child but never a day passes that I wouldn't willingly reject her handicap.'

Opinion is divided as to the significance of such feelings. Some still adhere to the view that ambivalence is an indication of unresolved grieving and that parents can only form a real attachment to their child when they have ceased to think of the 'normal' child they have lost (Parks, 1977, Opirhory and Peters, 1982). This has led to the suggestion that, where parents are still displaying signs of grief three months after the event, grieving has been 'unsuccessfully concluded' and intensive counselling recommended (Kennedy, 1970). Not all agree with this interpretation, suggesting that regret and sadness are a 'natural and understandable response to a tragic fact' and that, far from indicating rejection, these feelings often coexist with real pleasure and delight in the child's development and achievements. The term 'chronic sorrow' has been used to describe these feelings (Olshansky, 1962), acknowledging that acceptance is an ambiguous term in that it is often unclear just what the parents are being asked to accept.

Both of these approaches have implications for clinical practice. If one accepts that there should be a sequential progression through stages, then the involved professionals would expect to cease their intervention when acceptance had been reached. If, however, parents do experience 'chronic sorrow' then the expectation would be towards facilitating the parents' acceptance of these feelings and providing support (practical as well as emotional) at times of crisis.

This was investigated by Wikler et al. (1981) who used graphs and questionnaires to compare parents' self-report of feelings with those that social workers believed the family to be experiencing. The results lend support to the view that sorrow is, indeed, experienced over a considerable period of time but that it appears to be periodic rather than continuous, occurring mainly at periods of increased stress.

No parent reported constant, unchanging sorrow (although several social workers imagined this response). A more general finding was that, while social workers were aware of parents' feelings and did envisage distress occurring over time, there was a tendency to underestimate the degree of difficulty/distress occurring as the child grew older. It is possible, if not probable, that, with the further closure of large institutions and far more young adults remaining in the community, there will be an increase in the number of families experiencing more prolonged stress as a result and, therefore, in need of continuing support.

These points lead one to question the validity and use of the bereavement model in determining the response of parents to the birth of a child with a mental handicap.

In a comprehensive review of the research to date, Blacher (1984) not only addresses these points, but also raises the following questions:

1 How were such stages derived?
2 Are they reliable indicators of parental adjustment?
3 Is there an alternative approach which might, in fact, give more useful information?

As far as the first of these points is concerned, the stages appear to have been derived from a variety of sources and one of the difficulties in synthesising the available studies into a cohesive form is that different words are used to describe a similar reaction which leads to a slightly different interpretation of events. Whilst all describe an 'initial' response to the news that their child is handicapped, Drotar et al. (1975) place shock first, followed by denial, while Huber (1979) reverses the order, placing denial first. This difference in terminology may or may not be important in the overall context of the model but one cannot necessarily assume that the authors are, in fact, describing the same behaviour or response that this has predictive value for other families in the same situation.

Comparison between studies is further complicated by the differing research methodologies utilised which include observational studies, single case-studies, varying interview techniques and clinical case-studies. It is possible that these different methodologies are, in fact, measuring different responses and that there is not a predictable sequence of stages. Closer examination of the data also suggests that the stages are not time linked and can last from days through weeks and months, even to years, and may be just as applicable if the handicap is confirmed in later infancy after a long period of uncertainty as when the handicap is apparent at birth. The important factor seems to be a change in the way in which parents react to the current situation which can signal a movement between stages.

To summarise, it appears that, rather than clearly defined discrete stages, there exist three main categories of response which can be categorised thus:

Stage 1: *Initial reaction.* Includes shock, disbelief and denial of the diagnosis. May include rejection of the baby.
Stage 2: *Emotional disorganisation* during which parents variously report feelings of guilt, anger, sadness or disappointment.

Stage 3:   *Emotional organisation* which is a period of adjustment
            and acceptance, and the way in which this is viewed by
            society, which leads, as one parent commented, to 'Good
            days, bad days and days in which we just get on with
            it. . . .'

Perhaps, in the end, this is not so very different from the way in
which many cope as parents and could be seen as a reasonable
outcome.

The bereavement model therefore superficially appears to increase understanding of the processes involved in adjusting to the
birth of a child with mental handicap but, on closer examination, a
number of flaws are revealed. The stages themselves are derived
from a number of sources and do not, in fact, give a coherent
pattern, with different emotions being ascribed to different stages.
One would need to be cautious in the extreme in using the different
stages as *reliable* indicators of parental adjustment.

Parents of children with disabilities are not a homogeneous
group, and are, therefore, likely to show variability in their
response to the event. To expect all to respond in a predictable,
sequential manner carries with it the possibility that those who do
not respond in the expected manner may be designated as making
inadequate or inappropriate adjustments (Allen and Affleck, 1985).

If this happens then we are in danger of trying to fit parents to the
model rather than listening to what they are saying and accepting
their individuality of response.

Stress and adaptation

A more recent approach has been to use a cognitive–behavioural
framework with its recognition of the importance of factors *outside*
the family (as well as those *within*) in determining patterns of
adjustment. This model is based on the premise that all families
experience stress from time to time and the success with which this
is managed depends, in part, on the coping strategies open to the
family. One of the first to describe such a model of family stress was
Hill (1958) who proposed an ABCX model, the stress experienced
being an interaction between:

A   The stressor   Crisis
B   Family resources   →X   or
C   Family appraisal   adaptation

This acknowledges that there is unlikely to be a stereotypical response to a situation encountered, that families will show variance in their response, depending on the actual event, their coping skills and strategies and, to an extent, the way in which they construe the event.

Having a baby – any baby – almost always leads to stress! Some babies learn to live quickly and easily in the world, while others are much more demanding, taking time to settle. It is tempting to suggest that the latter are a much more potent source of stress than the former. However, while this may be so, the degree of stress experienced by the family will depend on the interaction of a multiplicity of factors. If the baby has special needs, then it is possible for this to become the main focus of interest and all resulting stress to be attributed to this event. Traditionally, families who have such a child have been seen as objects of pity, perhaps experiencing a tragedy from which they will only slowly recover and in which chronic sorrow is interspersed with periods of acute crisis (Summers et al., 1989; Olshansky, 1962).

Yet it is readily apparent that, on a day-to-day basis, many families do not fit this picture and, like the rest of us, get on with life in the best way open to them. Thus, each family deserves individual consideration: although their children may share the same or similar disability, this is not necessarily a good predictor of the functional ability of the child nor does it give any indication of the particular difficulties likely to be encountered, so that 'to assume the diagnostic label necessarily defines the problem' is an approach beset with pitfalls (McGowan, 1982).

In recent years there has been an increasing amount of attention devoted to family coping which is, in part, a result of the changes in the living patterns of those with a learning disability during the last 25 years. It is now no longer common practice to suggest institutional care as the first option, which means that more and more children with special needs are remaining with their families. However, community care will not succeed if the family experiences are not, generally, positive: if the care of the child becomes too stressful and if, as a result, the family ceases to cope.

Models of stress

Stress is arguably one of the most over-used words of the late 1980s. We all know what it is, are all familiar with it and probably all use the term, but it is also a general term and, as such are, at a disadvantage when a precise description is required. More work is needed to ascertain whether the word is being used as a description of internal feelings ('I feel stressed') or as a response to external events ('It was a stressful time') and, indeed, whether this is of clinical relevance.

Quine and Pahl (1989) found that parents of special needs children frequently describe a high degree of stress, the following events being seen as the most stressful:

1   behaviour problems in the child;
2   night disturbances;
3   social isolation;
4   adversity in the family;
5   multiplicity of child's impairments;
6   child's ill-health;
7   problems with appearance;
8   worries about money.

However, it has to be recognised that people vary in how they respond to events, so that reported stress is more than just the presence of the above factors, and the question that emerges is how this can be translated into a heuristic model of parental response.

Farran et al. (1986) propose a stress-adaptation model which considers the event, and associated changes, the individual and/or family's capacity to respond to the event and the eventual impact of *both* on the child. Their model, adapted from an earlier one can be described as illustrated in Figure 2.1:

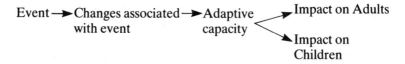

Figure 2.1

Although this model is linear, appearing to end with the impact on the family and child, it applies to situations of recurring crisis, a new cycle being triggered by any new event occurring within the family.

The initial event is the confirmation of disability but the way in which this is received by the family may well differ, depending on the circumstances. The news may follow an ultrasound scan, the birth itself, or it may have been preceded by a long period of uncertainty. In many ways the preceding factors are of lesser relevance when compared with subsequent events: whether the news comes as a 'bolt from the blue' or has been anticipated, it is still an 'event' and, as such, initiates a new cycle and is a source of potential stress.

However, other events are frequently associated with an increase in stress within the family. These may fall into one of two groups and are, therefore, foreseeable (Blacher, 1984).

1   Where there is a discrepancy between the parents' hopes and expectations and the actual achievements of the child. This can happen at any time from babyhood onwards. (For example, if the child fails to walk or talk at the expected milestones; it enters a special playgroup or school; when younger siblings overtake the handicapped child in development; or later with events surrounding leaving school/home.)
2   Those experiences which are *unique* to parents of handicapped children.

Many parents have to cope with events in the former category (though, perhaps, not to the same degree or frequency), but some concerns, regarding perhaps the need for residential care or who will care for their child after the death of the parents, apply *only* to those with a handicapped child (Wikler, 1986).

The changes associated with the event itself refer to both those that are immediate and also those that are long term. Some mothers have commented on the difficulty of sharing their child with the professionals involved. One woman described her feelings thus:

> In January 1987 C. was diagnosed as epileptic which required further readjustments on our part. It was also difficult to have to share C. with so many professionals. Each was concerned only with a specific part of him – his brain, his eyes, his gross motor skills. I felt totally redundant as a mother.

Others find that having a child with a handicap has an effect on both the self-esteem and career hopes of the mother in question, as well as on the finances of the family.

The extent to which any one family will be able to adapt to the demands made on them will again depend on a complex interaction of factors. Prior experience (either with their own or other handicapped children), support from friends and other family members, as well as the availability of other resources may all be involved. It is possible that such resources increase in importance with the age of the child and that certain services are of particular value at different times in the life of the child and thus need to be specifically targeted (Waisbren, 1980).

In a similar mode Crnic et al. (1983) incorporate stress, coping and family ecology in an interactive pattern. The handicapped child is assumed to be the source of stress (although, like Farran, they recognise that this is not constant), but that the amount of stress experienced by any one family is dependent on their individual circumstances and both the resources and the values of the society in which they live. Coping strategies also vary from family to family and involve the following:

1   parents' health, energy and morale;
2   their problem-solving skills;
3   social networks;
4   other resources, for example income; social class;
5   value system. (Crnic et al. 1983; Sloper et al. 1991).

At this stage of knowledge it would appear that this model provides a useful framework for considering parents' reactions to coping with a child with a learning disability. It recognises that adjustment is not a finite event and that new stresses can arise as a result of changes within the family and that new coping strategies may be needed as a result. By focusing on coping the situation is viewed in a positive light, emphasising the resources and skills already open to the family rather than concentrating on deficits.

One could not say more than it offers a useful framework and further research is needed to ascertain its relevance and usefulness in terms of service provision and service planning.

The way forward. . . ?

There is, despite the need for further research to clarify the processes involved, some important learning for clinical practice. As already discussed many parents do experience anger and disbelief at the news that their child has a learning disability yet one aspect that has received only minimal attention is the way in which this news is broken.

The majority of parents are quite certain that they wish to be informed as early as possible, as soon as those involved (nurse, obstetricians, paediatricians) are themselves aware that there is a real or potential handicap (D'Arcy, 1968; Berg et al., 1969). There seems to be little support for the once popular suggestion of withholding the news in order to allow parents to 'bond' with their baby (presumably to minimise the chance of rejection).

Obviously those concerned need to balance the possibility of creating what turns out to be unnecessary anxiety against the drawbacks of withholding very real concerns. In some cases suspicions are present at birth and can be confirmed or dispelled within a very short time.

However, in some instances where the delivery has been difficult with the baby requiring active resuscitation there may be a suspicion that some damage was sustained but the extent (if any) will only be revealed as the baby develops.

> Our son asphyxiated at birth and had numerous fits. He spent ten days in a SCBU having brain scans etc. At six weeks we were given the 'all clear' but at six months the bombshell dropped. . . . What makes me really angry is that both my health visitor and GP had concerns from about three months but chose not to share them. . . .

Many parents used words such as 'cheated' and 'deceived' to convey their reaction to the withholding of news and express the view that they have a right to share in any concerns of the staff involved. Many are also very critical of the way in which they are told.

> There is no good way of telling a parent that his or her child is handicapped but there are some which are bad or even worse . . . these should be avoided. In my case the Paediatrician stood by my bed – he didn't even fully close the curtains so everyone outside could hear. He just said that my son had Down's syndrome and then left before I could say anything. He hadn't even bothered to wait till my husband returned.

Other criticisms include the use of derogatory labels (for example, vegetable, idiot, mongol), being given a very negative picture ('don't overdo the therapy thing as it won't make much difference') or being given inaccurate and out-of-date information (Berg et al., 1969).

No doubt it is an extraordinarily difficult task and it is possible that there are inaccuracies in recall (Berg et al., 1969) but many parents were also quick to acknowledge a sensitive approach to the subject. The following points are the ones that parents themselves appear to value:

1 To be told when together rather than either the father or the mother being told on his/her own and then having to break the news to the other.
2 To be told in private where there is no chance of other parents overhearing.
3 To be given the information in understandable terms, avoiding the use of devalued words such as 'mongol', 'vegetable', 'not much use'.
4 To be given time to ask questions (and perhaps see the person the next day when the parents may have thought of more questions): to be given time to talk.

5   As far as possible to be given accurate information as to their baby's condition and possible development.
6   To be told where they might go for help – for example, specialist health visitor, portage, parent support group.
7   To be treated as adults and thus as equals. (Cunningham and Sloper, 1977; McConachie, 1991).

This will not take away the pain but it will accord a certain dignity and respect to the child as well as the parents and perhaps present the child in a more positive, valued way than that which frequently occurs.

At this stage it is not possible to say with any certainty whether or not parents would benefit from counselling. Undoubtedly some find that they receive sufficient support from each other, from family and friends while others welcome the opportunity to talk through their feelings with someone not so intimately connected with the family. All parents should have the opportunity to talk with someone if they so wish. This does not necessarily have to be formal counselling and could take the place of extra time with medical or nursing staff, health visitor or possibly psychologist or social worker. The main criteria are that the parents are given time to express their feelings, that they are listened to and that they are helped to work out the options involved for themselves in a non-judgemental manner.

Following this it should then be possible to identify those who could, perhaps, benefit from more systematic counselling and those who already possess the resources necessary for coping at home. It is also important not to minimise the need that parents have for information, not only with regards to their child but also about the practical help available (for example, portage, opportunity play-groups, family support groups). The information required will change as the child grows and it is important that services are coordinated so that parents are aware of the resources available at each stage of their child's development.

Many parents are also critical of the traditional services which still tend to convey a negative image of the child's potential. One observed that she had formed the erroneous impression that her child was unlikely to walk or talk because she had been told that he 'would just lie there and not be able to do much'.

This desire to emphasise the positive finds its support from studies of families who have chosen to adopt a child with a learning disability. These families overwhelmingly rate the experience as being a positive one, saying that they have become more tolerant and flexible as a result (Masters Glidden et al., 1988). Indeed, the shift in emphasis from family pathology to adaptation and coping is in itself positive as it focuses on what the family can do rather than emphasising its failures.

The important factor is whether or not these views are generally shared or if they apply only to a minority. If it is only a minority, then it would be useful to know which factors distinguish between those families that appear to adjust in a positive way and those for whom much of life is a struggle. Although the stages model is still used to describe parental adjustment, it does have, as discussed, many serious limitations. The initial confirmation of the news will probably always be associated with shock and distress of some degree but subsequent adjustment does not appear to follow a clear-cut finite path leading to acceptance and adjustment.

The coping/adaptation model makes it possible to consider adjustment over a longer period of time, and stresses the positive strategies open to the family. Further research with planned control groups is needed, not only to identify strategies associated with a positive outcome but also to shape service planning so that the needs of the individual and their family are met in full. In addition, it reflects the changes that have taken place in the last 25 years regarding the philosophy of normalisation. If children with a learning disability are to be seen and treated as people first, as valued citizens with the same rights and needs as anyone else, then this acceptance *must* start from birth. It would be unrealistic, especially with society as a whole placing a high value on success and achievement, not to expect parents to be shocked and saddened by the news that their child has such a disability. However, even at this stage the emphasis needs to be on what they have in common with other babies – the need for warmth, shelter, protection, food, comfort, affection, play and love, and for someone to value them. In this way parents of children with special needs are adopting the philosophy of self advocacy by saying they want their children to be seen as babies and children rather than as 'handicapped'. The change in terminology (from mental handicap to learning disability and/or special needs) is therefore not just an artefact but represents a real shift in the way in which the child is viewed. Services need to be geared to help meet both these and the subsequent needs of the family rather than, as at present, families having to fit in with existing resources to the best of their ability. Therefore, rather than adhering to a model of pathology, it is time to give more attention to the models of adaptation and coping; and to consider also what the child contributes in a positive way, rather than continuing to focus on the negative elements which exist, to a greater or lesser degree, in all families.

Acknowledgement

I would like to acknowledge the help of Bromley Portage in the preparation of this chapter and those mothers with whom I had contact and who were so generous with their time and feelings.

References

Aldrich, A.C. (1947) 'Preventative medicine and mongolism', *American Journal of Mental Deficiency*, 52: 127.

Allen, D. and Affleck, G. (1985) 'Are we stereotyping parents?', *Mental Retardation*, 23 (4): 200.

Berg, J.M., Gilderdale, S. and Way, J. (1969) 'On telling parents a diagnosis of mongolism', *British Journal of Psychiatry*, 115: 1195.

Blacher, J. (1984) 'Sequential states of parental adjustment to the birth of a child with handicaps: fact or artifact?', *Mental Retardation*, 22 (2): 55.

Byrne, E. and Cunningham, C. (1985) 'The effects of mentally handicapped children on families: a conceptual review', *Journal of Child Psychology and Psychiatry*, 26 (6): 847.

Crnic, K., Friedrich, W. and Greenberg, M. (1983) 'Adaptation of families with mentally retarded children: a model of stress, coping and family ecology', *American Journal of Mental Deficiency*, 88 (2): 125–38.

Cunningham, C. and Sloper, P. (1977) 'Parents of Down's Syndrome babies: their early needs', *Child Care, Health and Development*, 3: 325–47.

D'Arcy, E. (1968) 'Congenital defects: mothers' reactions to first information', *British Medical Journal*, iii: 796.

Drotar, D., Baskiewicz, A., Irvin, N., Kennell, J.H. and Klaus, M.H. (1975) 'The adaptation of parents to the birth of an infant with a congenital malformation: a hypothetical model', *Paediatrics*, 56: 710–17.

Farran, D., Metzger, J. and Sparling, J. (1986) 'Immediate and continuing adaptations of parents of handicapped children: a model and an illustration', in J. Gallagher and P. Vietze (eds), *Families of Handicapped Persons: Research, Programs and Policy Issues*. Paul H. Brookes Publishing Co.

Gath, A. (1972) 'The effects of mental subnormality on the family', *British Journal of Hospital Medicine*, 147.

Gath, A. (1977) 'The impact of an abnormal child upon the parents', *British Journal of Psychiatry*, 130: 405.

Hanson, M., Ellis, L. and Deppe, J. (1989) 'Support for families during infancy', in J. Singer and L. Irvin (eds), *Support for Caregiving Families*. Baltimore: Paul H. Brookes Publishing Co.

Hill, R. (1958) 'Sociology of Marriage and Family Behaviour 1945–56: A Trend Report and Bibliography', *Current Sociology*, 7.

Huber, C.H. (1979) 'Parents of the handicapped child: facilitating acceptance through group counselling', *Personnel and Guidance Journal*, 57 (5): 267–9.

Kennedy, J.F. (1970) 'Maternal reactions to the birth of a defective baby', *Social Casework*, 51: 410.

Kew, S. (1975) *Handicap and Family Crisis*. London: Pitman Publishing.

Kubler-Ross, E. (1970) *On Death and Dying*. New York: Macmillan.

Lonsdale, G. (1978) 'Family life with a handicapped child: the parents speak', *Child Care, Health and Development*, 4: 99–120.

McConachie, H. (1991) 'Breaking the news to family and friends', *Mental Handicap,* 19 (June): 48–50.

McGowan, M.P. (1982) 'Guidance for parents of a handicapped child', *Child: Care, Health and Development,* 8: 295–302.

McGubbin, A. (1979) 'Integrating coping behaviour in family stress theory', *Journal of Marriage and the Family,* 237.

Masters Glidden, L., Valliere, V.N. and Herbert, S.L. (1988) 'Adopted children with mental retardation: positive family impact', *Mental Retardation,* 26 (3): 119–25.

Menolascino, F.J. (1977) *Challenges in Mental Retardation.* Human Sciences Press.

Minnes, P. (1988) 'Family resources and stress associated with having a mentally retarded child', *American Journal on Mental Retardation,* 93 (2): 184–92.

Naidoo, R.M. (1984) 'Counselling parents with handicapped children', *British Journal of Projective Psychology and Personality Study,* 29 (1): 13–17.

Olshansky, S. (1962) 'Chronic sorrow: a response to having a mentally defective child', *Social Casework,* 190–3.

Opirhory, G. and Peters, G. (1982) 'Counselling intervention strategies for families with the less than perfect newborn', *Personnel and Guidance Journal,* 60: 451–5.

Parks, R.M. (1977) 'Parental reactions to the birth of a handicapped child', *Health and Social Work,* 2: 51–66.

Quine, L. and Pahl, J. (1989) 'Examining the causes of stress in families with severely mentally handicapped children', *British Journal of Social Work,* 15: 501–17.

Singer, G. and Irvin, L. (1989) 'Family caregiving, stress and support', in G. Singer and L. Irvin (eds), *Support for Caregiving Families.* Baltimore: Paul H. Brookes Publishing Co.

Sloper, P., Knussen, C., Turner, S. and Cunningham, C. (1991) 'Factors relating to stress and satisfaction with life in families of children with Down's Syndrome', *Journal of Child Psychology and Psychiatry,* 32 (4): 655–76.

Solnit, A.J. and Stark, M.H. (1961) 'Mourning and the birth of a defective child', *Psychoanalytic Study of the Child,* 16: 523–53.

Summers, J., Behr, S. and Turnbull, A. (1989) 'Positive adaptation and coping strengths of families who have children with disabilities', in G. Singer and L. Irvin (eds), *Support for Caregiving Families.* Baltimore: Paul H. Brookes Publishing Co.

Waisbren S. (1980) 'Parents' reactions after the birth of a developmentally disabled child', *American Journal of Mental Deficiency,* 84 (4): 345–51.

Wikler, L.M. (1986) 'Family stress theory and research on families of children with mental retardation', in J. Gallagher and P. Vietze (eds), *Families of Handicapped Persons: Research, Programs and Policy Issues.* Baltimore: Paul H. Brooks Publishing Co.

Wikler, L., Wasow, M. and Hatfield, E. (1981) 'Chronic sorrow revisited: parents v. professional depiction of the adjustment of parents of mentally retarded children', *American Journal of Orthopsychiatry,* 51 (1): 63–70.

3

Psychotherapy with the Siblings of Mentally Handicapped Children

Robert Wilkins

There is little doubt that the presence of a mentally handicapped person has an effect on all family members, including siblings. The difficulty is knowing its quality and extent. Because of the variety of compounding factors and variables, sibling research is beset with problems, but it assumes an ever-increasing importance as more and more parents opt to have their mentally handicapped children live within their natural families. The effect on siblings may be positive or negative, and may be caused directly, indirectly, or a combination of both. For instance, a sibling may enjoy helping to look after a handicapped brother or sister, may relish the sympathy bestowed on him or her by others, and may benefit from living in a family which has learnt to discuss problems in an open and frank way. On the other hand, another sibling may be reluctant to be seen in the street with a handicapped member of the family, may feel starved of parental attention, or may suffer as a result of marital disharmony generated by the stresses of rearing a handicapped child.

A large number of the early studies undertaken to investigate the effect a mentally handicapped child may have on siblings suffered serious methodological problems, especially the lack of adequate comparison groups (see Brody and Stoneman, 1983; Lobato, 1983; Stoneman and Brody, 1984, 1987). Faulty research design explains, to some extent, the bewildering and often disparate results that are to be found in the medical literature. But a little thought will highlight the enormous problems encountered by researchers when they attempt to control for all the factors which may be posited to have an influence on siblings. In 'single child' research the subject may be male or female, and consequently gender becomes a two-dimensional factor; in the simplest of sibling research there are necessarily four dimensions or combinations – two brothers, two sisters, an older brother and a younger sister, an older sister and a younger brother. The problems associated with research into larger units – more than a sibship of two – are geometrically complex.

Further, in research into the siblings of mentally handicapped individuals, such a sibling may be older or younger, and consequently the four dimensions become eight – older normal sister with younger retarded brother, and so on. And the problems do not end there since it can be predicted that the age difference is likely to be an important factor in either ameliorating or exacerbating the effects upon a sibling: a normal sister who is 16 years old when her mentally handicapped brother is born is likely to be affected in a different way from a normal sister who is only 2 years old at the time. Birth order can also be postulated to be an important variable.

Some insight into the logistical problems of controlled research can be gleaned if, say, one needed to match two Caucasian siblings where the older, 9 year-old child is a first-born, mentally handicapped male, who has a 7 year-old second-born normal sister. Matching for maternal marital status (married or single) and socio-economic status increases the difficulties still further and explains why many of the published studies relating to siblings report on relatively small numbers of children. And yet it is of paramount importance that such difficulties are overcome since these various factors undoubtedly influence the effects upon siblings: 'Unless these factors are addressed in their interactive combinations, the processes impacting the sibling relationship cannot be clarified' (Stoneman, 1989).

The effects on siblings that have been widely investigated include family stresses in general (Tizard and Grad, 1961; Lavigne and Ryan, 1979), aberrant sibling interactions (McKeever, 1983; Powell and Ogle, 1985), the burden of care-taking responsibilities (Breslau et al., 1981; Schwirian, 1976; Stoneman et al., 1988), lessened or altered patterns of parental attention (Holt, 1957; Schonnell and Watts, 1957; McAndrew, 1976; Simeonsson and McHale, 1981; Lobato, 1983; McKeever, 1983; Stoneman et al., 1987), the relative paucity of peer relationships and the risks of social isolation (Farber and Jenne, 1963), feelings of anger, guilt and so on (Farber, 1960; Grossman, 1972; Miller and Cantwell, 1976; Edmundson, 1985; Begun, 1989; Bromley and Blacher, 1989) and stigmatisation (Harvey and Greenway, 1984).

The number of studies reporting negative effects upon the sibling (Farber, 1960; Farber and Jenne, 1963; Cohen, 1962; Kaplan, 1969; Gath, 1973; Tew and Laurence, 1973; San Martino and Newman, 1974; Simeonsson and McHale, 1981; Lobato, 1983; Seligman, 1983; Harvey and Greenway, 1984; Ferrari, 1984) have generally outnumbered those which show beneficial effects, or else an absence of detrimental effects (Caldwell and Guze, 1960; Graliker et al., 1962; Gath, 1972; Cleveland and Miller, 1977). Simultaneous beneficial and detrimental effects have been cited by Grossman (1972) and Cleveland and Miller (1977).

Family and parental factors have been postulated as tending to ameliorate the effects of stressors upon the siblings, the most important of which have been parental attitudes of acceptance (Caldwell and Guze, 1960; Graliker et al., 1962); the degree of family integration and cohesion (Mink and Nihira, 1987); and the extent and efficacy of family support systems, both in the extended family and the wider social network (Dyson and Edgar, 1986). In a recent controlled study of 55 siblings, aged between 8 and 15 years, of developmentally disabled children aged below 7 years, Edgar and Crnic (1989) showed that a sibling's self-concept was directly related to the levels of parental stress. They also found that there were fewer behaviour problems in the siblings of disabled children in families which were seen as being mutually supportive, as displaying little interpersonal conflict, where free expression of feelings was encouraged, and where there was an emphasis on the importance of personal growth of individual members. In essence, families which were deemed well-functioning and harmonious were those in which the siblings showed optimal adjustment to the presence of a disabled member.

Miller (1974) postulated that siblings who are involved with the caretaking or training of developmentally disabled family members tended to become emotionally distanced and assume an 'affective' neutrality. This emotional disengagement replaced the more competitive, more intimate and stronger affective relationship seen in developmentally normal sibships. Such 'role confusion' of sibling caretakers is further exaggerated when a chronologically younger, normal sibling assumes the role of 'older' sibling to the disabled individual. In addition to confusion come feelings of anxiety, frustration and conflict (Grossman 1972; Farber, 1975; Simeonsson and McHale, 1981). Begun (1989) found partial support for the notion of 'affect neutrality' when she investigated 46 sisters of moderately, severely and profoundly developmentally disabled individuals. The age range of the siblings was 12 to 69 years, with a mean of 30 years, and the age range of the disabled individuals was 8 to 69 years, with a mean of 27 years. The relationship was compared to that of siblings who had a non-disabled sibling (age range 12 to 82 years, with a mean of 32 years). Unfortunately only about half of the disabled siblings resided in the family home at the time of the study. Despite the wide age ranges involved the relationships of the subjects with their developmentally disabled siblings were deemed to be relatively positive. Nevertheless, it was notable that adolescent subjects reported more conflict with their disabled siblings than did adults, and that conflict was highest where the age difference was less than three years. Further, in adolescents, disabled brothers induced greater conflict than disabled sisters.

Again in adolescence, the intensity of conflict was directly related to the degree of dependency shown by the disabled sibling and, not unexpectedly, was highest between siblings who lived together than when the disabled member lived away from home (see the 'sibling access' concept of Bank and Kahn, 1982). Begun also emphasises the less competitive and less intimate relationship which develops between a normal sibling and her developmentally disabled sibling. That the degree of disability has an important bearing on the sibling dyad is shown by Begun's finding that those 'relationships with least dependent siblings most closely resembled the affect, interactions and roles of normative sibling relationships'.

Conflictual relationships between mentally retarded children and their older siblings was investigated by Stoneman et al. (1988). Their work concentrated particularly on the household and child-care responsibilities of older siblings and the effects that such responsibilities may have on the siblings' peer relationships and out-of-home activities. Since Farber's work in 1960 and Gath's work in 1974, it has been assumed that the added caretaking roles would be given disproportionately to older sisters, rather than older brothers, which would then lead them to find less time for friends and social activities (see also Farber and Jenne, 1963). Stoneman et al. (1988) predicted that, despite the societal shift in the role of females that has taken place in the last quarter of a century, the onus of caretaking would still fall on the shoulders of older sisters rather than older brothers. It was also predicted that such child-care demands, made upon either sex, would engender tension, conflict and negativism towards the disabled individual. Such deleterious effects of child-care responsibilities were postulated to be more evident in lower socio-economic families (Farber, 1960; Gath, 1974; Grossman, 1972).

In a controlled study matched for age, gender, birth order and family demographics, which confined itself to same-sex siblings, Stoneman et al. (1988) looked at such child-care responsibilities as baby-sitting, monitoring of the handicapped individual's safety, and general assistance with feeding, dressing or bathing. The authors concluded that 'dramatic changes in the role of women in society appear to have had minimal impact on the disproportionate assumption of childcare responsibilities by older sisters of mentally retarded children'. True, older brothers did their share of baby-sitting, but in general they did not become involved in activities which included feeding, dressing etc. Encouragingly, it was found that the siblings' peer relationships did not appear to suffer: older brothers and older sisters showed normal, or even more frequent contact, with peers, and it did not seem, contrary to some beliefs (Parfit, 1975), that the presence of the mentally retarded individual stopped the sibling from bringing friends into the house.

Notwithstanding their small sample number (sixteen pairs of siblings, eight of each gender, each with a younger mentally retarded child), Stoneman and her colleagues (1988) demonstrated that with greater child-care responsibilities came greater conflict between the sibling and the younger mentally retarded child. This most often showed itself as increased resentment and dissension, and was less frequently observed in those better-off families which tended to place fewer child-care responsibilities on older siblings. The study also reinforced previously voiced concerns about the prudence of casting older siblings in the role of teachers to their mentally retarded siblings (see Crnic and Leconte, 1986; Lobato, 1983). For a longer discussion regarding optimistic and pessimistic views about siblings as teachers the reader is referred to Bronfenbrenner (1979) and Farber and Jenne (1963).

Earlier work, presumably on the same sample, by Stoneman et al. (1987) had reported on observations of the interactions of retarded children with their older, normal siblings, in a home environment. It was hypothesised that the rates of such interactions would be relatively low, that the activities would be such as to minimise the dyad's disparate skills, that the older sibling would assume the roles of manager (directing behaviour), teacher, helper and/or playmate, and that older sisters would be expected to take on these roles to a greater extent than older brothers. Such interactions were rated as being affectively positive or negative, and the extent of parental interactions with the older siblings was directly observed. The authors demonstrated 'a high level of interaction between retarded children and their older siblings', with the older sibling, especially older sisters, more likely to assume the manager/guidance and teacher/helper roles than older brothers.

An important finding of Stoneman et al. (1987) was that the predicted drop in the frequency and quality of parental attention given to the non-handicapped child was dependent on gender. Indeed, older boys actually interacted more frequently with their mothers when they had a retarded younger brother. Intriguingly, the interactions between fathers and older sisters of handicapped children was eight times *less* than the interactions between fathers and daughters in the comparison group.

Zetlin (1986), in her study of retarded-adult–normal-adult sibships, demonstrated that sisters played a greater role than brothers in providing for the needs of their retarded siblings, and that this was especially the case for siblings who were closest in age.

Therapy options for siblings

Although the main emphasis in this chapter is given to family therapy it must be borne in mind that there are a number of therapeutic options available to address the treatment of problems experienced by the siblings of mentally handicapped individuals.

Individual therapy can take many forms, from relatively uncomplicated and often short-term supportive therapy through to analytical psychotherapy spread over many years. Much would depend, among other factors, on the complexity of the problems being experienced by the sibling, the sibling's age and cognitive ability and the availability of professional help.

The most common approach is supportive psychotherapy, but with older, and generally more insightful siblings, analytical psychotherapy can be most beneficial. There is no one form of individual therapy which 'marries' with family therapy. Realistically, one is often constrained by the particular skills of the local therapists: i.e. you can only offer what is available. Some approaches may cover the entire range from behavioural through counselling and cognitive therapy, through to intense and prolonged dynamic psychotherapy. Research (for example, Sloane et al., 1975) has indicated that widely varying intervention strategies can be successful over the same range of difficulties and so, while it may be preferable to provide an intervention based upon a hypothesised model of the underlying process of the disorder, in practice one gets what the available practitioner is good at and this does not appear to be detrimental.

Family therapy and individual therapy are not mutually exclusive options and can often be combined with a beneficial effect which exceeds the sum of the parts. In the 1970s it was thought that the two approaches could not be used since to be told a secret in individual therapy, on the promise that it would not be shared in family therapy, placed a burden on the therapist which hampered resolution of the problems. Today, we are more enlightened and holding secrets does not necessarily fetter a therapist.

So why choose group therapy? Group therapy is an effective option in work with siblings because many of the emotions experienced by siblings are internalised like some guilty secret, and are not shared even with other normal siblings in the household.

The power of group therapy lies in the sharing of common experiences – experiences such as guilt, envy and fear which the siblings had previously believed to be unique to themselves. At its most simple level, group therapy rests on the adage that a problem shared is a problem halved. Such groups, which can be formed by professionals or parents, can cater for the needs of children and adolescents, and operate along the same lines as therapeutic groups generally. Everything should be done to facilitate the inauguration of such a group, and procedural issues must not be allowed to thwart initial enthusiasm. To paraphrase: 'If two or more are gathered together one has a group.' Expertise in running a group is obviously an advantage but valuable time must not be lost in painstakingly trying to acquire skills from others which can be more effectively obtained by actually starting such a group oneself. Group dynamics are invariably complex but the formation of a sibling group must not be shrouded in mystification, especially if the result is to ensure that such a group is never started, or, if started, is paralysed by a lack of so-called experts.

It is important to emphasise that family therapy, individual therapy and group therapy are not mutually exclusive. It is no longer fashionable to argue that individual and family therapy are incompatible and counter-productive. Nowadays it has become common practice for an individual to be seen individually as well as part of a family: such options may alternate or run concurrently (the sibling having a number of individual sessions followed by a series of family meetings). An eclectic and pragmatic approach, while disdained by purists, maximises therapeutic utility.

Family therapy for siblings: some preliminary thoughts

Family therapy has not always been best served by those who advocate its usefulness. All too often simple ideas and effective strategies have become shrouded in a spurious erudition which has obscured basic effectiveness. It is axiomatic that the birth of a mentally handicapped child poses profound and chronic problems for all the family members. It should be equally axiomatic, therefore, that many of these problems may be solved by facilitating the free exchange of ideas and emotions within a family. Ideally, all family members would attend and, with a little help from the therapists, they would begin to communicate with each other in a frank and open fashion. Unfortunately, ours is not an ideal world, and family therapists must expect to have to work with part-families whose members are very resistant to revealing their feelings. Happily the days are fast disappearing when therapists would refuse to work with a family unless every member committed themselves to 100 per cent attendance and total cooperation. Therapists must work with what they have and not forever be wishing for what might be. Siblings *can* be helped in part-families and it is unacceptable to withhold treatment just because, say, a father adamantly refuses to attend.

Minuchin (1974) has said that the most effective family therapists are those who have had the experience of both a family of origin and a family of procreation. Essentially, a therapist benefits from having children of their own, and experiencing life's vicissitudes first hand. Few can argue with this ideal, but it is an ideal that often cannot be met. This 'slings and arrows' premiss, applied across the board, would mean that one could only take on families who have experienced what you yourself have experienced. It is akin to saying that one cannot have a view about apartheid unless one has lived in South Africa, or that one cannot counsel someone who is terminally ill unless one is close to death oneself. Few therapists belong to families in which there is a mentally handicapped member, and they cannot therefore have experienced first hand the variety of emotions, positive and negative, generated by such an event. This affective ignorance – which rarely seems to be an obstacle to the proffering of bereavement therapy by one who has never been personally bereaved, or marital therapy by one who is single – frequently results in therapists who have no personal knowledge of mental handicap eschewing work with such families. This is to be regretted. (For a fuller discussion of caveats, see Wilkins, 1989a.)

A possible solution to a therapist's dilemma is to put oneself in the position of one who is there to learn as well as help. A junior colleague – successful, happily married and with no children, and yet a sensitive and effective therapist – put it to a family in this way:

> I do not know what it is like to have a disabled person in my family. You will have to try your best to tell me. But I am used to looking at various ways of expressing emotions – despair, anger, hatred – and trying to help you cope with these feelings. Our sessions will be a true exchange and not a one-way traffic. We'll all teach and learn.

She then looked specifically at the sibling, aged about 6 years, and said, 'I will learn a lot from you'.

The problems that siblings of mentally handicapped children sometimes experience can be an item on a hidden agenda that no one has given permission to be addressed directly. A child may be brought to a clinic because of behavioural problems and it is only by chance that the therapist learns that there is another sibling, mentally handicapped, who has not been brought to the appointment, and who lives in a residential facility. Now it could be that the sibling's behavioural problems are not related in any way with his mentally handicapped brother – but one cannot be certain. The situation is analogous to the ubiquitous hidden agenda of race and ethnicity. I have long been in the habit of saying something like this: 'I know you haven't come specifically to talk about Colin [the mentally handicapped son] but it could be that John's bad behaviour is somehow connected. If at any time you feel that Colin is relevant to what we're talking about, please do not hesitate to share your thoughts with me.' In this way 'permission' is given for the hidden agenda item to be made overt.

Open trading of feelings within a family, both positive and negative, goes a long way towards lessening the effects of covert and pernicious processes. Many parents are aware of negative feelings directed by a normal sibling towards themselves and the mentally handicapped individual, but are often taken by surprise at their sheer intensity. It is as well to be aware that 'things may get worse before they get better', since it is not uncommon that when such adverse emotions are first vented there is a temporary heightening of tension within the family. But ultimately, when these feelings are 'talked through', a better understanding usually develops among the family members.

Family meetings can be the vehicle by which a sibling owns a myriad of intense emotions and confusions: guilt that he is normal; anger when his mentally handicapped brother or sister scratches or bites him and fear of being more seriously injured; disgust and embarrassment at antisocial habits and behaviours, especially when out of the home; resentment at having to caretake, baby-sit or help with household chores. The worsening behaviour of one 6 year-old sibling was traced to 'boundary testing': he had set out to discover how naughty one had to be before he too was sent to live away from home – just like his mentally handicapped younger sister. In another family the sibling told of her fears of having a mentally handicapped child herself: these fears were openly discussed – and for the first time – by all members of the extended family who were encouraged to make use of genograms (family trees).

Many such anxieties are age related: a sibling's anxiety and embarrassment may peak when a mentally handicapped brother or sister attains adolescence and displays overtly sexualised behaviour, in and out of the home, and in front of a boy-friend or girl-friend; a mentally handicapped adult may pose great problems when alternative placements after the parents' death are contemplated.

All these problems can be tackled by open and frank discussion in family therapy sessions. Some would say that to call such an exchange of information 'family therapy' is somehow to aggrandise a simple idea. Ultimately, it matters not a jot what the process is called just as long as it takes place.

Varieties of family therapy

Family therapy is infinitely variable. Therapists should not fetter themselves or be bound to any rigid theoretical dogma. Students of family therapy often spend hours of their training debating the merits and demerits of systemic versus strategic approaches to treatment. Books have been written on this distinction – and the more that is written the more blurred it becomes. The systemic approach, naturally, involves a 'system', be it a family system, professional system or social system. It relies on relationships within the system, alliances, hierarchies and so on. The strategic approach is more covert and bowls round the wicket rather than delivering a full toss at the wicket. Strategic therapy is less obvious and less open, and consequently is more potentially dangerous.

The important message is that specialism is constricting and many successful interventions meld strategic and systemic approaches. Both strategic and systemic approaches can often be used in the same family with a beneficial effect which is greater than the sum of its doctrinal parts. Systems theory, concerned as it is with hierarchies, alliances, boundaries and so on, has an obvious application in many of the problems experienced by the siblings of mentally handicapped children. Strategic family therapy, and especially the considered use of paradoxical techniques, can also find applications to sibling problems.

The question about the extent to which a sibling can be used as a teacher to a mentally handicapped brother or sister is a contentious one, often depending on how the sibling's services are utilised: competence as an instructor, the subject matter and the sibling's motivation. Some mentally handicapped children benefit greatly from the sympathetic assistance of a sibling; others benefit much less. Such credit and debit considerations apply equally to the sibling. Optimal results often come about from a judicious balance of quality and quantity: how good a teacher the sibling is and how much time is given over to 'instruction' (whether by play or by more formal educative activities), and how much of the teaching is *mutually* enjoyable and beneficial. It is often the case that a sibling's enthusiasm to become a teacher to a mentally handicapped brother or sister generates profound anxieties in a family and is deemed inappropriate to both parties. And yet it can be very difficult to dampen down or redirect a sibling's enthusiasm. Paradoxical techniques can often be used with advantage in order to achieve a healthier balance: for example, encouraging the very behaviour one is aiming to attenuate.

However, the use of paradox is a sensitive business. It is generally used without the client being aware that the intervention is intended to be paradoxical. Its power therefore lies in the covert nature of its agenda and this places a considerable responsibility for caution and care upon the therapist. Beginning therapists using this technique are likely to need close supervision and support to help them to persist, to avoid collusion with others and to know when to terminate an unsuccessful attempt. The urge to share the paradox with another agent such as the GP must be resisted in order to avoid inadvertent sharing of it with the client. For a fuller discussion of paradoxical techniques see Wilkins (1989b).

Much depends upon the dynamics within the family, and it would be unwise to give the impression that paradoxical techniques can always be applied. Nevertheless, situations do arise in the treatment of siblings' problems, whereby to be seen to *encourage* a certain undesirable behaviour (such as too much instruction by a sibling or virtual ignoring by a sibling), marshals a resistance in the sibling which results in a diminution of that behaviour by paradoxical methods. The major practical obstacle to paradoxical techniques is to think up a believable reason for encouraging the very behaviour of which you have previously been known to disapprove. Paradoxical techniques, when used in family therapy, must take into consideration issues related to safety and ethics, and the experience of the therapist (Wilkins, 1989b).

Criteria for family therapy and individual therapy

There has to be an expressed need, an acceptance by the individual or the family members that help is needed, and motivation to resolve the problems. None of these is absolute: the need may be picked up by professionals (for example, teachers, General Practitioners) rather than spontaneously expressed; not all the family members need perceive the need to the same degree; it therefore follows that motivation among family members may vary – specifically, siblings may be coerced initially into therapy by their parents without admitting any personal need.

Nevertheless, in individual and family therapy, I believe *motivation* is the most important criterion in assessing prognosis. Contracts with families give clear indications of what to expect from therapy sessions, their course, content and process and so there is less likelihood of attrition although this cannot, of course, be guaranteed.

The frequency and length of sessions will be determined largely by such factors as family commitment and availability and constraints upon the therapist's time. It is often impossible to enter into lengthy treatment programmes but, generally speaking little is resolved in fewer than six family sessions. Traditionally, individual sessions are spread over a greater time span. I have never found that the venue is of great importance: sessions at the family home are, however, usually not considered cost effective in the use of a therapist's time.

Behavioural techniques in family settings

There seems to be a widespread assumption that behaviour therapy and family therapy are mutually exclusive treatment approaches. This seems to me to be mistaken. Indeed, family meetings are ideal settings for the 'nuts and bolts' of behavioural programmes to be discussed and agreed. Most behaviour programmes are focused on altering the unacceptable and/or undesirable behaviours of mentally handicapped individuals, and it is not unusual for the sensitivities of a sibling to be ignored. So often great resentment is engendered in siblings simply because they have been left out of a token economy or star chart programme. The sibling is left to muse over the seeming injustice of a disabled brother or sister receiving sweets and toys for good behaviours which they themselves display unprompted, consistently and without reward. It is the simplest thing in the world to design a simple star chart for use by a sibling who can thereby share in the largesse: for example, he or she might be asked to carry out simple tasks such as drying the dishes or walking the dog. And it is in the context of family meetings that hierarchies and rewards can best be discussed.

Role-play in family meetings

Children model themselves on adults: generally speaking the behaviours of parents, both good and bad, are mirrored by their offspring. And so should it be: 'a chip off the old block', as applied to a child, is generally a source of pleasure and pride to a parent. The birth of a mentally handicapped child can have widespread effects upon the parents' behaviour and attitudes and these will be reflected in their other, normal, children. If a parent cannot successfully negotiate feelings of guilt, disgust and anger, then neither will their children. It behoves the parents to become role models for their normal children in order for them to cope with the anxieties which mental handicap generates within a family.

Family meetings are the ideal vehicle for role-play. The therapists act as facilitators to encourage family members to share their social anxieties. A sibling may dread going shopping or going on holidays or eating in a restaurant with a mentally handicapped brother or sister. They are aware of people staring or looking away, of children pointing or laughing. An important way to prevent such social situations being the genesis of individual or family isolation is to initiate a role-play in a family meeting. It is not unusual for there to be an initial reluctance on the part of the family (especially fathers) to participate in such 'silly games', and this is where gentle persuasion on the part of therapists about the usefulness of the role-play is of vital importance. When this initial reluctance is overcome the role-play often moves rapidly along, fuelled by the enthusiasm of siblings.

Shopping expeditions are commonly chosen for role-play. A situation is enacted which has been identified as a source of problems in the past. Initially people may play themselves, with therapists taking the parts of shopkeepers or other customers. The action is frequently 'frozen' in order that people may share their feelings about some incident or other. Such feelings can either be discussed fully at that time or discussion can be postponed until later in the session. What is important for siblings is the growing awareness that they are not the only ones who are affected by an enacted situation but that the parents experience similar feelings which they have not openly expressed before. (It is analogous to junior nurses who suddenly discover in staff groups that a ward sister, whom they had previously assumed immune, shares their anxieties to an equal degree.) So often children believe that mum or dad cannot possibly feel the way they do, or that to express true feelings will be deemed weakness or disloyalty. Imagination is the only limiting factor in such role-play situations: 'model' reactions to taunts and teasing may be formulated and rehearsed by the sibling; roles may be changed whereby a sibling becomes mother, or father acts the part of the shopkeeper. Such role-play, which in my experience is invariably effective and beneficial, rests on the principle that a feeling felt should be a feeling expressed.

Role-play directed at treating a sibling must nevertheless be sensitive to the mentally handicapped individual. There is no reason why the handicapped child might not join in fully with what is being enacted. Equally there is no need to feel guilty if it is decided to exclude the mentally handicapped individual. Family sessions in general and role-play in particular have been found to be usful in facilitating the open expression of emotions in normal children whose parents are contemplating fostering or adopting a mentally handicapped child.

Setting up family therapy interventions

The choice of family therapy as a major intervention, perhaps in addition to individual work with the child who is giving cause for concern, depends upon a number of factors. These include:

1 the importance of family relationships in determining the sibling's attitudes and problems;
2 the willingness of family members to examine their role in the family, the willingness to accept individual and corporate responsibility, and the willingness to attempt change;
3 the availability of therapists willing to work with whole and part families.

Some examples

'An act of God': the case of Gilbert
Quite frequently the power of family therapy rests solely in its facilitation of information exchange between family members who are not normally in the habit of communicating with one another. The therapists have merely acted as catalysts.

Gilbert, who was 10 years old, had an older sister, Samantha, aged 12 years. Samantha had Down's syndrome and was profoundly mentally handicapped. Mother was a busy housewife and her husband was a hospital porter working the night shift, and sleeping most of the day. Despite a multitude of stresses the family appeared stoical and accepting. They had been referred to the clinic because Gilbert had begun to steal money from his parents, to be aggressive at school, and had changed from having a cheery disposition into being sulky and truculent. The referrer, the family's General Practitioner, had mooted the idea that Gilbert was perhaps being teased on account of Samantha.

When the family was seen first the major part of the session was taken up gathering information. Gilbert was asked about his school and whether he was teased. The therapists seemed reluctant to broach the relationship that Gilbert had with his sister, and during a break this omission was pointed out by the supervisor (who had been observing through a one-way screen). The second half resumed with questions related directly to family functioning as a result of Samantha's mental handicap. Gilbert vehemently denied that he was teased. His parents agreed and mother said about

Samantha, 'It's an act of God, and we can do nothing about it'. Father smiled and nodded his head, Gilbert looked bemused and angry, and Samantha continued playing happily with a puppet.

It was then decided that Gilbert should have individual sessions with one of the therapists so as to give him the opportunity to express any anxieties that he might be reluctant to voice in the family meeting. It was hoped that if any such anxieties were divulged, a method may be found of sharing them with his parents as a first step to neutralising any pernicious effects. It was not until the third session that Gilbert spoke about Samantha as 'an act of God', but it became immediately clear that Gilbert saw his sister as some form of divine retribution for an undisclosed sin committed by either his mother or his father – or himself. Samantha was the embodiment of a family punishment which, in Gilbert's belief, was likely to affect his own children. He shrank from talking to his mother because of his fear that he himself shared responsibility for Samantha's condition. This was the explanation of his changed behaviour.

The next family session was the denouement of the problem. Gilbert was helped to share his misconceptions with his parents. Mother was taken aback at such a literal interpretation of her ideas about providence. Gilbert was assured that it was only 'a figure of speech'. The family continued in therapy for six more sessions in order to capitalise on the freer exchange of ideas and feelings between Gilbert and his parents. To date, six years on, Gilbert appears to be a well adjusted teenager, able to give and receive in his relationship with Samantha.

An absent father

Tom was 7 years old when his younger brother Ben was born. The marital relationship was fraught long before Ben was diagnosed as autistic. Indeed, the parents had discussed separation and divorce, and the diagnosis of autism had tempted father to stay and abandon plans to marry another woman. Mother, seemingly anxious that one of them should find happiness, encouraged her husband to follow the dictates of his heart rather than those of his conscience.

Tom was bereft at his father's leaving and reacted violently and angrily at what he saw as a situation brought about by the birth of Ben. Initially it was agreed between the parents that Tom would spend alternate weekends with his father but these were soon abandoned when Tom took to 'acting out' in a dangerous fashion: running off across a busy main road or threatening to jump from the window of his father's first-floor flat. Tom's behaviour became even more reckless and impulsive in the company of father's fiancée, Jill.

Finally, when after three months, the opportunity for a sabbatical year abroad presented itself, father accepted with alacrity.

On hearing that his father was going to America, Tom tried to drown Ben in the bath. Mother decided not to tell father, hoping that, in time, things would settle down and Tom's behaviour would gradually settle down. It did not. Although Tom never tried again to get rid of Ben in so permanent a fashion, his general behaviour, at home and at school, became more and more unacceptable. It was at this time that a referral was made to the local Child Guidance Clinic with a request for a Multi-Professional Assessment (MPA) – a preliminary assessment of a child's educational needs, a procedure which commonly results in the recommendation of special schooling, often in a residential environment. It was decided that the psychiatric input to the MPA would be information obtained from a series of family meetings. The family consisted of mother, maternal grandmother, Tom and Ben, but on the first visit to the Clinic mother had decided not to bring Ben. During that visit it was clear that mother had no regrets about the separation from her husband and was deeply involved with another man, James, whom she hoped to marry some day. Unfortunately Tom had not taken to James and refused to entertain the idea of his mother marrying this new man.

At this first meeting many issues were discussed in a preliminary fashion. It appeared that Tom's father wrote and telephoned regularly; he also sent lavish gifts at birthdays and Christmas. It was suggested by one of the therapists that *two* empty chairs be set out for the absent father and James. Whenever the opinions of these absentees was sought, the therapists would look at the empty chair and say, 'Now what do you think James would say about that if he were here?' It was this ploy, more professionally termed 'strategy', that provided the first clue to the reason why Tom was behaving so badly. The consensus view on Tom's behaviour had been that he was acting in this way in order to revenge himself on his father for leaving, and his mother for allowing father to leave. A chance remark of Tom's laid this lie: pointing from one empty chair to the other Tom said, 'My Dad will come back and beat James up!'

Over the next three sessions it became increasingly apparent that Tom had conceived a plan to compel his father to return to live with his mother. In the simple world view of a 7 year old, it was merely a matter of behaving so badly that the combined concern of his natural parents would be bound to bring them together again in order to prevent Tom from 'upping the ante' in ever more dangerous ways. If parental anxiety were sufficiently high, Tom reckoned, then his father would be certain to return in order to prevent a catastrophe. This new interpretation of Tom's behaviour had given insight into the working of a child's mind. It was Ben who had driven his parents apart; it would be Tom who would effect their reunion and live happily ever after. In family therapy terms, Tom was giving the wrong answer to the right question: he was attempting to reconcile his parents (the right question, from Tom's point of view, being 'What can I do to bring Daddy back?') by inappropriate means – become a bad enough person and force his parents together (the wrong answer). It was beyond Tom's ken to realise that such paediatric solutions to adult problems rarely, if ever, succeed.

In the sessions, with one of the co-therapists speaking on Tom's behalf, it was affirmed that this was indeed Tom's master plan. He had got the idea from a friend whose father, so it was said, had returned to live at home in order to ensure that his son went to school regularly. Tom even admitted that he had contemplated bunking school but had decided against it because he liked his class teacher too much. In the third session one of the two empty chairs was filled: James joined the group. It was quickly apparent that, in other circumstances, Tom and James would have got on very well since they shared many things in common. It was unfortunate that James was regarded as a usurper, and an obstacle to Tom's natural father's return to the family. As sessions continued, the bond between Tom and James seemed to deepen and, concomitantly with this improved relationship, came a more tolerant attitude shown by Tom towards Ben. Ultimately, after some ten family meetings it became clear that the facilitation of the exchange of feelings, both positive and negative, had had beneficial effects on family functioning: Tom was blaming mother less for allowing father to leave; Tom was beginning to play with his younger brother; mother and James were openly talking about setting up home together; and Tom, almost against his better judgement, was beginning to become fond of James.

Father remained the fly in the ointment, since Tom's fundamental loyalty was towards him and the goal of his return: a goal which was likened by one of the therapists to the quest for the holy grail, an ideal that could never materialise. It was mother who suggested a way to unravel the skein of enmeshed emotions and loyalties. She proposed that father, whose sabbatical had ended, should join the meetings and find a way of explaining to Tom the concept of right questions and wrong answers. The idea was unanimously agreed and father, who had been kept abreast of developments, readily agreed.

The meeting was one of the most poignant the therapists had ever witnessed. Tom's ambivalent feelings were evident; drawn by love to his father, and repulsed by feelings of profound betrayal. In an emotional and painful session, father explained that he would always love and care for Tom and Ben, but that there was nothing that Tom could do which would bring mother and father back together again. It was explained that father (and Jill) desperately wanted to have regular access to Tom and Ben (who had long since joined the sessions), and mother loved James and he was going to join the family. In an unscripted moment, father implied that continued contact between he and Tom might be dependent on Tom's *good* behaviour and may be put in jeopardy by Tom's *bad* behaviour. These sentiments of behavioural blackmail provoked anxiety in every member of the team, but Tom seemed to accept them realistically.

When last contacted, Tom's behaviour was back on an even keel: he no longer blamed his mother, he had grown attached to James, he had even 'tolerated' Ben, and no longer blamed his brother for his father's leaving home. Tom and Ben spend alternate weekends with their father and his new wife – and the newly born twins.

'Back to school'

Brenda, a serious-minded 8 year-old was always eager to teach her 4 year-old mentally handicapped sister, Joyce. Initially the parents were gratified that the two sisters got on so well together and took such pleasure in each other's company. It seemed a bonus that Brenda appeared to delight in trying to teach Joyce simple tasks. Brenda loved to play 'school' in which she took the role of teacher, with Joyce as the 'pupil'. Very soon, however, things became more formalised with Brenda setting Joyce inappropriately complicated problems and delighting in chastising any poor performance or lapses of attention. Not unnaturally Brenda's didactic approach soon began to make Joyce frustrated and aggressive. Mother attempted to limit such 'school' play to once a day, and closely to supervise what was going on. Unfortunately such supervision upset Brenda who started displaying temper tantrums whenever she was thwarted. The problem was raised in a family therapy session, one of a series of family meetings originally convened to focus on marital problems.

A paradoxical approach was mooted whereby mother reckoned that if Brenda was enjoying the role of teacher so much, and Joyce was enjoying the role of pupil, then it followed that everyone else in the family would enjoy playing school – mother would be teacher and Brenda would be the pupil. In fact, so as not to leave father out, he would also join in, teaching Brenda at weekends. Father, a computer programmer, would teach Brenda her sums. Brenda's face was seen to register undiluted horror at this suggestion. Brenda's protestations were connoted by the therapists as unselfishness, an attempt on her part to 'give' rather than 'receive' pleasure. The family resolved to cancel their visit to the zoo and, instead, spend the weekend enjoying games of school. Brenda was to show her parents how to play properly. Brenda's profound reluctance and lack of enthusiasm for weekend school – especially with her as pupil, and sums as the lesson – was apparent to all. Her parents feigned bemusement and again focused on her unselfishness. Ultimately Brenda had to exercise her independence by openly and actively resisting all suggestions of school play, whether between she and Joyce or she and her parents. Brenda's enthusiasm to teach Joyce went into precipitous decline and was replaced by a more relaxed and mutually enjoyable relationship between the sisters. Appropriate teaching activities were encouraged in moderation but were closely monitored by the parents. Brenda received fulsome praise and cuddles for all the help she was giving Joyce.

Conclusion

It is important that the very real needs of the siblings of mentally handicapped children are identified and met. Family therapy has been shown to be an extremely effective and versatile way of tackling a sibling's problems.

References

Bank, S. and Kahn, M. (1982) *The Sibling Bond*. New York: Basic Books.

Begun, A. (1989) 'Sibling relationships involving developmentally disabled people', *American Journal of Mental Retardation*, 5: 566–74.

Breslau, N., Weitzman, M. and Messenger, K. (1981) 'Psychologic functioning of siblings of disabled children', *Pediatrics*, 67: 344–53.

Brody, G. and Stoneman, Z. (1983) 'Children with atypical siblings: socialization outcomes and clinical participation', in B. Lahey and A. Kazdin (eds), *Advances in Clinical Child Psychology*. New York: Plenum Press, pp. 285–326.

Bromley, B. and Blacher, J. (1989) 'Factors delaying out-of-home placement of children with severe handicaps', *American Journal of Mental Retardation*, 94: 284–91.

Bronfenbrenner, U. (1979) 'Contexts of child rearing: problems and prospects', *American Psychologist*, 34: 844–50.

Caldwell, B. and Guze, S. (1960) 'A study of the adjustment of parents and siblings of institutionalized and noninstitutionalized retarded children', *American Journal of Mental Deficiency*, 64: 845–61.

Cleveland, D. and Miller, N. (1977) 'Attitudes and life commitments of older siblings of mentally retarded adults: an exploratory study', *Mental Retardation*, 15: 38–41.

Cohen, P. (1962) 'The impact of the handicapped child on the family', *Social Casework*, 43: 137–42.

Crnic, K. and Leconte, J. (1986) 'Understanding sibling needs and influences', in R. Fewell and P. Vadasy (eds), *Families of Handicapped Children*. Austin: Pro-Ed.

Dyson, L. and Edgar, E. (1986) 'The self-concept of siblings of handicapped children – an exploratory study', paper presented at the Council for Exceptional Children annual international convention, New Orleans (Eric Document Reproduction Service No. ED 268 767; EC 182 371).

Edgar, L. and Crnic, K. (1989) 'Psychological predictors of adjustment by siblings of developmentally disabled children', *American Journal of Mental Retardation*, 3: 292–302.

Edmundson, L. (1985) 'The "discovery" of siblings', *Mental Retardation*, 23: 49–51.

Farber, B. (1960) 'Family organization and crisis: maintenance of integration in families with a severely mentally retarded child', *Monographs of the Society for Research in Child Development*, 25 (1).

Farber, B. (1975) 'Family adaption to severely mentally retarded children', in M. Begab and S. Richardson (eds), *The Mentally Retarded and Society*. Baltimore: University Park Press.

Farber, B. and Jenne, W. (1963) 'Family organization and parent–child communication: parents and siblings of a retarded child', *Monographs of the Society for Research in Child Development*, 28.

Ferrari, M. (1984) 'Chronic illness: psychosocial effects on siblings – I. Chronically ill boys', *Journal of Child Psychology and Psychiatry*, 25: 459–76.

Gath, A. (1972) 'The mental health of siblings of congenitally abnormal children', *Journal of Child Psychology and Psychiatry*, 13: 211–18.

Gath, A. (1973) 'The school-aged siblings of mongol children', *Journal of Child Psychology and Psychiatry*, 123: 161–7.

Gath, A. (1974) 'Sibling reactions to mental handicap: a comparison of the brothers and sisters of Mongol children', *Journal of Child Psychology and Psychiatry*, 15: 187–98.

Graliker, B., Fishler, K. and Koch, R. (1962) 'Teenage reaction to a mentally retarded sibling', *American Journal of Mental Deficiency*, 66: 838–43.

Grossman, F. (1972) *Brothers and Sisters of Retarded Children: An Exploratory Study*. Syracuse: Syracuse University Press.

Harvey, D. and Greenway, A. (1984) 'The self-concept of physically handicapped children and their nonhandicapped siblings: an empirical investigation', *Journal of Child Psychology and Psychiatry*, 25: 273–84.

Holt, K. (1957) 'The impact of mentally retarded children on their families'. M.D. Thesis, University of Manchester.

Kaplan, F. (1969) 'Siblings of the retarded', in S. Sarason and J. Doris (eds), *Psychological Problems in Mental Deficiency*. New York: Harper & Row, pp. 186–208.

Lavigne, J. and Ryan, M. (1979) 'Psychologic adjustment of siblings of children with chronic illness', *Pediatrics*, 63: 616–26.

Lobato, D. (1983) 'Siblings of handicapped children: a review', *Journal of Autism and Developmental Disorders*, 13: 347–64.

McAndrew, I. (1976) 'Children with a handicap and their families', *Child Care, Health and Development*, 2: 213–37.

McKeever, P. (1983) 'Siblings of chronically ill children: a literature review with implications for research and practice', *American Journal of Orthopsychiatry*, 53: 209–18.

Miller, N. and Cantwell, D. (1976) 'Siblings as therapists: a behavioral approach', *American Journal of Psychiatry*, 133: 447–50.

Miller, S. (1974) 'An exploratory study of sibling relationships in families with retarded children. Unpublished doctoral thesis, Columbia University Teachers' College (quoted by Begun, 1989).

Mink, I. and Nihira, K. (1987) 'Direction of effects: family life styles and behavior of TMR children', *American Journal of Mental Deficiency*, 92: 57–64.

Minuchin, S. (1974) *Families and Family Therapy*. Cambridge Mass.: Harvard University Press.

Parfit, J. (1975) 'Siblings of handicapped children', *Special Education/Forward Trends*, 2: 19–21.

Powell, T. and Ogle, P. (1985) *Brothers and Sisters: A Special Part of Exceptional Families*. Baltimore: Brookes.

San Martino, M. and Newman, M. (1974) 'Siblings of retarded children: a population at risk', *Child Psychiatry and Human Development*, 4: 168–77,

Schonnell, A. and Watts, B. (1957) 'A first survey on the effects of a subnormal child on the family unit', *American Journal of Mental Deficiency*, 61: 210–19.

Schwirian, P. (1976) 'Effects of the presence of a hearing impaired preschool child in the family on behavior patterns of older "normal" siblings', *American Annals of the Deaf*, 121: 373–80.

Seligman, M. (1983) 'Siblings of handicapped persons', in M. Seligman (ed.), *The Family with a Handicapped Child: Understanding and Treatment*. New York: Grune & Stratton.

Simeonsson, R. and McHale, S. (1981) 'Reviews: Research on handicapped children: sibling relationships', *Child Care, Health and Development*, 7: 153–71.

Sloane, R. B., Staples, F. R., Cristol, A. H., Yorkston, N. J. and Whipple, K. (1975) *Psychoanalysis versus Behaviour Therapy*. Cambridge: Harvard University Press.

Stoneman, Z. (1989) 'Comparison groups in research on families with mentally retarded members: a methodological and conceptual review', *American Journal of Mental Retardation*, 94: 195–215.

Stoneman, Z. and Brody, G. (1984) 'Research with families of severely handicapped children: theoretical and methodological considerations', in J. Blacher (ed.), *Severely Handicapped Young Children and Their Families*. New York: Academic Press.

Stoneman, Z. and Brody, G. (1987) 'Observations of retarded children, their parents and their siblings', in S. Landesman and P. Vietze (eds), *Living Environments and Mental Retardation*. Washington, DC: American Association of Mental Deficiency.

Stoneman, Z., Brody, G., Davis, C. and Crapps, J. (1987) 'Mentally retarded children and their older same-sex siblings: naturalistic in-home observations', *American Journal of Mental Retardation*, 92: 290–8.

Stoneman, Z., Brody, G., Davis, C. and Crapps, J. (1988) 'Childcare responsibilities, peer relations and sibling conflict: older siblings of mentally retarded children', *American Journal of Mental Retardation*, 93: 174–83.

Tew, B. and Laurence, K. (1973) 'Mothers, brothers and sisters of patients with spina bifida', *Developmental Medicine and Child Neurology*, 15 (Supplement 6): 69–76.

Tizard, J. and Grad, J. (1961) *The Mentally Handicapped and Their Families*. London: Oxford University Press.

Wilkins, R. (1989a) 'The King and his Fool', *Journal of Family Therapy*, 11: 181–95.

Wilkins, R. (1989b) *Behaviour Problems in Children: Orthodox and Paradox in Therapy*. London: Heinemann.

Zetlin, A. (1986) 'Mentally retarded adults and their siblings', *American Journal of Mental Deficiency*, 91: 217–25.

4

Secondary Mental Handicap as a Defence

Jon Stokes and Valerie Sinason

In 1980 The Tavistock Clinic, a major National Health Service training and treatment clinic, formally embarked on providing psychoanalytic psychotherapy for mentally handicapped people. This was due initially to Neville Symington, a psychoanalyst and clinical psychologist in the Adult Department who became so interested in the impact of psychotherapy with one mildly handicapped adult that he formed a workshop. His first paper (Symington, 1981) aroused further interest both in psychotherapists and in those already working in a psychodynamic way in mental handicap. Professor Joan Bicknell, Dr Sophie Thompson and Professor Sheila Hollins of St George's Hospital were among the first visitors to the new workshop and have remained the core of a growing psycho-dynamic network.

From 1985 to 1988 the workshop was co-convened by the two of us and there was an expansion of clinical work, psychotherapy research and cross-fertilisation with colleagues in the mental handicap field. We decided to hold an open workshop once a month to which other professions were invited and started ten-week introductory courses on psychodynamic thinking in mental handicap. In addition, we found ourselves giving papers, lectures and providing training days at an increasingly fast rate as other professions became aware of the use of psychoanalytic psychotherapy both as a treatment and as a body of knowledge that could be usefully applied. Since 1988 the workshop has been convened by Mrs Valerie Sinason, child psychotherapist and Dr Sheila Bichard, clinical psychologist, and the research and clinical programme has expanded.

Although the Tavistock Clinic only became involved in 1980 there has been psychoanalytic interest in mental handicap from the 1930s onwards. However, the interest never generalised so that there seem to be pockets of concentrated work with long gaps between them. Pierce Clark (1933) and Chidester and Menninger (1936) were the most significant figures in the 1930s in England and America. In the 1950s and 1960s Harold Bourne in England and Clifford Scott in Canada heralded further progress. Our own involvement in the 1980s is matched by similar colleagues in Sweden, Denmark, France, Italy and America. The work has been expanding steadily and has nearly reached a decade and we have every reason to believe it will now be properly established.

Clinical work

The workshop is treating approximately 25 individuals, children and adults, for long-term psychoanalytic individual or group psychotherapy, couple or family therapy. In addition, we provide over 30 assessments a year and, from the courses, reflect on over 60 case presentations a year from our students. In the first few years of its existence the workshop mainly treated people in the mild handicap range (IQ 50–75), while now many clients are not only profoundly mentally handicapped but are also managing physical handicaps and mental illness. The psychotherapy carried out is essentially unmodified psychoanalytic psychotherapy as would be offered to non-handicapped children or adults, generally once-weekly sessions of 50 minutes using the transference situation to understand the internal world of the individual client. Adult group therapy is for one and a half hours once a week.

Our understanding has developed along a number of lines and we would like to provide a general psychodynamic understanding of the difficulties for professionals and parents in caring for mentally handicapped individuals, while focusing in detail on particular issues to do with handicap as a defence. Our workshop and courses are multi-disciplinary and we strongly support the need for cooperation in the extended family of professionals that a handicapped individual requires. Within that context, the contribution we are able to make to the multi-disciplinary team is derived from our own psychoanalytic psychotherapy training. It is important to stress that our knowledge comes from treating people with a mental handicap who have been referred to us for their emotional problems. The points we make in this chapter apply to our specific population although they are likely to be of wider relevance.

A note on terms
When Neville Symington formed the workshop it was called the 'Subnormality Workshop' which was the accepted term at that time.

After a few years the term 'mental handicap' came into practice and the workshop was pressured to change its name. Now, of course, the term 'mental handicap' is criticised and new terms like 'mental disability', 'learning difficulty', 'learning disability' and 'special needs' have appeared. While upholding the need not to use dehumanising labels and to call clients by the name they prefer, we would like to point out the defensive aspects involved in changing a term every few years (Sinason 1989c, 1989d; see also Szivos and Griffiths, Chapter 5). Quite apart from the genuine hope engendered by new terms there can also be an irrational hope that the irrevocable organic handicap could go away if its name were changed.

We use the term 'Mental handicap' as defined by the World Health Organisation (1980) to mean the disadvantage that results from an impairment or disability that limits or prevents the fulfilment of a role that is normal (depending on age, sex, social and cultural factors) for that individual.

We use the term 'secondary Mental handicap' to indicate the emotional sequelae of the primary impairment.

Guilt, loss and separation problems

Having a handicapped baby is usually a trauma for the parents, the baby and the community. However much love develops later between parents and handicapped baby, there is often a difficulty in making an attachment at the start. This is not surprising when we consider that there is a strong biological wish to have a child at least as healthy as yourself. To have a baby who is damaged in some way is a blow to the self as a procreating being and usually evokes a reaction of rejection that could be in part instinctive. Similarly, the handicapped individual can represent all the damaged aspects of ourselves we want to be rid of. Hence the wish, despite recent moves towards community care, to hide handicapped people away from the rest of the community. The actual lack of adequate facilities in the community contributes to this distancing process.

The parents, in addition to their distress and shock, may find the handicapped baby more difficult to parent. Without the reassuring reward of normal developmental milestones, emotional resources can be rapidly depleted. To deny their hurt or anger and their feelings of guilt at having any negative feelings towards their child, some parents can become over-concerned and encourage an excessive dependency. What we as psychotherapists often see is an individual who is referred when the prospect of separation between mother and child, or institution and adult, is impending and feared by all concerned. Sometimes, this is because the separation is equated by both parties with rejection and even death. The unspoken question of the child, 'Why was I born like this?' and of the adult, 'Why were you born?', although hidden and unspoken, often come to the fore at these times. As we stressed earlier, our experience comes from working with those who have suffered emotionally. There are likely to be people with a mental handicap who have been spared these processes. Nevertheless, we consider that the issues involved in the cross-section of clients we see have a wider relevance and application.

The psychoanalyst D. W. Winnicott (1971) has described the early stages of development as involving a process of 'disillusionment'; the illusion which is initially fostered is that the baby and mother are one so that the baby does not have to experience all the pain of separation and in the best circumstances the experiences of separation and frustration are introduced in tolerable doses. That is, the illusion that baby and mother are one is gradually disillusioned. This situation of gradually facing increasing degrees of separation and adversity encourages learning and development.

This process of disillusion is often disturbed in the case of a baby born with a mental handicap (Symington, 1981) and the proper separation of mother and child does not occur. Part of the original illusion is the feeling that the mother has that she has the 'ideal' baby. This necessary idealisation is threatened if the baby is evidently damaged. Failure to develop out of this stage is connected with a fear of new experiences and a stifling of curiosity. This in turn adds to the original handicap. One child commented (Sinason, 1989b), 'It's like those dolls inside dolls. They want to come out, but if they do they won't be inside a mummy and they won't have a mummy.' The child understood that if he did separate and show he was a separate, though handicapped being, he would face the rejection that was cushioned by the collusion that he was unborn or still a baby.

Among the reasons why parents or workers may avoid separation are:

1   Parents with an adult handicapped child may not be able to give up their parental role. Sometimes, the only way they can stay bearing a parental function while other parents are slowly freed of it is to bond in a way that they did with much younger children. Without this, they would not be able to stay attached. Similarly, workers knowing that some adults will always have to be washed, dressed, fed and taken to the toilet can only bear this

by treating their clients as babies. 'She can't do a thing for herself, bless her' said a worker of a 35 year-old handicapped woman.

2   To separate means facing the loss of the normal child they did not have. Bicknell (1983) has described the failure to mourn that forms part of the parents' difficulty in helping a handicapped child grow up and leave. Separation would thereby uncover the depression in having had such a child. 'It doesn't even feel like an empty nest' said one mother when her 25 year-old handicapped son left for a hostel. 'I'm feeling it was not a real nest in the first place because it wasn't a proper baby.'

3   A handicapped child can become the receptacle of all handicapped, unwanted and stupid parts of every member of the family. The child provides a useful place to locate incompetence, damage, depression and pain. Separation would mean re-owning these projected aspects of each family member. 'We can't come out, you know we have to look after Tommy, he can't manage on his own.' When Tommy finally found a boarding placement the family had to recognise that their own inability to maintain relationships had been hidden under the excuse of 'caring for Tommy'.

4   Semi-fusion and non-separation provides a haven and retreat from the painful facing of the actual handicap and the real limitations. Sometimes these are not as great as are feared but because they remain unexamined can be terrifying for both individual and family.

5   Handicap is not curable and workers and parents can feel so guilty that they cannot make it right that they feel they have to devote themselves entirely to the handicapped individual.

In our experience, handicapped individuals are often more aware and more ready to try to face some of these profound problems than parents or professional carers. Foremost among these is often the anxiety associated with the painful matter of who will care for the severely handicapped person when the parents die. It is for us almost a rule of thumb that these questions are in our clients' minds when we first meet them. Experience from discussions with workers and parents in educational and residential settings would suggest that these anxieties are widespread.

The traumatic effects of handicap on the personality

The Office of Health Economics' paper on mental handicap (1973) describes mental disability as the product of three factors: inherited constitution; modification or injuries caused by pre- or postnatal injury or disease; and conditioning and training of the intellect. We cannot be sure of the exact nature of organic limits on any handicapped individual, or indeed on ourselves. Indeed, there is often such a discrepancy between each of us as we are and each of us as we might be if we did not undermine our own capacities, that the question of finite capabilities rarely seems very meaningful. However, we do find it useful to distinguish between cognitive intelligence and emotional intelligence.

While an academically brilliant individual might be emotionally out of touch or undeveloped, the reverse can be true; a mentally handicapped individual with limited cognitive abilities can be capable of emotional understanding and knowledge. There seems no clear one-to-one relationship between cognitive and emotional understanding. An interprofessional link between psychoanalytic psychotherapy and clinical psychology helps to understand this further.

For example, a 14 year-old severely handicapped boy could not recognise the picture of a knife in a word recognition test given by Dr Sheila Bichard (who now co-convenes the Mental Handicap Workshop). The quality of this non-recognition was not to do with consciously withholding knowledge but a quite powerful unconscious blocking of a traumatic memory. In therapy with one of us (Valerie Sinason) the week before he had described cutting his wrist with a knife.

Another client (Stokes, 1987), a 24 year-old woman with Down's syndrome, illustrates the quality of emotional intelligence and articulacy possible while still not functioning highly on performance intelligence. On the session following her birthday she described her feelings about her birth.

> I just wanted to be inside my mummy's tummy again. I wondered what was the point of coming out – I am pushed around on the underground and they make me feel small. I think it was nice in there. I was thinking why was I born and why did my mother bring me up like this.

Birthdays are powerful occasions for all of us and bring back different memories according to whether we experienced ourselves as wanted or not. Birthdays are particularly painful for many handicapped individuals as it reminds them of their birth and the response to it. The words of the client described above were not only virtually indistinguishable from a non-handicapped client, they were more emotionally in touch than many ordinary people are able to be.

Handicap as a defence against trauma

Freud (1920) defined trauma as

> any excitations from outside which are powerful enough to break through the protective shield. . . . Such an event, as an external trauma, is bound to provoke a disturbance on a large scale in the function of the organism's energy and to set in motion every possible defensive measure.

The experience of trauma, in our experience, is a common one for handicapped individuals and their families and carers. The smile of the handicapped child or adults we find often to be not of happiness but rather of appeasement and fear towards an aggressor. It seems that the handicapped baby tries to help the parents by being friendly and dependent even though disturbance breaks through. Many of our referrals begin 'X is a charming boy. He is really happy and smiles all the time. It is just that he keeps attacking staff or banging his head.' We have found that the experience of trauma is so difficult to process that manic smiling and activity from the client or care staff is a mechanism put into play to avert depression. The fantasy that handicapped people are friendly as a group (rather than that some individuals are and some are not) is part of the denial of grief. The moment beams are returned only by an ordinary smile, the moment hugs are gently withdrawn from and a hand is offered instead, we see the smile turn into depression and rage.

The earliest reference we have found on handicap as a defence against trauma is from Clark (1933), who wrote a book on the way in which regression to a severely handicapped state can be a retreat from traumatic experiences at birth and later of not being wanted. A disturbing contemporary finding (Sinason 1986, 1988a, 1988b, 1989a, 1989d; Buchanan and Oliver, 1977; Cohen and Warren, 1987) is the link between sexual abuse and handicap. In several cases, mental handicap seemed to provide a screen against acknowledging the reality of sexual abuse, a matter which first came to light during the course of psychotherapy. The 'screen' of mental handicap provides a state of not knowing about, as a protection against the terrible feelings of abuse and rejection. Long-term psychotherapy has provided some significant improvements in the ability to function as the traumatic events are gradually faced. It is well established that learning difficulties, quite apart from mental handicap, are a regular feature of sexual abuse and physical abuse (Bentovim, 1987). This is not surprising. If knowing and seeing involve knowing and seeing terrible things, it is not surprising that not-knowing, becoming stupid, becomes a defence (Sinason, 1991).

However, it is a mad defence as it takes away the possibility of communication and gaining help or understanding.

Maria (Sinason, 1988b) was a 5 year-old girl with learning difficulties. Once she was able to express more of her experience of abuse, more of her intelligence returned to her. In one session (p. 104) she tore the head off the father doll. 'Stupid daddy, I've thrown his head away. Now he is only a body. He can't see, hear or know. He doesn't know what I am doing to him because he had no mind.' She threw him across the room and laughed angrily and then did the same with the mother doll. She wanted me and her parents to know what she had felt like, deprived of her head, her sight, her intellect. Maria, however, was not mentally handicapped. It was easy to see that her learning difficulties had an emotional base.

However, our own clinical work and that of colleagues has clarified instances where the primary mental handicap is actually caused by abuse. As a consequence of trauma a mentally handicapped state of mind can be used as a defence against the memory of physical or sexual abuse. Buchanan and Oliver (1977) also point to abuse and neglect as an actual *cause* of mental retardation in certain cases. Recent American research (Cohen and Warren, 1987) also links abuse with acquired disability.

Pioneering researcher Oliver (1988) in fact coined the term 'VIMH', violence-induced mental handicap, concluding that 'Ill treatment in the home accounts for such conditions [mental handicap] in 5% or more of all handicapped people'. Although these figures are new, the knowledge is not. For example, ever since psychoanalysis began, the link between trauma and handicap has been regularly examined.

It is not just physical, sexual and emotional abuse that create trauma. As already stated, the Office of Health Economics (1973) describes mental ability as the product of three factors, 'inherited constitution, modification or injuries caused by pre- or postnatal injury or disease and conditioning and training of the intellect'. The environment itself can be traumatagenic. Child psychiatrist Michael Rutter (Rutter et al., 1970) has shown that poverty, psychiatric illness, unemployment and large numbers of siblings are relevant to mild mental handicap.

Exaggeration of handicap as a defence

We have a simple organising principle that we have found useful in our work (Stokes, 1987). This is to distinguish between a handicapped and a non-handicapped self. The distinction derives from Wilfred Bion's (1967) differentiation between psychotic and non-psychotic functioning in the same person. We therefore find it helpful to think of a distinction between the handicapped person in a state in which handicap is predominant and another state in which a more perceptive and less damaged self is predominant. In seeing handicap as a state which people move in and out of (Stokes, 1987) we also acknowledge that according to the severity or organicity of the handicap, the unhandicapped mode might only be seen rarely. However, we feel that with nearly all our clients there is extra potential that is not being fulfilled.

One factor which impedes development is the exaggeration of secondary handicap as a defence. A bright middle-class undergraduate told her friends she was sure she had failed her degree. Her real fear was that she had not gained a first or an upper second. Her hurt at not doing as well as she wanted in terms of her own high expectations was denied through exaggerating the extent to which she had fallen short. Sometimes, the gap between what is wanted and what the reality is can be so painfully narrow that it is unbearable. One client (Sinason, 1986) had a speech defect that came from his cerebral palsy. It was a mild one. However, he found the difference between his voice and a normal voice so unbearable that he exaggerated the level of his defect.

In the course of therapy, when the therapist became suspicious that the distorted voice was a facsimile and commented on this, he revealed the real sound of his voice. Only then could his hurt at his handicap be thought about. Similarly, his contorted physical position proved an equal exaggeration. We now ask all workers to consider carefully whether their clients are exaggerating their difficulties.

Another client (Stokes, 1987) was a young mildly handicapped woman who had cerebral palsy as a result of perinatal anoxia. She was referred because she was hitting other clients at the day centre she attended and also scratching herself severely and smearing herself and her clothing with faeces (self-injurious behaviour and violence are the most common causes of referral). At the first meeting her pigeon-toed walk and odd lilting voice encouraged a view of her as stupid and childish. In the course of the first meeting she muttered 'It is too late'. When the therapist wondered aloud if she felt it was too late to repair her handicaps her voice changed to a more normal tone. She was then able to say she had thought there would be an operation to make her 'look more pretty like other girls' but now she knew that was not possible. When the therapist suggested she must feel quite hopeless and angry she agreed, saying that was why she attacked and scratched her body. When it was then suggested that she got some satisfaction from this as it expressed her rage with her parents for giving her a handicapped body she returned to her false lilting voice. When this was commented on she spoke in a more normal voice saying 'I am angry'. The amount of anger that is encapsulated within exaggerated secondary handicap is enormous. Dealing with the secondary handicap means having to deal with the rage and grief that follows.

When 10 year-old Barry (Sinason, 1986) exaggerated his handicap so as to be virtually inaudible he enjoyed the fact that the normal population was being fooled. Instead of being the victim of his handicap he had found a way of handicapping others. Every person who spoke to him and struggled to hear him was turned into an idiot. Similarly, when 12 year-old Mary who had Down's syndrome aggressively cuddled everyone she met she was somewhere enjoying the violence of abusive physical contact.

To have a handicap is to have something that happened that was out of anyone's personal control. If that trauma is not worked through there is instead a wish to resort to omnipotent thinking. To make up for the loss of self-determination, a new facsimile handicap is made or a real one is exaggerated. This provides a sense of control, albeit a self-abusive one. This furnishes an omnipotent fantasy that if some of one's handicaps can be deliberately created or distorted then the real handicap could similarly be removed at will. As shown by the example of the undergraduate, this defence is not confined to handicapped people. Often, school pupils who are performing badly prefer to say 'I only failed because I didn't work hard enough' rather than feel they could not have done much better.

Another important use of handicap in this way is to cling on to an immature way of being or relating, as a defence against dangerous impulses such as sexual or violent feelings. Another way relates to Cohen's (1986) concepts about physical handicap – it can be more acceptable to see oneself as deficient than as hostile or sexual.

Opportunist handicap

Finally, there is the concept of opportunist handicap (Sinason, 1986) which covers a more pernicious use of handicap to express hostility and envy. If we think how a minor illness, like a cold, can become a vehicle for carrying infantile aspects of the self, it is not surprising that handicap should do the same. If someone is bearing the burden of a handicap on a daily basis, it clearly depletes many internal resources leaving the individual prey to inner disturbance. Depending on how lucky the individual is with their own constitution, the handicap can either deplete inner resources or, more seriously, not only deplete resources but excite and attract disturbance. The handicap can become a magnet for every emotional difficulty and disturbance the individual has. In this difficult constellation we regularly find envy of normality, hatred for parental sexuality that created them and refusal to mourn or acknowledge the loss of the healthy self. Howard (Sinason, 1988c), a violent young man who was multiply handicapped, ferociously demanded 'a woman'. He did not want to think about his problem or to consider that a sexual relationship was part of an emotional connection. His unworked-through self-disgust at his handicap was projected on to handicapped women. He wanted a 'normal' woman in the absence of any real relationship. Once he became clear that therapy would not give him a woman, but would allow him the space to understand his difficulty in relating to anyone, he could not bear the pain.

A handicapped young man treated by Joan Symington would lift his hand only a tiny amount when he wanted a bus to stop. Inevitably the bus driver did not see, and drove on, leaving him repeating statements on how unfair the world was. One aspect of this complex situation is a self-inflicted attack on his own capacity which allows him to remain in a disgruntled angry state in which he can claim there is nothing good in the world. That which could be good and give him something he needs has been spoiled by a violent reaction. This can be an envious response to the self who is capable of asking for help as well as a denial of the need for anything outside of himself.

Envy, with its effect of spoiling, mocking and devaluing that which is good (Joseph, 1986), is an essential component in opportunist handicap. Most of us have had fantasies of becoming an Einstein, Austen or Beethoven, which slowly dwindled as realism grew. Some of our adolescent admiration for our heroes and heroines might have been tinged with jealousy, which still allows us to recognise something good. Jealousy is quite a distance from envy, however. If we all find it hard to struggle with our limitations it is not surprising that this is more painful for the handicapped individual. To face such limitations without being destructively envious is extremely difficult.

One client (Stokes, 1987) would regularly ask questions that made the therapist feel stupid and uncertain because he neither knew why the client was asking or what the answer was. For example, in the room where the therapist sat with his back to the window the client asked in a silly voice 'Is it sunny outside?' Another client (Sinason, 1990a) would ask 'What's your name Valerie?' In instances like this, the client was wanting the *therapist* to feel confused and stupid. In addition there was an aggressive, envious and mocking quality in these questions.

Conclusion

Handicap is a blow to the sense of the self and a blow to the family and the community, however lovingly responded to. This means that it automatically involves loss, grief and trauma. As a way of struggling with these emotions many handicapped individuals find defensive ways of surviving. These can involve both denial and exaggeration of the handicap to foster the illusion of control. Handicap deals a severe blow to the personality which becomes weakened in its struggle with the envious and destructive aspects of the self. Through an understanding of the unconscious psychological factors influencing handicap, it is now possible to provide psychoanalytic psychotherapy for mentally handicapped people. Such understanding is also of use in helping workers in various settings to better orientate themselves towards their clients and, indeed, in clarifying the nature of attacks on intelligent thinking in everyday life for everyone.

References and further reading

Ammerman, R. et al. 'Maltreatment of children and adults with multiple handicaps', *Journal of the Multihandicapped Person*, 1 (2).

Bentovim, A. (1987) 'The diagnosis of child sexual abuse', *Bulletin of the Royal College of Psychiatrists*, 11: 295–9.

Bicknell, J. (1983) 'The psychopathology of handicap', *British Journal of Medical Psychology*, 56: 167–78.

Bion, W.R. (1967) *Second Thoughts*. London: Heinemann.

Buchanan, A. and Oliver, J. (1977) 'Abuse and neglect as a cause of mental retardation', *British Journal of Psychiatry* 131 (November): 458–67.

Chidester, L. and Menninger, K. (1936) 'The application of psychoanalytic methods to the study of mental retardation', *American Journal of Orthopsychiatry*, 6: 616–25.

Clark, P. (1933) *The Nature and Treatment of Amentia*. London: Bailliere.

Cohen, S. (1986) 'Sense of defect', *Journal of the American Psychoanalytical Association*, 34: 47–56.

Cohen, S. and Warren, R. (1987) 'Preliminary survey of family abuse of children served by United Cerebral Palsy Centres', *Developmental Medicine and Child Neurology*, 29: 12–18.

Freud, S. (1920) *Beyond the Pleasure Principle*. London: Hogarth.

Hollins, S. and Evered, C. (1990) 'Group process and content: the challenge of mental handicap', *Group Analysis*, 23 (1).

Hollins, S. and Grimer, M. (1988) *Going Somewhere, People with Mental Handicaps and Their Pastoral Care*. London: New Library of Pastoral Care, SPCK.

Hollins, S. and Sireling, L. (1989) *The Last Taboo*. A Video on Death and Mental Handicap. Available from St George's Medical School, London.

Joseph, B. (1986) 'Envy in everyday life', *Psychoanalytic Psychotherapy*, 2: 13–22.

Office of Health Economics (1973) *Mental Handicap*. London: OHE.

Oliver, J. (1988) 'Successive generations of child maltreatment', *British Journal of Psychiatry*, 153: 543–53.

Rutter, M. et al. (1970) *Education, Health and Behaviour*. London: Longman.

Scott, Clifford, W. (1963) 'The psychotherapy of the mental defective', *Canadian Psychiatric Association Journal*, 8 (5).

Sinason, V. (1986) 'Secondary mental handicap and its relationship to trauma', *Psychoanalytic Psychotherapy*, 2 (2): 131–54.

Sinason, V. (1988a) 'Dolls and bears; from symbolic equation to symbol. The use of different play material for sexually abused children', *British Journal of Psychotherapy*, Summer.

Sinason, V. (1988b) 'Smiling, swallowing, sickening and stupefying. The effect of abuse on the child', *Psychoanalytic Psychotherapy*, Summer.

Sinason, V. (1989a) Chapter on 'Sexual abuse', in H. Wolff et al. *UCH Handbook of Psychiatry. An Integrated Approach*. London: Duckworth.

Sinason, V. (1989b) 'Mental handicap and sexual abuse', in A. Craft and H. Brown (eds), *Thinking the Unthinkable*. FPA and BIMH.

Sinason, V. (1989c) 'The psycholinguistics of discrimination', in *Crisis of Identity*. London: Free Association Books.

Sinason, V. (1989d) 'Psychoanalytical psychotherapy and its application', *Journal of Social Work Practice*, 4 (1).

Sinason, V. (1991, forthcoming) *The Sense in Stupidity: Psychotherapy and Mental Handicap*. London: Free Association Books.

Stokes, J. (1987) 'Insights from psychotherapy', paper presented at International Symposium on Mental Handicap, RSM, 25 February.

Symington, N. (1981) 'The psychotherapy of a subnormal patient', *British Journal of Medical Psychology*, 54: 187–99.

Symington, J. (1985) 'The analysis of a mentally handicapped patient' (unpublished).

Winnicott, D. W. (1971) *Playing and Reality*. London: Tavistock.

5

Coming to Terms with Learning Difficulties: The Effects of Groupwork and Group Processes on Stigmatised Identity

Susan Szivos and Eileen Griffiths

Introduction: learning difficulties as stigmatised identity

'Stigma' is defined by Goffman (1963) as the discrepancy between a person's actual and virtual identity: that is, the difference between how one actually is (for example, having learning difficulties) and how one is normally expected to be by society (i.e. competent, independent and so on). Several writers have testified that many people with learning difficulties are aware of stigmatisation and its negative consequences. Edgerton (1967), for example, found that the ex-patients he studied expended considerable energy in trying to 'pass' for normal and attempted to 'deny' their handicap. Gibbons (1985) and Zetlin and Turner (1984) reported that friendships were problematic for many people with learning difficulties such that, although often rejected by non-disabled people, they considered other people with learning difficulties as inferior candidates for sharing social activities. This almost certainly contributes to the social isolation experienced by many adults with a learning difficulty (Donegan and Potts, 1988; Gilkey and Zetlin, 1987).

Similarly, the dominant service philosophy of normalisation or social role valorisation (we refer to the version expounded by Wolfensberger [1972, 1983, 1984; Wolfensberger and Thomas, 1983], rather than the versions developed by Nirje, 1969 or O'Brien, 1987) seems to be an approach which endorses 'passing' in Goffman's sense. Put briefly, this philosophy endorses accruing socially valued roles and status to people with learning difficulties by enhancing their image and competencies. This twin emphasis on image and competency enhancement implies a reduction in the discrepancy between actual and virtual identity. In so doing, normalisation and social role valorisation theorists assume that if the behaviour and images of handicapped people are improved, public attitudes and the quality of life of such people will also be improved. Wolfensberger and Thomas' (1983) discussion of the 'conservatism corollary', in which they state that a person at risk of devaluation in society should be encouraged to take on additional positively valued trappings (such as suits and ties) in order to balance their devalued role, and Wolfensberger's (1988) distrust of specialist services, are examples in which the need to 'pass' is given particular prominence in image-making. The same could be said for the emphasis throughout the normalisation and social role valorisation writings that friendships with non-disabled people are to be valued more than friendships with disabled people (for example, Wolfensberger, 1972).

Given these emphases on image and competency and their consequent de-emphasising of the individual's subjective sense of self and well-being (for further discussion see Briton, 1979 and Corbett, 1988), it is not surprising that people with learning difficulties experience the difficulties in forming friendships that they do. Our aim as therapists was therefore to explore the potential therapeutic benefits in *not* 'passing for normal' or 'denying' disability, but in exploring alternative methods of understanding and coping with a 'spoiled' identity.

Alternatives to 'passing': consciousness-raising and the literature on loss

According to the literature on social identity (Tajfel, 1981) and consciousness-raising, 'passing for normal' has unwanted psychological and social consequences: it may exacerbate a sense of shame at belonging to a stigmatised group; it perpetuates the notion that bearers of the stigma are inferior potential partners for social activities; and it does not mitigate stigma for the group members who do not succeed in passing. In other words the assimilationist perspective does not necessarily make the discrepancy between actual and virtual identity any more positive. The experience of other stigmatised groups has been that an alternative to passing has been to acknowledge and rally round the stigma, whether it be skin colour, gender or sexual orientation. The aims of this alternative, which we refer to as Consciousness-Raising (CR), were overtly political and involved bringing attention to the ways in which stigmatised people were subject to prejudice and exploitation.

However, it was soon realised that CR also had therapeutic benefits (Kravetz, 1981). Through exploration of the meaning of the stigma, disadvantaged group members have been able to develop a strong and positive group identity, thereby ridding themselves of the feelings of shame attached to their group membership. Unlike normalisation, which seeks to minimise the use of labelling and group cohesion, the positive use of labels has been a noteworthy feature of CR, and slogans which re-evaluated the status of the group such as 'Black is beautiful' enabled individuals to feel positively about their group identity. CR can be further contrasted with normalisation in that it attempts to re-evaluate the existing discrepancy between actual and virtual identity as something positive.

Thus, the CR paradigm implies that there might be benefits to people with learning difficulties in talking openly about their stigmatised identity. As well as being able to revalue self and others with disabilities, benefits might also include: reducing the confusion which is generated when individuals encounter unclear labels and stigmatising behaviour together with 'polite' disavowal that there is anything wrong; making more realistic attributions about one's abilities and disabilities, including reducing feelings of blame about the disability; increasing self-esteem by improving the status of the group, and by increasing individuals' sense of responsibility towards initiating action which might benefit the group.

As regards the Loss paradigm; handicap, conceptualised as a discrepancy between actual and virtual identity, implies a 'minus' or a loss of the perfect identity one might have wished to have. In growing up, the stigmatised individual learns the 'normal' view-point, then experiences loss as he or she realises that he or she in some way falls short of it (Goffman, 1963).

Elisabeth Kubler-Ross' (1970) book *On Death and Dying* suggested that in coming to terms with death, individuals experience emotional stages of shock, denial, anger, sadness and acceptance. Her original paradigm has been extended to many other kinds of loss: bereavement, health, and the loss parents may experience to the expected 'normal' child when a handicapped child is born (for example, Byrne and Cunningham, 1985; Friedrich et al., 1985; Murray-Parkes, 1971; Suelze and Keenan, 1981).

The Loss paradigm similarly implies that there are potential benefits in talking openly about the stigma and loss associated with disability. Talking about these matters should enable the individual to come to an understanding and acceptance of the emotions associated with loss; to recognise that these emotions are part of a normal rather than a pathological process; to allow alienating and defensive behaviour to be dropped; and to achieve self-acceptance.

Running a group for adults with a mild learning difficulty

Our experience in learning difficulty services convinced us of the feasibility of trying to run a group to explore the issues and processes described above. The rest of the chapter describes our efforts to do so; as far as we know, these paradigms have not been applied to people with learning difficulties before. We wished to see whether forging a positive identity and exploring the emotions associated with loss as an alternative to 'passing' are feasible ways of working with people with learning difficulties.

After consultation with local service providers who were asked to nominate individuals with low self-esteem who might benefit from taking part in a group, we selected seven young adults who were at the mild end of the continuum of learning difficulties. These individuals had sufficient verbal skills to enable them to take part in the group, and agreed to do so. Four of the group members were women; three were men.

The group was facilitated by two members of the local Community Mental Handicap Team (including the co-author), and ran for 13 weekly sessions, each lasting one and a half hours. The group sessions were videotaped to allow a more leisurely analysis of the processes which took place.

Throughout the group, the facilitators stressed that the members could share experiences concerning their disability and how it affected their lives. They emphasised that by bringing topics of a potentially painful nature to the group, members could gain support from others, validate their experiences, and discuss new ways of coping with problems in the future. The facilitators took the lead from the group members in the topics that were discussed: most of the group members introduced items of concern to them such as work, relationships, family, and how they found out that they had a disability. The facilitators' primary role was to ensure that for each topic every group member was encouraged to make a contribution. They also attended to the smooth running of the group in stressing that group members should support each other, and in managing any behaviour that might have become disruptive to the group.

The group processes

From the rich material which emerged from the groups, we identified six different ways in which the group members talked about their handicaps. We called these Denial and Resistance; Statement; Discovery; Exploration; Meaning; and Acceptance. We now give a short description of the main characteristics of each way of talking about handicap before going on to describe and illustrate them more fully. For brevity we will describe each of these ways of talking about handicap as a 'phase' that the group members went through. Later we will discuss more fully whether these phases showed any therapeutic progression, as do Kubler-Ross' stages.

1   *Denial and Resistance*: The individuals resist coming to the group, deny any common group membership, and avoid discussing anything related to that membership.
2   *Statement*: Group members may make a bald statement concerning membership of the stigmatised group. The label is seen as imposed; the language is that of other people. The individual has not explored the personal meaning of the label.
3   *Discovery*: In this group the members broached the subject of disability by describing how they first found out about it. They expressed feelings of shock and disbelief in talking about the impact this had on their self-image.
4   *Exploration*: The group members continued to explore the impact of disability on their lives. Some of them expressed confusion around the contradictory ways in which others responded to them: sometimes colluding in their 'passing'; sometimes subjecting them to stigmatising experiences including isolation and rejection, lack of trust, privacy and autonomy.
5   *Meaning*: Having explored the various themes associated with living with an identity which includes disability, the group could arrive at an understanding of what their learning difficulty meant for them. This often meant changing a global label or evaluation of themselves to a more specific one, thereby making their overall self-evaluation more realistic and positive.
6   *Acceptance*: Arriving at a meaning of disability that was not globally negative facilitated the group members' acceptance of themselves as people with specific areas of disability. This acceptance was manifested in several ways. The first cluster relates to their acceptance of each other. The second cluster relates to their ability to acknowledge and 'own' the emotions associated with their disability and loss.

What now follows is a series of illustrations of each of these phases. Wherever possible we have given these in the words of the group members themselves. Where names are given, these have been changed to protect the group members. 'Fac.' stands for facilitator.

Denial and Resistance
Acknowledging any sort of group identity was extremely difficult for the group members. This surfaced in a variety of ways: some people, although physically present, resisted participating in the group and distanced themselves from it. Jay and Abe, for example,

complained that the group was 'boring', refused to answer questions, and giggled and pushed each other. They also remained silent for long periods, including maintaining silence when asked a direct question. That this was defensive was inferred from the fact that this behaviour occurred at 'difficult' times – for instance, when they were asked if they had anything in common with the others, and when the conversation was about feelings of anger and rejection.

This was the most difficult behaviour to deal with in the group. The facilitators confronted the giggling and pushing by saying that this was unfair to the others and unacceptable, and gave Jay and Abe the option of leaving the group. They chose to remain and this stopped further 'horseplaying' and complaints about the group being boring. However, their long silences did re-emerge periodically throughout the groups and were very difficult to deal with, although both responded well when they had the attention of the group on matters that were of great concern to them.

The facilitators also overcame a certain amount of resistance by stressing that the group 'belonged' to the group members. If they wanted to just come and chat and pretend everything was alright, they were at liberty to do so, but this might not be the best way to use the group time. Much time in the earlier sessions was spent in establishing an environment in which group members could start talking about relatively 'safe' topics, such as work, and indeed as the group progressed, all of the group members overcame their reticence and talked openly about their problems for most of the sessions.

Despite the other members clearly finding the idea of the group attractive, there was also some initial difficulty in recognising a shared focus or experience among the group members. Paul agreed that they had 'some sort of problem', but didn't know what it could be. Initially, Paul claimed not to be able to remember anything about his childhood, although later it became clear that he had good reasons for not wanting to remember it: he had had many painful experiences of bullying, teasing and feeling guilty about having to be protected and causing his parents anxiety. Likewise, Rick claimed not to remember any label like 'handicapped' being used to refer to him. In most cases, the establishment of a trusting environment, and the modelling provided by both the group members and the facilitators in talking about their feelings helped the group members to talk about their feelings and experiences.

One of the group members, Eve, used denial much more fully. For the duration of the group she denied having any problem that could be referred to as a 'handicap': she would only describe herself as 'shy'. We learned, during the group, that she was supported in this self-conception by her parents, so this type of denial is more far-reaching than the initial resistance of joining the group, and will be discussed further, later.

Beth, while not using denial as completely as any of the others, had considerable insight into why it could be useful:

> *Beth*: It's hard to talk about that just now because, I must say, if I think about all that too much it just won't help me to cope . . . it won't help me to concentrate on the work I'm doing. It won't help me to . . . try to make the most of the life . . . that I've got.

Statement

We have defined this as the phase in which group members acknowledged having been labelled, but the discussion of the label makes it clear that they are using other people's words, not their own. There is recognition of a problem, but also denial that it impinges on the individual's sense of self. Given the intensely personal nature of the labelling experience, this can be seen as a defensive process akin to intellectualisation in which the problem is 'split off' from 'me' and is displaced into the realm of abstract categories. Beth and Gwen talked in this way of places where they had stayed so that the label seemed almost to apply more to the buildings than to the people within them:

> *Fac.*: Can you tell the other people what it is, because they won't know?
> *Gwen*: It's a Camphill Trust with main buildings, sheltered workshop, for mentally handicapped and those who have, like, mental and nervous breakdowns.
> *Beth*: Sort of 'rehabilitation', yes. There are the occasional ones that won't really benefit a lot, but they will benefit a bit, so they keep them there. . . . It's a sort of training centre.

In this phase talking about handicap is done through the medium of what other people have said to them rather than through examining their own experience – for example, being told they were 'difficult' children or classified as 'disabled' or 'handicapped'. The acknowledgement of the label is curiously devoid of emotion; what emotion is shown is carefully detached and displaced as though to show it for oneself would be to expose one's most private and painful vulnerabilities, for instance:

> *Paul*: My parents have told some people that I'm mentally handicapped or brain damaged.
> *Fac.*: . . . What do you think about it? . . . Do you see yourself as having difficulties?
> *Paul*: Not really, don't know.
> *Fac.*: Not sure?
> *Paul*: No.

This seemed almost to serve the function of 'testing' the group's response. When people weren't shocked, and when others talked about the labels that had been used on them, Paul went on to talk about what the labels meant. This phase therefore seemed to facilitate the later phases of exploration and meaning.

Beth also projected her feelings of anger and sadness on to the more abstract categories of a physically handicapped girl whom she had known and other children with Childhood Autism (her own diagnosis):

> *Beth*: . . . At home my family know a girl called Freda, and she's far more handicapped . . . than any of us because she can't use her arms and legs. . . . She's very angry that she's been born like that at all because she's got a reasonable intelligence and yet she can't do half the things that we can do simply because she can't use her fingers and arms and legs. . . . I think it must be very difficult because all her sisters are normal, and if she had been normal it would have been quite marvellous because there would have been two identical twins, and instead she's had to put up with a tragedy. . . . It's almost double the handicap because not only is she handicapped but it probably affected her sister as well. And I just find it very very sad, you know.
>
> *Beth*: . . . there are children in hospital that can't say anything at all; I think sometimes it's because of government cuts and things like that they're denied the chances of getting some therapy to help them talk a bit. And they might . . . never learn to say anything because they might find it too difficult to do so without help; that makes me feel a bit angry because then they're just locked inside their own little worlds and they just can't communicate with other people and I think there's some that would . . . very much like to be able to talk to other people.

The parallels became clear in later sessions: Beth also has a sister (who had to grow up very quickly because of having a sister like Beth), and had a mother who had to work very hard to 'get through' to her.

Discovery

This way of talking about disability is the one which impinges most on the Loss paradigm. For all the group members who could remember when they first learnt about their handicap, this discovery was a time of considerable emotional stress, and Kubler-Ross' stages of shock, denial, anger and sadness were expressed by the group members.

Also, there was not necessarily a single occasion when this occurred; some group members reported several instances on which the news came to them; as with the conveying of any kind of bad news, they simply needed time to assimilate the information and its import to them. The repetition of this 'discovery' is also an indication of the amount of shock, disbelief and confusion that was involved in learning of their stigma, but it also mirrors certain life transitions (like going to school) in which the individual's status is reconfirmed, pointing to the need for counselling at each life transition rather than once and for all. So, for instance, Beth spoke of finding out about her handicap as a series of events:

> *Beth*: I think in a way I realised it when I was little, when I was in Guy's Hospital, but I wasn't really sure what to think. Then I was older I suddenly got . . . ill for some reason . . . I got very depressed . . . I had a lot of drugs and then I went to hospital for 18 months because I was quite ill. And I think . . . it must have been round about when I was 13 that I realised that I had something – that something wasn't right . . . I was at this school with other girls that were handicapped. . . .

The shock experienced by some of the group members was exacerbated by the fact that some of them learnt about their disability in rather a heartless way. For instance:

> *Gwen*: (In hospital) they used to make notes about people in general, and I saw that on mine they'd written 'certain char . . . certain characteristics of Down's syndrome', anyway. And that just got me thinking.
> *Fac.*: Had . . . anybody said 'Down's syndrome' to you before that?
> *Gwen*: Not like that, not at all, no.
> *Fac.*: So that was the first time that you . . . heard that you might have some of those characteristics?
> *Gwen*: Yes it was. 'Cause I can see that Henry and John [group home members] have got it because they really look it . . . you can tell just by looking at them that they've got it. But I just, I couldn't believe it, I just couldn't believe what I was reading.

We witnessed almost at first hand this stage in people's lives when Eve came to the group extremely angry and confused that she'd received a letter inviting her to a meeting for 'mentally handicapped'.

> *Fac.*: Eve, . . . does it affect how you feel about yourself when you get letters like that? Do you start to question?
> *Eve*: Sometimes I do, like I did last night.
> *Fac.*: What sort of things do you start to wonder about then?
> *Eve*: I wondered why I wasn't, er, if I wasn't handicapped why they sent me one. And I told my Mum about it, and she said I'm not; she said they made a mistake; they probably sent everyone those letters.

The group members' testimony indicates the emotional turmoil involved in learning of one's handicap. This raises many questions for therapists. The first is clearly one of sensitivity. Gwen (and other of the group members) did not learn about their disabilities in a supportive and accepting way. As we will see, this did not help her future adjustment to her feelings about her disability and her beliefs about the way people would respond to her.

The next question is, can such news ever be communicated in a supportive and accepting way, or is it best to allow the individual to remain unaware of his or her handicap? Eve did not wish to discuss handicap, preferring instead to think of herself as shy. Should she have been told unequivocally that she had a learning disability or not? This is a complex issue which we will return to later, but for now we will leave the reader with a quotation from Beth which most fully vindicates our assumption that there is a need to talk things through:

> *Beth*: Well, I wish I had time to talk about it when I needed it before, but no one ever offered it. I don't think anyone ever realised just how hard it is to come through something like being ill, [having Childhood Austism] and trying to come to terms with life again.

Exploration

In this phase we have put the group members' descriptions of their daily lives as they are affected by their handicaps. A common feature in the group members' lives was the lack of autonomy and other ways of being treated that would be associated with a much younger child. Not having their aspirations reacted to with seriousness was a problem that became acute for two of the group members, Jay and Abe, when they contemplated marriage. Jay relates the first reactions of her fiancé's parents:

> *Jay*: Well, first of all we were talking to Abe's [fiancé] Mum and she was all for it. She said if she had the money she'd give it to us. She told Abe's Dad, and he got really angry so we stopped saying we wanted to. . . . My Mum would always tell me what was said, but Abe's Dad, he wouldn't say anything; he'd tell Abe's Mum, but she was always being told not to tell us, but she did.

Despite their parents' attempts to hide it from them, both Jay and Abe were aware that it was their handicap that presented the real difficulty for their parents to their hopes for marriage:

> *Fac.*: . . . What do you think your parents would think about it if you were all somebody who. . . .
> *Jay*: What, normal?
> *Fac.*: . . . Do you think they'd take it more seriously?
> *Jay*: I think so, yes.

Many of the group members felt excluded from important decisions that were made about their lives by parents and professionals. In Rick's case, following his last review he was told that what had been discussed was none of his business:

> *Rick*: I've just . . . had one and I didn't attend. I was in the workroom . . . I asked my Mum what it was about, she said 'Oh, it's nothing to do with you'. And I'm going into a home this Christmas.
>
> *Fac.*: . . . What do you think of that? It'll affect you a little bit, doesn't it, where you live?
>
> *Rick*: . . . It'll be a bit strange because it'll be the first time I've been away from home.

The theme of stigmatisation and the need to 'manage' stigma arose several times throughout the groups. Every group member had been teased at school; for some, this continued to be a problem. Teasing is a stone which sends out many and far-reaching ripples in people's lives. Quite apart from the isolation and lack of confidence experienced by all the group members, it sets up its own tension within the family. For instance, the parent is put in the dilemma whether to protect or not to protect the teased child; siblings behave in ways which express both their jealousy for the 'favoured' child, but also their awareness of their role as 'protectors' themselves. In Paul's case this contributed to feelings of resentment and distance on the part of his older brother.

The parental dilemma of how to respond to their child's obvious vulnerability has other far-reaching consequences. Paul acknowledged that he felt he was overprotected, and realised that this was because his mother felt 'scared' for him. Both he and Eve were trapped in a dynamic of having to protect their parents' fearfulness by being shy: for both, the shyness itself and the functions it fulfilled became extremely handicapping.

A final intrapsychic consequence of teasing is the feeling of always being an outsider, of not fitting in, of being rejected. Sometimes this feeling comes from the world 'outside' the disability, sometimes it is experienced as not fitting into the labelled group. For Gwen, being handicapped means 'being different from all the rest of the family', but also feeling out of place wherever she goes; Beth felt herself to be left out of things by her brothers and sisters, and a work placement kept her in a constant state of feeling not quite right:

> *Beth*: I found that for some reason or other whatever I did in that bakery there was a sort of air of dissatisfaction, they were not always too happy with what you'd done, I don't quite know why.
>
> *Gwen*: I thought I'd learn to accept it and try to be at X [the group home] . . . but I still feel as if I'm being rejected. . . . A lot of them are very handicapped and I just feel that I don't belong, some-

how . . . I want to try and find somewhere where I can fit in and be like everybody else.

A further contributory factor to the group members' unease and isolation was the tension between the uncertain success of 'passing' and the shame of revealing biographical information that is part of the stigma management. Disability is a highly taboo topic. Even within the group, people found it difficult to articulate the very words 'handicap' and 'disability', prefacing them with hesitations, or replacing them with circumlocutions. How much more should this be so 'outside'. When the source of the person's rejection can never be directly tackled, the result is confusion and a feeling of grasping for a difference that is both intangible and unmentionable.

This tension between telling and passing is strongly illustrated in the way Gwen talks about her disability; despite her considerable competence, the fear of being discredited is never far away:

> *Gwen*: But a while ago . . . I think it was when I first started the cooking class that I thought it was beginning to show, for other people seemed to be looking rather anxiously at me.
> *Fac.*: You say you thought it was beginning to show? Can you tell me how? Or can you tell other people what was beginning to show?
> *Gwen*: Well, I think it was mainly because I had to ask . . . because I was having trouble with my – I can't explain, but I just felt awkward. So I thought they knew I was handicapped . . . they probably just guessed, or whatever. A lot of people, one person in particular . . . at my English class, when I said about being handicapped and so on, she said to me 'You're not handicapped'. I just couldn't believe it . . . now I'm not sure whether I'm handicapped or not.

In Gwen's case, her experience of being suspected of having Down's syndrome is important in understanding her fears that the handicap is somehow visible:

> *Gwen*: I can see that Henry and John have got it because they really look it. But I just couldn't believe it. . . . 'Cause it's obviously important to know what that means, to know how another person feels about you, especially someone like me who gets very close to friends: we talk about all sorts of things like problems, mostly problems, but we just talk like good friends.
> *Fac.*: Do you think . . . it's important to know about that to know how they feel about you; do you think that some people would feel differently about you if they knew you had some characteristics of Down's syndrome?
> *Gwen*: I think some people would, actually. They might feel pretty bad themselves. . . . They might not want to get involved with anyone like it – when they already have.

Clearly the fear of being discredited (Goffman's term for having an invisible stigma 'found out') can provide barriers to all kinds of social interactions: initiating a conversation, asking for help or advice, starting a friendship. For Gwen, this stigma has been so great that she has carried her knowledge of her handicap as a guilty secret all her life; even to close friends, she has never revealed her anxieties.

Meaning

As with denial, this phase of talking about handicap was partly characterised by a rejection of imposed labels of 'handicap'. However, it differs from denial and statement in its terminology of personal self-assessment, as individuals explored areas of difficulty in their lives.

The sorts of difficulties that were acknowledged included social and emotional problems. Abe and Beth both talked about emotional problems:

Abe: I don't think I am handicapped or, um, because of my handicap. . . . I'm just a bit slow. It takes a while for me to understand; I'm very emotional, very easily upset.

Beth: I used to get these moods and I found it very hard to control them. I think it's probably almost the same as for an average person, except the average person, because they have more . . . finds it easier to calm down; they don't have to think about it so much.

Beth: There are certain things I have to cope with . . . like Arthur [group home member]. . . . He can be a bit annoying at times, the way he talks to people. And I find it strange that they expect me to be calm all the time, because it is not that easy when I have to work with someone like him.

We felt that psychological growth was shown by these two group members; for Abe this consisted in the fact that within the safety of the group he could acknowledge that he found it difficult to understand things and that this was perhaps the reason for his emotionality. Beth's increasingly mature perspective on her moods as a normal reaction to a difficult living situation is perhaps due to the fact that within the group she was able to describe both her moods and her home environment for the first time.

Others mentioned social difficulties: Abe and Paul felt shyness was a problem, Eve, that it was her major problem: 'It means I can't think of what to say.' Abe admitted to feeling nervous and afraid of looking silly. Other problems were of a more specific and practical nature. Paul felt he needed help in 'organising my life', and in making arrangements to go to places. Jay acknowledged that she was not very good at money, and Eve that she might be 'perhaps slow at some things'. It was important that in the group we did not focus on negative things. For instance, Abe also spoke positively about his abilities:

> *Abe*: 'Cause I mean, I've got a lot going for myself, really. 'Cause I'm more capable than what they are at X [the ATC]. I mean, I've helped Jay [girlfriend] along with her money, you know, when she's been buying things; as soon as she's used up her silver to put her other money to one side. And she's been grateful for the help.

We felt it was especially important for people to have a clearer conception of what their disability meant to them where the 'syndrome' they had been diagnosed as having was itself confusing. Thus, for example, being told, as Gwen was, that 98 per cent of her cells was normal and the other 2 per cent had Down's syndrome was not something that she could attach much sense to: did she 'have it' or not? Similarly, Beth had been told she had 'Childhood Autism', but that mental handicap was something you did not grow out of; now that she was grown up, did she still have it or not? In these cases it was especially important to build up a personally meaningful picture of what their disability entailed.

Nobody mentioned being clever or intelligent (or not) as something that distinguished them from others. This may be because the concept of intelligence is a rather abstract one and the group members were used to thinking in more concrete terms; also a focus of the group was to specify particular areas of competence or incompetence, which would tend to encourage the use of concrete rather than abstract terms. It is also true that in society generally we do not have any easy way of talking about intellectual differences: the subject remains taboo whether one has learning disability or not.

This, then, may be an opportune point at which to examine what the global label 'mental handicap' meant to the group members. (Despite the term 'learning difficulties' having been in use among professionals for some years, the group members were not familiar with the term, and used the terms 'mentally handicapped' or 'disabled' when talking about themselves and others with learning difficulties.) Although most of the group members did not accept the term 'mentally handicapped' for themselves, they did acknowledge difficulties, like 'being slow at some things', that most of us would think of as characterising someone with a mental handicap (or learning difficulty). In order to understand this apparent contradiction it is necessary to see what meaning the label carries for the group members.

It became clear that for the group members the term 'mental handicap' referred to a condition that was clearly visible, often physical, and certainly more severe than any difficulties they had experienced. For Eve, someone who is handicapped is someone who 'acts a bit funny. You can tell by the look of them that they are mentally handicapped.' Abe concurs, 'I think it's the ones that are in wheelchairs that are handicapped. . . . You can tell by the look of them that they are, um, pretty bad . . . some of them are far worse . . . than . . . someone like me or Eve.'

For Gwen and Beth the definition of handicap is something more cognitive (although Gwen, because of her experience of Down's syndrome, maintains the idea that it 'shows').

> *Gwen*: . . . they just don't understand what's really going on. Specially Joe [group home member], for instance. . . . I don't know if he can hear or what, because he's had hearing tests and all this sort of thing, and you can't really tell whether they are listening. . . . They're so different from everybody else. It's hard to tell whether they can understand or not.

Beth has a more complex view of the nature of handicap: 'Some of them are very able and have a fairly normal intelligence, and some of them can't do anything very much at all . . . they can't talk or things like that.' But even for her, the label tends to evoke extremely severe disability:

> *Beth*: You can't really talk to [them] . . . because unfortunately many of them don't really have the ability to hold a sensible conversation . . . a lot of them can't work things out in a logical way because I think their minds just . . . don't seem to work properly.

Acceptance

For us, talking about disability in an accepting way meant two things: self-acceptance and acceptance of others with a disability.

As regards acceptance of other handicapped people, this was manifest in several ways. There were many examples of group members recognising that their support, sympathy and advice would be valued by others in the group. Some group members were able to show compassion and understanding for those more handicapped than themselves, rather than using their presence as an opportunity for downward comparison or derogation. Gwen felt that it would be unfair to criticise a severely handicapped person for not performing certain tasks very well; Jay felt that whatever the degree of handicap, a person still had the right to attend their reviews and to know what was going on in their lives.

There was also evidence that the group members became more comfortable with the idea of seeing other in-group members as peers, friends or possible marriage partners:

> *Fac.*: Do you think it's easier to think about having a relationship with somebody who's got difficulties as well?
>
> *Abe*: I think so.
>
> *Fac.*: About having relationships with 'normal' people, do you think it's easier to have a relationship with somebody who's also . . . got difficulties?
>
> *Jay*: Yes, 'cause then you've got, you're both the same, then . . . it's easier to talk with the person because we're both handicapped or . . . we're both disabled, I suppose.

There was also some comfort acknowledged in having people 'like oneself' around at home and at work. In contrast to Gwen who felt different from all her family, and Paul who found it difficult growing up with a cleverer brother, Abe commented, 'I'm lucky, because my sister's the same as me'.

However, such acceptance was not complete. There were also opportunities for downward comparison that occurred when talking about their relative strengths and weaknesses that were taken up. For example, Jay took the opportunity to taunt Abe about his tendency to fall asleep and not follow what was going on during a temporary absence of the facilitators when the video was left running.

The second kind of acceptance that we consider is self-acceptance. This includes the acknowledgement of one's areas of disability, strengths and weaknesses that we discussed in the previous section on meaning, and of the emotions associated with disability. We have indicated that in the phases of denial and statement, painful emotions are split off from the individual's situation by being displaced on to some other target, denied completely or converted into some more easily experienced emotion such as anger.

Several of the group members were quite angry; Beth at the plight of autistic children; Jay and Abe at 'nosy' professionals and at the facilitator for running the group and bringing issues about disability into salience. While some of this anger is a legitimate part of the mourning process as conceived by Kubler-Ross, we could not help having the impression that some of it was also displaced. The CR paradigm teaches us that when people can acknowledge the source of this anger it can be used more effectively to change discriminating and stigmatizing practices. Dealing with and appropriately expressing anger is one of the pivots around which both the CR and the Loss paradigms turn.

Another way in which emotional acceptance might be shown is in the individual's ability to acknowledge their sadness, as when Gwen comments that 'Being handicapped means I am different from everyone else in my family'.

This provokes the question as to whether the group members expressed acceptance towards their disability in that they were able to say they felt positively about it. Given the way that the group members viewed mental handicap and given the stigma associated with it, it seems unrealistic to ask members to be happy with their lot. Instead, the most 'positive' kind of acceptance that we found was a kind of 'comparative' acceptance in which the person takes comfort in the feeling that 'At least I'm better off than many others', or 'Things could be worse'. For example:

> *Beth*: I think compared to some people I'm very lucky because a lot of them, they can't do things that we take for granted like being able to read a book or . . . being able to go shopping on their own. I was quite lucky because a lot of autistic people don't get better.

There is also a sort of 'compensatory' acceptance; for example, Gwen feels that her grandmother probably liked her best because she was born handicapped, and Beth feels that even though she hasn't got a proper job she can at least contribute to the community 'in a way that's almost as important as a proper job'.

Do the CR and Loss paradigms 'work', and what can we learn from them?

The group did not address the more overtly political aims of CR, but focused instead on its therapeutic implications. We felt justified in this approach for a number of reasons. The group members did show stronger affiliations within the group as it progressed, including less denial and resistance, greater willingness to share advice and experiences and to consider each other as friends, and more compassion for others less well off than themselves. This culminated, towards the end of the group, in an attack by some of the group members on the injustices of the review system which excludes many handicapped people from taking an active part in many major decisions concerning their lives.

As such this vindicates the assumptions of CR in that raising the esteem of the group is a necessary precursor to making the group and its members seem worth fighting for. It also seems to vindicate our assumption that self-acceptance is central to the individual's belief that he or she has both the right and the responsibility to assume greater control in his or her life.

However, it must be said that in-group affiliation was limited. Some group members continued (at times) to reject each other and people with more severe disabilities. No doubt this is due to the low esteem in which people with learning difficulties continue to be held in society: we do give more rewards, power and status to people who are attractive, independent and competent. Thirteen weeks cannot be enought to undo 20 years and more of adverse value judgements (see Baumhardt and Lawrence, 1983).

For CR to succeed fully, therefore, it is critical that people with learning difficulties (and we) be taught to value each other for what they are, rather than merely for the normative images and competencies we try to impose on them. One important task to this end is to explore with handicapped people suitable words, labels and images that would help them to feel positively, rather than negatively, about the 'discrepancy between their actual and virtual identity'. We believe that groups such as the one we have described have a useful part to play in this endeavour.

We also believe that the Loss paradigm provides a sensitive and humane way of working with people with learning difficulties. All the emotions of shock, denial, anger, sadness and acceptance identified by Kubler-Ross were evident in the group members' responses to their disability, especially when they recounted first learning about it, but also in subsequent life transitions, of which joining the group was one.

Furthermore, there were other considerable benefits to the group members in being 'allowed' to acknowledge their disability. It helped clarify much confusion that group members experienced around their status: some group members had had contradictory messages as to whether they had learning difficulties or not, or had been diagnosed as having confusing 'syndromes'. The opportunity to talk through their emotions was seen as valuable by some of them. There is the additional benefit of learning that to talk about disability need not automatically invite embarrassment and rejection, but can be an acceptable part of oneself. Being accepted by others, and in turn, accepting them, helps remove some of the shame and stigma associated with disability, enabling the individual to shed the defence of derogating other handicapped people. Further, by clarifying the extent of the disability, individuals are enabled to make more realistic attributions about themselves, empowering them to take a more active role in determining their lives.

However, there was an important difference between the ways in which the group members talked about accepting their disability and the ways in which Kubler-Ross' patients talked about accepting their death.

We have to question whether, given the stigmatised status of learning difficulties, acceptance is completely possible for a person with learning difficulties who is aware of that status. In the group we witnessed only 'comparative acceptance' ('I'm lucky, I could have been worse') and 'compensatory acceptance' ('At least, one person loved me better for being as I am'). No one had anything positive to say about being as they were; instead, an acknowledgement and acceptance of the emotions associated with disability, such as sadness or tolerance, was as close to acceptance as they could get.

However, it should be said that the individuals were selected for the group on the basis of their apparent low self-esteem. As with the CR paradigm, a crucial next step is to explore ways in which handicapped people can be helped to feel positively about the particular contribution that they make to society.

Given our provisos about the possibility of accepting a stigmatised identity, what of the 'phases' that we described? Is there a therapeutic progression or not? In the group there certainly was a sense of progression: certain phases pave the way for others; for example, statement seemed to set the scene for meaning; a territory cannot be explored until it has been discovered; you cannot accept something until you know what it means, and so on. Moreover, the group seemed to have to go through phases like denial and resistance as part of the process of checking out whether the group would be a safe environment to which to bring personal problems.

Progression for individuals was less dramatic. Some of the group members seemed locked into a pattern of anger or of denial in coping with their disability. Nevertheless, even these individuals (like Jay and Eve) demonstrated change over time. It is interesting that after the group, Eve, who had never had a friend before because she rejected disabled people and was too shy to talk to non-disabled people, developed a friendship with one of the other group members. Jay also learnt to deal with her anger sufficiently to feel protective towards other handicapped people, and was reported as being much less surly in her supported job in a shop. We felt that the group forum was useful in that the shared trust which developed and the 'modelling' of different ways of talking about disability helped the group members to experiment with different ways of feeling about and coping with disability. This in turn helped them move on a little even in the brief time-scale of the group.

This brings us to the next point about how, and indeed whether, to talk to people about their disability. We think that the theoretical reasons given for attempting the group have been justified, but that the process of thinking and talking about disability could begin much earlier. This is exemplified, although negatively, in Eve's assertion that she was not handicapped, just 'shy'. This self-imposed label paradoxically handicapped her more than a realistic appraisal of her abilities and disabilities might have done. By keeping her aloof from other disabled people, her defence of 'shyness' kept her socially isolated and lonely. The same was found in Zetlin and Turner's study (1984) in which people with learning difficulties whose families had tried to deny that there was anything 'different' about them experienced more restricted and lonelier lives than those whose parents had acknowledged disability to them openly, since childhood. There is also the finding that people (like Gwen) will hear the contradictory messages anyway, and become isolated and confused because of them.

However, the problem of stigma throws some doubt on the full applicability of both paradigms. Acceptance and a positive group identity are not easily achieved for people with learning difficulties as a group, however much one may optimistically argue that equally stigmatised groups have successfully overcome similar problems. As regards people like Eve, the process of exploring the personal meaning of handicap must always be client led. We would not advocate tearing away her defences, leaving nothing in their place. Instead, by providing her with models and experiences for valuing other handicapped people, we would hope that in time she would feel valued enough herself no longer to need to claim to be 'just shy'.

We are also not certain about the wisdom of changing labels, such as substituting 'learning difficulties' for 'mental handicap'. Time may prove us wrong, but we suspect that substituting new euphemisms for old labels may not be the answer. New terms quickly become pejorative and may do little or nothing actively to destigmatise the concept of handicap. Pretending that such categories do not exist by eliminating labels altogether, as is also occasionally advocated, does not seem to be the answer either, since the source of the rejection and unhappiness experienced by people with learning difficulties is often the objectively existing disability itself and informal labelling can take place when the formal labels are removed. What is important is that any labels or images which are used should be ones which the people involved can feel positive about using but which do not downplay their particular contributions to society. Like the rest of us, people with learning difficulties need to be valued for their differences as well as their similarities to other people.

References

Baumhardt, L.A. and Lawrence, S. (1983) 'Transforming negatively labelled student groups into support groups', *Social Work in Education*, 5 (4): 229–40.

Briton, J. (1979) 'Normalization: what of and what for?', *Australian Journal of Mental Retardation*, 5: 224–9.

Byrne, E.A. and Cunningham, C.C. (1985) 'The effects of mentally handicapped children on families: a conceptual review', *Journal of Child Psychology and Psychiatry*, 26 (6): 847–64.

Corbett, J. (1988) 'The quality of life in the "Independence Curriculum"', *Disability, Handicap and Society*, 4 (2): 145–63.

Donegan, C. and Potts, M. (1988) 'People with a mental handicap living alone in the community: a pilot study of their quality of life', *British Journal of Mental Subnormality*, 66 (34) (1): 10–21.

Edgerton, R.B. (1967) *The Cloak of Competence: Stigma in the Lives of the Mentally Retarded*. San Francisco: University of California Press.

Friedrich, W.N., Witurner, L.T. and Cohen, D.S. (1985) 'Coping resources and parenting mentally retarded children', *American Journal of Mental Deficiency*, 90 (2): 130–9.

Gibbons, F.X. (1985) 'Stigma perception: social comparisons among mentally retarded persons', *American Journal of Mental Deficiency*, 90 (1): 98–106.

Gilkey, G.L.-M. and Zetlin, A.G. (1987) 'Peer relations of mentally handicapped adolescent pupils at an ordinary school', *British Journal of Mental Subnormality*, 64 (33) (1): 50–6.

Goffman, E. (1963) *Stigma: Notes on the Management of a Spoiled Identity*. Englewood Cliffs, NJ: Prentice-Hall.

Keogel, P. and Edgerton, R.B. (1982) 'Labeling and perception of handicap among black mildly retarded adults', *American Journal of Mental Deficiency*, 87 (3): 266–76.

Kravetz, D. (1981) 'Consciousness-raising and self-help', in A.M. Brodsky and R.T. Hare-Mustin (eds), *Women and Psychotherapy: An Assessment of Research and Knowledge*. New York: The Guilford Press.

Kubler-Ross, E. (1970) *On Death and Dying*. London: Tavistock Publications.

Murray-Parkes, C. (1971) 'Psychosocial transitions: a field for study', *Social Science and Medicine*, 5: 101–15.

Nirje, B. (1969) 'The Normalisation principle and its human management implications', in R.B. Kugel and W. Wolfensberger (eds), *Changing Patterns in Residential Services for the Mentally Retarded*. Washington, DC: President's Committee on Mental Retardation.

O'Brien, J. (1987) 'A guide to lifestyle planning', in B. Wilcox and G.T. Bellamy (eds), *A Comprehensive Guide to the Activities Catalogue. An Alternative Curriculum for Youth and Adults with Severe Disabilities*. Baltimore: Paul H. Brookes.

Reiss, S. and Benson, B.A. (1984) 'Awareness of negative social conditions among mentally retarded, emotionally disturbed outpatients', *American Journal of Psychiatry*, 141 (1): 88–90.

Suelze, M. and Keenan, V. (1981) 'Changes in family support networks over the life cycle of a mentally retarded person', *American Journal of Mental Deficiency*, 86 (3): 267–74.

Tajfel, H. (1981) *Human Groups and Social Categories*. Cambridge: Cambridge University Press.

Wolfensberger, W. (1972) *The Principle of Normalization in Human Services*. Toronto: National Institute on Mental Retardation.

Wolfensberger, W. (1983) 'Social role valorisation: a proposed new term for the principle of Normalisation', *Mental Retardation*, 21 (6): 234–9.

Wolfensberger, W. (1984) 'A reconceptualization of Normalization as social role valorization', *Mental Retardation*, 34 (2): 22–6.

Wolfensberger, W. (1988) 'Reply to "All people have personal assets"', *Mental Retardation*, 26 (2): 75–6.

Wolfensberger, W. and Thomas, S. (1983) *PASSING: Normalization Criteria and Ratings Manual* (2nd edn). Toronto: National Institute on Mental Retardation.

Zetlin, G. and Turner, L.T. (1984) 'Self perspectives on being handicapped: stigma and adjustment', in R.B. Edgerton (ed.), *Lives in Process: Mildly Retarded Adults in a Large City*. Monograph No 6, American Association on Mental Deficiency.

6

Psychotherapy with People with Learning Difficulties

Rosalind Bates

Working with people with learning difficulties in a psychotherapeutic endeavour is only different from working with non-handicapped adults, adolescents or children in the sense that the processes through which one works have a different time span and rhythm. The changes in rhythm require the skills of a detective – I have been working in this field for nine years and still regard myself as a learner.

Referrals

People are referred to me by residential agencies, social service workers, members of the Community Mental Handicap Team (CMHT), General Practitioners or other psychiatrists. As with any new case, a decision has to be made whether to offer individual work or whether to work with the family or carers, or if drug treatment is appropriate. No one approach excludes the others and a combination may be tried.

Selection

The majority of people I offer to work with individually are young, between 18 and 30, with mild or moderate learning difficulties and thus fairly good language skills. I have learned from strenuous experience that if a person is living in an adverse milieu (and is aware of this), it will be impossible to help sort out the emotional turmoil until this problem has been ameliorated. I am also aware that changing the person's place of living for another place may not do more than re-locate the problem, but one may have some months' grace in which to work, so that if problems re-emerge this can be acknowledged and worked through.

If people refer themselves and are capable of travelling to see me on time, this is an ideal starting-point. Such people are often capable of living independently and deserve to be seen without referral to others except at their request or with agreement after discussion. When someone who wants help cannot attend alone but has an advocate willing to accompany them to sessions, this provides the dual function of getting the person to my office on time, and providing some background information about progress between sessions.

Although I try to assess whether I feel there is a willingness or ability to change, I am often influenced by the dire straits the client may be in, for example, likelihood of exclusion from day care or residential facility. If the need to preserve the person's way of life is so great that the appearance of 'something being done' may be given by an offer of individual work, I will take on someone for whom I have little hope of conventional change. Such cases are sometimes men who show sexually unacceptable behaviour. In my experience these may turn out to be unexpectedly successful and rewarding, although my method of working with them may not be exactly pukka.

Sometimes after months or years of working with someone in the presence of other workers or a parent, I find I can begin individual work, as certain barriers have been overcome and both of us feel such interaction can be useful. On other occasions the process of 'individual' work may need to be carried out in the presence of another person, perhaps because the person is too timid or inarticulate to work without an advocate. If someone has persecutory tendencies and misinterprets what is said, it is helpful to have a care giver present, who can rehearse the contents of the discussion and correct any fantasies. It may also help care workers to see how their clients respond to a non-judgemental outsider and in such cases I may be able to act as a role model for staff in dealing with provocative language and threats uttered by a person who is upset at being asked to discuss areas of difficulty.

The conduct of each session

Like most social contacts, I try to open each session in as friendly a fashion as possible. 'Well-trained' clients may rush in and after the usual 'hellos' deliver 'the problem for today's discussion'. If necessary I will introduce other topics which we should discuss. Another satisfying aspect of the work is how, even after a session in which tough issues have been aired, it is often easy to end the session on a positive and cheerful note. People with learning problems are often so glad of attention, and are so used to being 'advised' and critically evaluated, that they are quite forgiving of the distress which might have been a necessary part of the session.

So every session begins on a cheerful note and ends as far as possible with an expression of reinforcement of the positive aspects of the client's behaviour, so that we part on friendly terms.

Presenting problems

As one would expect with a case load which could be regarded developmentally as adolescent, people present with emotional difficulties due to poor adjustment, or to the greater insight which adolescence brings to their position of being 'learning disabled'. They may have relationship problems with family or with peers and many have sexual problems. Lack of assertiveness with resultant passivity or aggression is common. Depression, bereavement, severe anxiety and intermittent psychosis may be presenting symptoms. Individual sessions provide the opportunity for an extended diagnostic period and this is sometimes extremely humbling, when I suddenly tumble to a diagnosis I should have made a lot earlier. There are parallels in my work with the psychiatrist operating in the field of adolescent psychiatry, where the patient is referred by other people such as parents, schools and so on to another authority figure – a doctor, for goodness sake – who is sitting in an office, in a suit. Fortunately people with learning difficulties welcome one-to-one attention and this may be overcome so that resistance does not become insurmountable. It also helps that there is a subculture among people with learning difficulties, so that all we members of the Community Mental Handicap Team are well known and the client group boasts proudly of their own worker – the therapist as status symbol.

Method – engagement

The process of therapy is infinitely variable. I like to 'feel my way' at the beginning to try to find the 'key' to a successful engagement. Engagement is the primary goal and may take a long time. For me this involves getting people to accept me as a valid person, one benignly intended, who is prepared to give time regardless of how they behave towards me. There has to be an 'alliance' so that we may each feel able to speak freely, to face any situation or facet of the problems. This implies a considerable loosening of the person's defences, the development of a dialogue and a shared vocabulary at their level of understanding. Some of the difficulties in engagement may thus be due to my need to 'find the right level' and many approaches may need to be tried out during this process.

Engagement may come about quite suddenly, even after a number of sessions in which the person may have been hostile or belligerent, and may take the form of an expression of a personal interest or concern for some aspect of my life. I may be given directions across the borough to a day centre or, on one occasion, instructions in minute detail of how to get to the Lake District by a route which would certainly have reached Land's End!

Goal setting

Once comfortably engaged, the opportunity exists for an exchange of views about the problem and so it is possible to set a number of goals for future work. This cannot be done in too mechanistic a fashion, as the client may not be able to understand the concept of goal setting. It may therefore be a goal-setting exercise for the therapist, as a discipline, or it may be necessary to face the fact that goals must be very limited. The expectation of the referring agent may include the abolition of undesired behaviours, or that the person's emotional suffering should be eased. While these aims are laudable, they tend to be rather long term and the goals need to be more modest and internal to the individual. I am more concerned about personal growth and the development of awareness which will help to reduce untoward behaviour or emotional unease.

Defining the 'problem'

The first and most obvious goal for the therapist is to agree with the client what is the main problem. Careful history taking on the first and subsequent interviews will have elicited this from the viewpoint of the carers and others significant to the individual. However, it is for the therapist to puzzle out and mull over with the person what are the factors giving rise to the difficulty from their point of view. The problem will need to be aired in an attempt to make it quite safe to talk about it. Sexual difficulties are particularly challenging in this respect. The young people I see find it very difficult to discuss sexual issues because of reticence, embarrassment, guilt feelings and especially because they are repeatedly reminded in every setting that sex in both the anatomical and physiological sense is 'private'. Most young people nowadays are aware of their entitlement to sexuality whereas the older ones are generally repressed.

It is an oversimplification to assume when working with clients that there is only one identifiable problem. For instance, a young person who may be engaging in sexual exhibitionism will need to discuss this but the underlying problem may be that this person does not have sufficient judgement to be allowed out unchaperoned. It is therefore necessary to try to identify what is the problem for discussion with the client and sometimes a separate agenda may need to be set for the carers. The ensuing paragraphs will need to be read in the light of this and it must be remembered that the focus for discussion may vary once the person begins to bring current problems to the session.

Describing the 'problem'

One has to try to develop a language for use with each person. This can be formulated over time, depending on the level of understanding of the individual, their use of language and maturity of thinking. Concreteness of thinking means that the use of analogy, parable or role reversal has to be taught painstakingly, in order for work to continue.

If someone has problems of concentration, it takes much repetition and continual 'bringing back to the point' to produce a dialogue. Some people are perseverative and keep asking questions which can deflect the therapist. These questions have to be gently but firmly conditioned out of the conversation. I enjoy the challenge of trying to cut through these 'background' utterances to communicate at a deeper level.

People with learning difficulties are sometimes incapable of describing feelings or are unaware that they have, or are entitled to have, feelings. With time many such people can learn to describe quite overwhelmingly painful emotions and to put a name to them such as 'frightened', 'cross', 'sad' or 'miserable'. Empathy, labelling and personal description can facilitate this process.

Overcoming resistance

Since the person with a problem has usually been referred by people at work, day centre or home, they may defend against admitting to any problems at all. Denial is probably the strongest defensive position and may be a well learned skill.

Workers in this field are accustomed to meeting clients of day centres who do not know that these facilities are for people with learning difficulties. They may not have faced the truth that they attended special schools. Much of this may have emanated from the parents and relatives denying that the pupils have learning problems, or through altruism on their part, wishing to spare their child's feelings. It is not unusual to find parents blaming the school or the teachers for their adult child's failure to achieve anticipated social or educational goals.

Members of our Community Mental Handicap Team have to explain the term 'mental handicap' to our clients, who may be astonished to feel included in such a client group. The term 'learning difficulty' is easier for people to acknowledge, but one does not entirely wish to collude with the denial of the handicap with which our clients are living (see Szivos and Griffiths, Chapter 5). The handicap vs. disability debate is beyond the scope of this chapter, but it is important to remember that problems with learning are not necessarily handicapping of themselves.

It may therefore happen that I am the first person who has ever discussed the above concepts with someone. However, mildly disabled people often stay in short-term or long-term residential facilities alongside severely disabled or physically handicapped people. They meet people with a range of disabilities at social clubs and sports facilities and so the notion of handicap or disability can be addressed in the context of comparison. It is interesting that occasionally I have to tell people that they are *not* handicapped by a learning difficulty. Again even in these cases I may be the first person to broach this to someone who has been hiding for many years behind a label of educational handicap, who may have been socially underdeveloped instead. I have even met parents who were none too pleased to have to readjust to this idea, as it is easier to accept that a child is 'backward' rather than poorly adapted.

So the seeds of denial may have been implanted early and some basic negotiation of the adolescent task – who am I, what am I, where do I fit in? – has to take place, before one can start to work on the solution to 'the problem'.

Inducing awareness
Once there is agreement about the identity of the problem, the next stage is to help the person to understand its meaning in a social context, for instance bullying of parents by an overcontrolling and overbearing adolescent, or supercilious attitudes to fellow day-centre clients. Rigidity of thought may allow people to feel that, as they are 'handicapped', there is an expectation that staff, relatives and even the general public should be kind and helpful and make allowances, while it is perfectly all right for them to bully, kick, swear, obstruct or be demanding in a childlike way. Discussions around this topic are usually very stormy but can be quite fruitful. For this sort of work a strong engagement between the therapist and client is clearly vital, as the tenor of discussion could leave the individual feeling heavily criticised. I find it helpful to use humour and ridiculous analogies or ideas of role reversal to make these battles more light hearted and acceptable to the recipient. If both parties can stay the course of the first of such skirmishes, subsequent discussions of difficult areas can be easier and eventu-

ally the person may actually present self-critical descriptions in order to check out their social implications.

Overcoming language difficulties

As therapy progresses certain problems of language use may become apparent. The most common of these is the tendency to give expected answers, particularly by institutionalised people, and in those who are by nature passive. This can be detected by asking a question in one way to obtain the answer 'yes' and then reframing the same question to obtain the negative. There is then no point in continuing the discussion until the person is persuaded to relinquish this position, if that is possible.

Comprehension difficulties abound and I frequently have to check whether or not the client knows the meaning of the words they have agreed to. For example, 'rape' may mean 'to be hit', while 'hostile' can mean 'doing something I shouldn't' because of the *tone* in which these words are delivered by all the authority figures known to the person with a handicap. There is often a gap between expressive language, which may appear to be very good, and comprehension and abstract reasoning ability. This is one of the biggest traps for anyone working in this field. Many people are taken in by a person's apparently good speech, which in fact is made up largely of learned utterances culled over years from other adults. This puts the handicapped individual in a position of constant failure because they cannot live up to other people's expectations. They will therefore often be blamed for being 'lazy', 'resistant' or 'rebellious' while actually performing optimally.

Weighing up the cost of the problem and seeking solutions

Once the crux of the person's difficulties has been teased out and has been admitted to the conversation, it is important to assess awareness of the difficulty and of its *cost* to them in personal or relationship terms. I use the following techniques which I have borrowed from more conventional forms of therapy.

The use of imagery

'Cost' is quite an abstract area which many people with mild learning difficulties have problems in grasping. Over the years I have developed a number of concrete analogies to try to bring home the message. These examples are often very popular with my clients and can be cited in future sessions. Sometimes they use the analogy back to me when describing everyday events and difficulties they are proud to have overcome. The images I use are powerful and vibrant and examples are cited below for different problems.

a) *Lack of self-control*
If an aggressive adolescent talks of aggressive or destructive behaviour as if it is something that is uncontrollable, not belonging to them (an example of splitting), I may use the 'driver of the bus' analogy.

> Think of yourself as a large red bus, going along the High Street. If the bus is travelling along on automatic pilot it will keep crashing, and will fail to stop to pick people up. Q. 'What does this bus need?' A. 'A driver.' Right, so *you* are this large red bus – who is the driver? . . .

One man with whom I discussed this said that sometimes he felt he was a Sherman tank and sometimes a ramshackle old stage coach with tired horses in front.

People with a psychoanalytical leaning will see how useful this analogy is with people in adolescence! If the client can respond to this approach it is quickly internalised and can be used as a reminder of the need for self-control.

b) *Irritability and outbursts of rage*
For people who exhibit rage in the form of temper tantrums or swearing in response to minor difficulties, the powerful image of 'World War III' can be both productive and amusing:

> So someone poured tea into *your* mug and drank from it. I see. And you did what? You jumped up and down and shouted and swore? Mm, I see. What else did you do? You threw a chair across the room? Oh.
> What was it about someone drinking out of your cup that decided you to declare World War III?

Discussion can ensue about grossly over-reacting to a minor slight and how one incurs everyone's rancour in the process.

c) *The oversensitive person – the easy 'wind up'*
People living in new group homes are often selected for compatibility on simple measures such as self-care and language skills. Until a home opens it may not be clear how they will settle down together. As they tend to be young people, newly left home, there are difficulties in being one of three or four people with only one or two 'parental' figures who may be untrained and as young as themselves. There will inevitably be friction and competition between residents. The oversensitive person will soon exhibit unhappiness or rage.

My favourite analogy for this is that of 'insulation' – either of electrical wires or of a 'cool box'. Having established what insulation is, it is possible to explain how a thick wall of insulation will stop the other person's behaviour from hurting. Often staff tell such people – 'Go to your room' or 'Go outside'. This may be helpful but it tends to reinforce avoidance of conflicts so that individuals do not learn to stand their ground and control or face their feelings. Imagined insulation may help to cultivate 'deafness' or 'blindness' or prevent the person from hitting out or slamming doors.

d) *The bereaved person*

If it has been established that the loss of a parent (often the loss of a home too) is causing depression or leading to depressive equivalent behaviour, the recommended mourning techniques of grave visiting, seeing the old house and looking at photographs of family may not always alleviate the problem. Sometimes talking about the loved one without a defensive strategy makes the bereaved person feel more lost or more depressed. It is helpful to establish the person's ideas of what happens to people when they die. Nearly every one of the clients I have worked with on this sort of problem has an idea that the loved person is 'in heaven' or 'gone to Jesus'. This avowed atheist then swings into the 'happy angel' routine, whereby an explanation is given of the idea of 'Mother up there watching over you' – with the suggestion that it would be better for Mother to see you having a really *good* time and a *nice* life – wouldn't she be a proud and happy angel to see you doing so well – and so on. The look of delight on a recipient's face is enough to reinforce my behaviour and I find the best response to this comes from the *more* able people.

e) *Persistently offensive behaviour – denigrating the symptom*

Men who show perverse or unacceptable sexual behaviour take a great deal of persuasion before they will relinquish it. In order to show behaviour such as sexual exhibition, it must be either very compulsive or the person must be splitting himself off from it. Thus it is likely to be very deeply ingrained. Frequently such men are referred after ordinary attempts at counselling and therapy about sexual matters, sexual mores and sex as part of a mutual relationship have seemingly failed. The defences against therapy are many and the most powerful is to suggest that some kind of specialised effort (that is, not *mine!*) is needed. Most of my clients who exhibit are grossly inadequate people who cannot relate at all to women, and could sometimes be assumed to be expressing aggression or hostility to women in their actions. Having established exactly what the man does in public and what his private sexual fantasies and capabilities are, a more directive approach has to be taken – i.e. telling him that sexual fantasies have to be private and getting him to perceive and explore his impoverished relationships with women. But these approaches are unlikely to stop the behaviour until the client *sees* the behaviour as a problem for *himself*.

I accidentally stumbled on an image which would help when, with my first such client, after he had told me how well he was doing, I asked him 'Tell me then – done any flashing lately?' The effect on him was amazing – he began to see the behaviour as quite ridiculous, appears to have relinquished it and cannot understand why he or anyone else could carry out such a stigmatising act.

Other such denigrations include 'bossy-boots', 'the whopper department', 'the home-wrecker' and 'the volcano', for bullying, lying, destructiveness and explosive rages respectively.

However, it is necessary to know the person extremely well and have had a few good skirmishes with him before embarking on mockery.

Other strategies   People with poor imaginative or language skills, severe egocentricity or dysmaturity cannot respond to the use of imagery. They require a simplified approach which may include the following strategies.

a) *Directive suggestions*
Where people repeatedly show unacceptable behaviour but no capacity to understand the effect it has on others, it may help to dwell more heavily on the cost to *themselves* of the behaviour, such as loss of day-centre or residential placement or involvement with the police or courts. This is particularly useful with immature or egocentric individuals who have no development of conscience. Developmentally they may be fixated at the punitive stage and so it is necessary to be more direct – for example, 'If you do that you will get into trouble with the police' or simply 'People don't behave like that in public'. Most care workers have experience of the planned use of the local police when there has been a spate of theft in a home or a resident wanders out at night and is thus in danger. My technique is a less frightening use of the same idea and I am relying on a degree of suggestibility and sometimes on the person's desire for my approval.

b) *Teaching about feelings*
People who have poor empathy and severe egocentricity tend to have a narrowed range of feelings. These can be opposites – feeling good or bad, very tense or calm, or negative emotions such as anger, hostility or rage. The emotional range may be shallow, with catastrophic outbursts of rage over small discomforts and an

immediate return to calm once the feeling has been expressed. Such people are always in trouble, either at home or in day facilities or work. They remind me of an electric toaster with settings only for 'underdone' (1–2) and 'burnt' (9–10) and no 'normal' or comfortable emotional settings in between. In talking to these people I become aware that sometimes they do not know the difference between 'angry' and 'upset'. Everything is 'anger'. Such a conversation unfolds as follows: Q. 'If I went into your bedroom and looked into your cupboards and personal possessions, how would you feel?' A. 'Angry'; Q. 'If I found you in my office reading letters and papers about my other clients and I told you off very crossly, how would you feel?' A. 'Angry'. It seems therefore that people like this spend a lot of their time reacting at the burnt toast end of their emotional rheostat.

I spend a great deal of time trying to elicit the bodily sensations the individual has when angry, tense, sad or upset to try to help them become aware of the difference between these emotions. Such individuals find the task difficult, being outside their experience and tend to direct the conversation with inappropriate questions or statements, often needing to be brought back to the task. After a number of sessions I sometimes notice a loosening of emotion when people describe unpleasant experiences. There may be tearfulness when describing a remonstration or an expression of extreme hurt after breaking off a relationship.

c) 'Naggotherapy'

This term was coined by myself and entered the vocabulary of our CMHT some years ago. People who try to help difficult clients who persistently behave inappropriately, by giving advice which is constantly ignored, find themselves indulging in a repetitive, nagging and directive approach. Mothers of normally untidy rebellious children will recognise the problem. I felt it was sometimes important to maintain a stance in which the client could not avoid, deny or slide out of accepting ownership of untoward behaviour. Perhaps because I often have people referred to me after other workers have been unable to achieve this, I have developed a tough-minded approach.

First I have to exclude depression or psychosis as a possible cause of inappropriate behaviour. Then I discuss the problem from as many angles as I can muster, sympathising with the person's inability to recognise the difficulty in advance and lack of strategy to pre-empt it. Strategies and 'scripts' can then be offered, often by giving out tips on assertiveness, for example, 'You don't have to answer other clients who ask you personal questions' and teaching people, if necessary by rote, what to say. This is a much stronger, more repetitive variation of the directive approach. Such work is occasionally rewarded when after a long time the person begins to use, with conviction, expressions which they have been taught.

Other considerations

It has to be borne in mind that people with learning difficulties seen for psychotherapy are in contact with many other helpful people. They have homes with parents or staff, day centres or jobs with staff interested in their welfare, plus a galaxy of professionals – social workers, community nurses, students, speech therapists, psychologists and doctors. All of these significant people bring the techniques of their own disciplines and their personal attitudes to clients to bear on the person's problems on a much more regular basis than a therapist who may only have a peep at their personality once a month. People attending day centres are sometimes subjected to annual reviews in which they have to listen to every worker's opinion of their work, dress, personal hygiene, time keeping and character in front of their parents or carers. This may be a devastating experience for some people but a positive outcome can be that clients are having things said to them which may be conflicting or hurtful or helpful and they can discuss their feelings about these with me. Solutions to well founded criticism can be discussed and comparisons drawn between how the individual feels in this situation and how other people may feel when on the receiving end of that person's own frank remarks.

With less communicative, less aware or denying clients, one relies on liaison with other workers to hear how they are coping. This is possible through written reports or reports relayed by an advocate (usually a social worker or community nurse). The CMHT meetings provide a useful forum for this. If, however, I am the only worker who knows the client, I may have to meet with carers and day-centre staff to get a full picture.

Written reports are not so helpful as they can tell me more about staff attitudes or how fed up the client makes everyone than about the actual behaviour or its circumstances.

One drawback of the multiple agency contact is that of multiple advisory contacts being offered to a client who may 'shop around' for a preferred solution or use one person's advice to contradict another. It can take some time to detect people who do this but fortunately, it is nearly always possible to plug the gaps and minimise any adverse effects of this strategy.

What is success?

If the goals of therapy set at the beginning have been realistic, success can be seen as occurring when the client comes to an acceptance of the problems and as good a resolution of them as can be expected. There is no magic in recognition of this – as with ordinary troubled people, the client becomes calmer, easier to get on with and less tempestuous or less depressed or anxious. Expressions of anxiety or desperation from parents or staff become fewer and the person's level of functioning improves.

When to cease or reduce contact

Many people make this decision for themselves and if I feel we have done as much work as is helpful for the time being, I agree to end contact. When I feel there is more work needed, I may negotiate a number of further sessions.

Sometimes a client begins to show slight improvements in self-awareness, but remains in need of further contact. I begin to reduce the frequency of contact and explain that we have spent a lot of time together and perhaps now we need to meet less often.

Some people require a short, sharp approach with a contract of 4–6 sessions and then we agree to stop, with an offer of further help if required. Further meetings with well motivated clients like this are usually confined to one or two sessions as the barriers are already removed and short cuts established.

Those whose disability prevents the development of awareness and with whom after some time I begin to feel I have seen this cycle through twice already, with little or no improvement, are problematic. It may be possible to cease work by mutual agreement, or pass such a client to another worker, in the hope of a fresh approach being of help.

Frequency of sessions

Realistically, I find it difficult to offer regular sessions on less than a four-week frequency. Sessions last between 30 minutes and an hour depending on the tolerance and ability of the person to concentrate. More able, more troubled clients need more sessions. If someone is emotionally upset I can usually fit in two sessions at two-weekly intervals before relaxing to a four-weekly schedule. For most people four weeks is a reasonable spread and even intervals of 6–8 weeks do not seem to interrupt the rhythm too much once engagement is established. Of course there are those with whom interruptions are unhelpful and upsetting, especially people with Asperger syndrome. Some people have to be restarted at almost every session as they cannot hold the relationship between sessions. This usually improves with time.

The above description of strategies is far from complete. There is always room for the development of further ways of understanding and translating people's cognitive and emotional processes in order to help. Some cases will be described to try to illustrate the process of therapy in people with different kinds of causes for their problems, although the presentation may be similar.

George

I first met George when he was 19. He was a tall, good looking man who had totally failed to live up to his parents' expectations of him. His voice boomed, he moved awkwardly, he was dishevelled and ate all the food from the fridge just prior to visitors coming. His frustration and outbursts of aggression were largely confined to home, and his parents took to having weekend guests, because in the presence of outsiders George would keep his temper.

There were few outbursts of aggression at his day centre because it was made clear to George that this would not be tolerated. Unfortunately the aggression escalated at home, driven by his egocentricity, lack of empathy and extreme oversensitivity to criticism. George could sense his parents' criticism and only had to be in his mother's company for a very short time before being overwhelmed by feelings that she was criticising him.

When George left home it was because he stabbed the family dog, and was not deemed safe to remain in the family home. He was unwilling to leave, and it was fortunate that the local psychiatrists were willing to give him a bed in a ward of a large psychiatric hospital. His parents were advised to take an injunction against his coming home, and to our extreme relief they did so. This had a curbing effect on George's behaviour, as he has a great respect for the law.

For the next two years a considerable amount of work was carried out by a psychologist in tandem with a social worker, and George gradually learned to live away from home, which reduced his outbursts of aggression and gave him scope for developing his many domestic and social skills. Over the years I have seen him from time to time, but gradually I 'inherited' him as first the psychologist and then the social worker left the district to further their careers.

At the beginning of our relationship George regarded me as an extremely authoritarian figure who had the power to have him removed to hospital. This proved a helpful perception, as I was always there in the background if his behaviour should get out of hand. In this way I became his 'conscience' and however angry he may have been with me at the beginning, there has always been a great respect between us.

Once I became the only remaining long-term adviser to George, the ability that he had developed to talk about his feelings with other workers became something which we could share more or less exclusively. He was able to bring material to every session which showed a developing insight into his difficulties. One day he appeared very upset because someone had told him 'Pipe down, you've got a voice like a fog horn'.

I had always been aware of George's booming voice, but had considered that as part of his make-up and had never discussed it with him. The adverse feelings engendered in him by these remarks were useful. He became aware almost for the first time of how intimidating he could be although for years he had been shouting at people in order to get his own way and had of course found that this had worked. I was able to introduce him to a speech therapist, who taught him voice control. He now speaks in a quieter voice and expresses his appreciation of her help.

In order to help to accept responsibility for his behaviour, 'the driver of the bus' analogy was used, to his great amusement. Once he got the hang of being responsible for his own behaviour, he could describe incidents of misbehaviour in a wry and insightful way and this problem has improved considerably. He has long since relinquished blaming other people for his difficulties.

To try to help him with his extreme oversensitivity I have used the insulation analogy. This has helped to a certain extent, but I am still having to work on this as it may be more difficult for him to preserve himself. Recently I have switched to a more transactional approach, advising him to reply to criticism by agreeing with it. Therefore when he meets his mother on the doorstep and sees her disapproving look followed by the comment 'your jumper is dirty', I am trying to teach him to reply 'Yes it is rather grubby isn't it?'

One insight which I have developed with George is a backlash to the 'when you feel overheated why don't you go to your bedroom' approach. This is advocated by workers in many settings, particularly those involved with residential care. Although going away from the situation has a good effect in the situation at the time, I now feel that it does not help people to develop an ability to stand there, accept their feelings of anger and frustration, however strong, and find a way of coping with them *in situ*. Telling people to go away when they are angry may only reinforce an avoidance of accepting the real cause of their difficulties and teach them to run away from uncomfortable, overheated feelings. I am therefore trying to teach George strategies as set out above to use in each situation where his frustration and anger are aroused. I actually give him a script, help him rehearse it and ask for feedback.

To date George has not attacked anyone, does still look quite fearsome when crossed, has difficulty in making friends and so falls back too frequently for his own good on his family of origin when he is lonely, but he has learned to live in a very independent setting, with some quite difficult residents. My work with him continues. It is fascinating to hear the insights he has developed and how he is able to learn from adverse experiences in his daily life.

Matthew

Matthew, aged 25 years, came to me following a short admission to psychiatric hospital. His cognitive abilities place him above our usual level for considering clients, but his social impairments were so severe that we felt he could be construed as 'mentally handicapped' and he had clearly elected to be one of this client group.

Because of his good verbal skills, he came with a lot of imaginative descriptions about himself. He had attended a school for 'maladjusted' boys, was explosive at home, and since he could travel about the borough unescorted, his parents found him hard to control. He was placed out of the borough two years previously and had returned to a semi-independent setting within the borough at his request.

Matthew described feelings of fear of attack by others in the street (some of which was based in fact) and fears of being a demanding, violent and explosive person – 'like a Sherman tank'. He was defended and withdrawn at first, and it was difficult to get him to talk about his past life. He had a fear of never being able to 'make it' with a girl but refused to discuss his sexuality, even with a male community nurse in a series of sex education sessions. He had depressive symptoms, which were partly relieved by antidepressants. Because he could not cope with his living situation or his day centre, he sometimes 'went mad', which resulted in his admission several times to hospital. The histrionicity of his presentation resulted in reinforcement from his carers and admission to hospital seemed to crown this.

Gradually, with the help of a social worker, his support needs were recognised and after several attempts a suitable placement was found with a good understanding of the needs of people like himself. He was treated with a tranquilliser which reduced his severe anxiety and stopped his tendency to appear as a 'psychiatric hypochondriac'. He had a flirtation with physical hypochondriasis and on one occasion took an overdose of tablets.

With discussion and explanation that he could get attention for his emotional needs without these displays of 'sick' behaviour he relinquished all this. His progress was maintained until one day he began to show symptoms of a severe anxiety state and confided to a woman carer, who is professionally trained, that he was suffering from severe sexual guilt. She referred him to me, as an emergency, and I set up a series of sessions in which he poured out a sad history of homosexual exploitation by other young men and older acquaintances, dating from his boarding-school days until about three years before I met him. He described his extreme vulnerability to such predations, his anger at being exploited, his guilt for enjoying much of the physical activity and self-blame for acts which were instigated by others. These symptoms are characteristic of the abused child, and had been flagged up over the years by him, but could not be released until he was ready to trust people enough to tell his story.

Since that time Matthew has become calmer, warmer and softer. He is beginning to see the reality of his situation and does not construe himself as an active homosexual. The Sherman tank analogy of sexual aggression has left him. He has no fear of attack by others. Work continues to try to assess his true sexual alignment, to help him address the complexity of sexual relationships and to try to wean him off his psychotropic medication.

John

John was referred to me at 19 by a community nurse who was trying to work with him and his family. He has suffered from epilepsy since early childhood and has mild learning problems. His social interaction is impaired, he has obsessional ideas and compulsions, lack of empathy, egocentricity and he is immature. John can be very persuasive but impossible to persuade. His parents, the community nurse and his day centre were all experiencing difficulty with this young autistic man, as people were trying to reason with him because of his useful, if often unusual, language.

My first interview with his parents, himself and the community nurse was fairly bizarre but dominated by his intention to learn to drive and his parents' intention to collude with this desire to reduce his demands upon them. I was able to observe the full range of his disabilities. As a new observer, of course, this picture was striking, while to those used to him, he may have appeared less abnormal.

It was first necessary to be strictly directive about driving. I informed his parents of the illegality of teaching him to drive and, as gently as possible, of how dangerous was their intended collusion. They ceased discussing the matter with John, said 'No, you can't learn to drive' and the item completely disappeared from John's conversation.

Since then I have been trying to help John to cease his continual handling of people, his displays of childlike overexcitement and his obsessions with particular professional workers. I use a directive approach and he no longer lets his obsessions enter our discussion. At last, after some years of work, he has been able to describe how upset he feels at times if he believes he has been criticised by respected figures.

Problems in working with him include a short attention span, rigidity of thinking, abnormal use of language, problems of comprehension and a tendency to ask the meanings of words, possibly as a defence against the discussion. He no longer tries to listen to his Walkman during sessions, does not wear two watches and keep consulting them, and is making a great deal of use of our sessions. He is slowly beginning to mature.

7

Transactional Analysis as a Theory of Interpersonal Behaviour and as a Psychotherapeutic Model

Joanna Beazley-Richards

Introduction

This chapter aims to give a practical guide to using Transactional Analysis (TA) with clients who have learning difficulties (the phrase that I shall use for people called 'mentally handicapped'). It focuses on practical applications. What theory I do include is to give an understanding to practice, and is described very briefly. While most TA therapists use groups, there was not room here to include groupwork, and so I concentrate on working with individuals. The reader is referred to *Born to Win* by James and Jongeward or *TA Today* by Stewart and Joines, for a general introduction to TA. Here, I have selected the areas of TA which I believe are of the most immediate, practical use for working with people with learning difficulties.

About TA

Transactional Analysis is an approach to psychotherapy pioneered by Dr Eric Berne. One of its major virtues in working with people with learning difficulties is that it uses relatively straightforward language, and concepts which can be readily understood (indeed there is a TA book for TOTS!). I work regularly with people with profound and severe learning difficulties, and find that they respond well to the approach – especially as the non-verbal behaviour is so explicit. It is also contractual, and goal directed, so it is very appropriate for use within traditional settings for people with learning difficulties, as well as for working with clients who are not in such settings.

TA is based on a number of assumptions:

– people are OK;

- everyone has the capacity to think;
- people decide their own destiny, and these decisions can be changed.

Set squarely in the humanistic tradition, TA believes that at core all people have worth, value and dignity. Their behaviour may not be OK, nor their circumstances, but *they* are OK. TA practitioners believe that they must retain their *own* OK-ness as well as respect the OK-ness of their clients.

In TA we believe that everyone, except the most severely brain-damaged person, has the capacity to think. Thus, clients can indicate in their own way of communicating what they want from the therapy. TA is a model of behaviour which believes that people decide their own thoughts and feelings, and ultimately their own behaviour. Children are seen as deciding their responses to environmental pressures, and can re-decide how to respond later. Thus, patterns of behaviour are originally selected by clients, including people with learning difficulties, and can be changed by new decisions. We see clients as being able to decide to change, also to make profound changes, and to sustain these changes. The goal of TA, therefore, is to enable the clients to move towards personal autonomy; that is towards the ability to meet problems and situations using their full resources, responding to the present in the present, instead of repeating self-limiting ways of being from the past. TA therapists and clients meet as equals, and the therapist is there to assist the client towards achieving the goals that she selects for self-change. At present, three of my clients with learning difficulties have these goals: client A's contract is 'To control my temper when I can't get my own way'; client B's contract is 'To feel calm and not worry for a week'; and client C's contract is 'To have a boyfriend and have regular good sex with him'.

Clients state what they want to achieve, and I say whether I'm willing to help them work towards that. If I agree, I contract to offer my best professional skills to them during our time together. I also always 'close the escape hatches' and require clients to undertake not to kill or harm themselves or other people or to go crazy while we work together. The other contract is the *business contract* in which we agree administration details such as times, place and dates, fees or other means of reward, programmes and what sort of sessions. With people with severe learning difficulties, I explain it all very simply – always assuming that at some level everyone is able to think.

We also contract for confidentiality. I guarantee confidentiality to all clients, including those with learning difficulties, except where I believe that someone will harm self or others, or where they reveal serious law breaking. The sort of situation that has arisen is where a client with severe learning difficulties revealed that she was pregnant and that she hadn't told the hostel staff. Believing that she and her baby were at risk, I told her that she must tell the hostel staff within three days and that I would phone after that time to check they knew. Another testing situation was when a man wouldn't state that he wouldn't hurt anyone – he said he was going to hurt his mother, perhaps kill her. I refused to work with him and told the police.

Ego states (structural model)

Central to TA theory and practice is the concept of ego states. Berne observed that at times people behave as they thought, felt and did in the past, particularly as they did when they were young children. When someone does this, it's said they are in their Child ego state (note the capital letter to denote the ego state). At other times, a person may behave think or feel as she has observed others to do, and has copied (usually not in awareness). When she is behaving as someone in her past did, we say she is in her Parent ego state.

When the person's behaviour is neither their own past ways of feeling, thinking or doing, nor a copy of someone's way of feeling, thinking or doing, but is a direct response to what is actually occurring, we say she is in her Adult ego state. We all have three ways of expressing our personality; each way is defined by an observable set of behaviours, and will be constantly accompanied by a set of thoughts and feelings that are typical of that ego state. The terms Parent, Adult and Child, thus, are names given to three distinct sets of feelings, thoughts and behaviours.

Therapists can learn how to diagnose which ego state a client is in by looking at behavioural clues, namely facial expressions, gestures, posture, tone of voice, words used and so on. This is *behavioural* diagnosis.

When someone is in Parent, they will say and look as the person did *whom* they are copying. Sometimes I catch myself sounding like my Aunt Jean, and people who know me and her say I'm quite like her when I'm in my 'Jean' Parent ego state.

Another way of telling when someone is in a particular ego state is by *social* diagnosis. Here the therapist observes the responses she makes to how the client is, and if possible, the responses that others make to her. Thus, if I and everyone around the client is responding in a nurturing, parental way, the chances are that the client is in their Child ego state.

Another source of data as to which ego state someone is in is from *historical* information. This is done by asking the client about her childhood and the significant people who featured in it. Ask questions like 'I notice you're hunching your shoulders and putting your head down – did anyone do that around you when you were little?' (seeking confirmation of Parent ego state) or 'When you were little, did you behave as you are doing now?'

Finally, TA therapists use *phenomenological* clues. Here clients re-experience situations as if they were happening in the present, and we have a chance to diagnose their ego state phenomeno-logically. Thus, if during a counselling session, a client gets angry when talking about childhood abuse, then she is not only showing behavioural clues to Child, but re-experiences the feelings experienced at the time of abuse and the entire childhood scene.

Ego states are represented diagrammatically or illustrated in Figure 7.1. These three ego states can be reliably distinguished from one another by observation and questions. As therapist, you are able to determine whether they are replaying their own childhood (Child); replaying material borrowed from parent figures (Parent), or responding directly to the here and now (Adult). And by monitoring your own ego states, you can be in the appropriate ego state for the here-and-now situation.

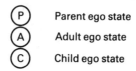

Figure 7.1   *Structural model of ego states*

Switching ego states is a skill which we can learn to do deliberately. Once clients can recognise their ego states, they can switch to another one in order to cope better with a situation (go into another ego state). For example; if a client who loses their temper realises that this is how their parents reacted to frustrations, by learning to cathect Adult, and choose in the here and now what to do instead of angering themselves, then they have a range of new choices available. I do this in role-play very often, so that clients *experience* their new control over feelings, thoughts and behaviours. Or if clients realise that when they are folding up in fear and embarrassment when criticised it is actually their Child reaction to criticism, and that they are an adult who can and has the right to assert themselves, they can go into Adult and choose not to crumple. The Adult ego state refers to immediate, apparently spontaneous behaviours, but in fact integrates all the person's experiences and uses these in a fresh way anew in any situation. Unlike the Parent and Child, it does not have a set pattern of feelings, thoughts and behaviours since the Adult responds anew in every situation.

Ego states (functional model) and transactions

Ego states are also important because of the way they influence relationships or transactions with other people. Each person has a Parent, Adult and Child ego state, and each is brought about by certain, predictable situations. We were all innocent, self-pleasing children at one point (Child ego state); we all observed and imitated our parents (Parent ego state) and we all have to make new sense of the world (Adult ego state). When we describe transactions between people, we diagram it as if nurturing and critical/controlling behaviour comes from the Parent ego state, analysing and problem-solving from the Adult ego state, and rebelling, conforming or childlike emotional expressions come from Child ego state. In fact, we saw above that any behaviour can come from any ego state in the *structural* model, so we call this way of describing transactions the *functional* model (see Figure 7.2). Transactions do not need to be verbal, and we readily experience other people's ego states for their non-verbal language; people with severe learning difficulties are frequently very perceptive about ego states.

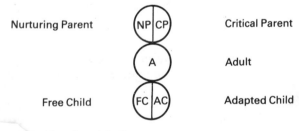

Nurturing Parent   NP | CP   Critical Parent

A   Adult

Free Child   FC | AC   Adapted Child

...nctional model of ego states

another adult, our communication will ...ate, and we can expect a complementary response from the Adult of the other person. For example, you ask the electrician how much her work costs, she tells you £10 per hour.

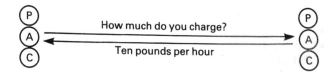

At other times, you may behave towards others in a Parent–Parent way, as in 'Aren't those others awful, leaving their litter all over the place' – 'Yes aren't they'.

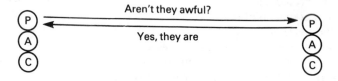

Other transactions may be Parent–Child with a Child–Parent reply – such as 'The grass needs cutting' – 'Leave me alone!'

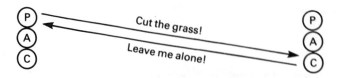

Complementary transactions are messages where the reply comes from the ego state addressed, and address the one that addressed them.

Complementary transactions can go on indefinitely, unless someone cathects a different ego state.

Complementary transactions have a quality of expectedness about them. If we give a Controlling Parent message to someone we *expect* them to reply in Adapted Child way. Many conversations consist of a chain of complementary transactions, such as from father to his son with learning difficulties:

Father: Ronald, stop dribbling! (P–C)
Ronald: I can't help it! [*whining*] (C–P)

Father: Yes you can! [*sounding cross*] (P–C)
Ronald: It's really hard for me Dad! (C–P)
Father: Don't come that, you know you can stop it if you want! (P–C)
Ronald: No, I can't, it's 'cause of my mouth! [*whining*] (C–P)
Father: I'm not going to listen to all that, I just want you to stop it! (P–C)
Ronald: Oh, Dad. . . ! (C–P)

Notice I said that complementary transactions *can* go on indefinitely, not *will* do so. In order to break the flow or create a change, someone needs to move into, or cathect, another ego state. When they do this, and use a different ego state, especially if they also *address* a different ego state in the hearer, we will have a *crossed* transaction.

Crossed transactions

If Ronald, above, instead of his whining replies from Child to his father's Parent had cathected another ego state and replied from that, the conversation might have been very different. In fact, I've found it the most powerful tool that self-advocates have in their repertoire. Let's imagine that instead of going into his Child ego state, Ronald had cathected Adult; he may have crossed the transaction thus:

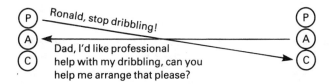

or by cathecting Parent himself, Ronald might have replied

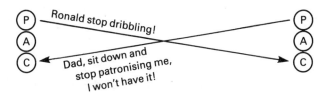

or, to lighten it, he might have addressed his Father's Child from his Child:

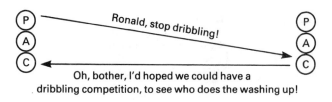

Oh, bother, I'd hoped we could have a
dribbling competition, to see who does the washing up!

Of course, replies don't have to be verbal, and Ronald could have stood up and shouted from Parent, or giggled and thumbed his nose from Child.

Any time that the reply does not come from the ego state addressed, or addresses a different ego state from the one addressed, we say that it is a *crossed* transaction. It cuts the flow of communication. When a transaction is crossed, the chances are that the person receiving the cross will shift into the ego state that the crosser has invited. She will then likely as not move into a parallel transaction from the new ego state. When a transaction is crossed, a break in communication results and one or both individuals will need to shift ego states in order for communication to start again. The break in communication may be felt as a jolt, or it may result in a deep emotional response.

Uses of complementary and crossed transactions
As therapists, we can use these rules of communication in a number of ways. First, we can teach about ego states and transactions so that clients can understand what is involved when they are having problems communicating with people around them. For example, someone I work with found herself getting more and more depressed by the moaning (about hostel life) that staff *and* residents engaged in (in Transactional Analysis we call that playing the game of 'Ain't it Awful!'). Once she realised that unless someone crossed the transactions it could go on indefinitely and everyone would feel more and more pessimistic, she decided to cathect Adult, and say, 'Let's look at what we can *do* about this place, where shall we start?' or 'I feel depressed when we talk like this, let's stop and look at some things to do about it', she felt much more potent, and people started to be more constructive. Another client, who had some physical difficulties too, used to get ribbed by the young people who lived near her and teased her for her disabilities. She began to say 'I feel hurt when you say things like that, please stop!' instead of folding up and crying or avoiding walking down the street as she used to.

We can also use Transactional Analysis in our communication with clients. We can, for example, help clients to relate to us from the range of ego states and to practise addressing different ego states in ourselves. Sometimes they are in the habit of transacting to everyone who doesn't have learning difficulties from Child. By practising the other options, they can gain confidence to communicate with a wider repertoire outside the therapy situation.

Ulterior transactions
Whenever a message is conveyed socially, there is also a psychological message being passed too. While the social level message is overt, the psychological one is covert or hidden. While the social level messages may well be Adult–Adult, the psychological message is frequently Parent–Child, or Child–Parent.

Eric Berne believed that the outcome of an interaction is determined at the psychological and not the social level. Thus when people are communicating at two levels, what actually happens is likely to be the outcome of the psychological level.

In therapy, for example, a client may apparently be functioning from Adult ego state and addressing our Adult, but at an ulterior level, they are addressing our Parent from their Child. Recently, I had a session which went like this:

Joanna: What do you want from today's session?
Sue: I can't think of anything I want to talk about.
Joanna: How are you feeling as you tell me that?
Sue: I'm not feeling anything, I'm OK.
Joanna: What does OK mean for you?
Sue: Oh, fine, I'm feeling fine.
[At that point, I realised I was feeling angry, and I said so. . . .]
Joanna: Sue, I'm feeling angry, I'm wondering if you are feeling angry too?
Sue: Yes, I don't want to be here.
Joanna: So you don't want to be here?
Sue: No, I wanted to cancel my session, but Lorraine [the officer in charge] said as you were coming, I had to be here.
Joanna: So do you want us to finish there? Or shall we talk about why you didn't want to come today?
Sue: I was angry, because I can't go home this weekend.
Joanna: You were feeling angry because you couldn't go home this weekend. . . .
Sue: Yes, and I felt angry with you.
Joanna: Because. . . .
Sue: Because last time you wouldn't let me smoke.

and so on. . . . By picking up the ulterior level, namely a message to me of 'I won't. You can't make me', I was able to bring out the process between us, and we went on to look at what was happening in general in our relationship. She had had many years of being told what to do, and had originally found that resistance was the best way of responding. Actually, she wanted to find other ways of reacting to Critical Parent behaviour, and has now started to say what she's feeling and ask for what she wants.

Symbiosis

According to Jacqui Schiff, a symbiosis occurs when two or more people behave as though between them they form a single person. In a relationship like this, the people concerned will not be using all their ego states. Frequently, one will be using more Parent and Adult functions than Child, and the other will be using more Child than Parent and Adult. In services for people with learning difficulties, it is not uncommon to find that users of the services take the Child role, and the staff seemingly almost automatically take the Parent and Adult.

For example, I know of a hostel where the staff had traditionally made all the decisions about what clients would eat, what times people did things, including when they went to bed, got up, went out or whatever. As a result of attending a workshop which was run by some self-advocates with whom I work, they all realised that clients were being held in passivity by this routine, and all voted to change it, thereby enabling all concerned to use all ego states.

When working in therapy with a client, you may encounter a psychological invitation from them to enter into a symbiotic relationship. Clients may expect you to do more than half the thinking, and to come up with the ideas, and to take the initiative. When this happens, mention it – open up the situation for discussion. The following comes from a session not long ago:

Joanna: So what do you want to change today?
Silvia: I'm fed up with living here. [*changes what is meant*]
Joanna: So what do you want to get from this session?
Silvia: I want to leave this place.
Joanna: Silvia – I've asked you twice what you want to get from this session, and you've not told me yet.
Silvia: I want to get out of here. [*sounding very angry*]
Joanna: Silvia, you won't be able to leave by the end of this session – but you can change yourself – what do you want to change about yourself by the end of the session?
Silvia:You help me get out. [*avoiding responsibility*]
Joanna: I hear you want your place you live in to change, and you want to leave here – now what can you do in this session towards leaving?
Silvia: Bloody fucking shithouse.

> *Joanna*: What do you want?
> *Silvia*: I want to make up my own mind.
> *Joanna*: OK – so you want to make your own decisions – about what?
> *Silvia*: I don't know why I have to stay here.
> *Joanna*: So you want to make your own decisions, and you want to leave, but it's not up to you at present.

The above example is my unsuccessful attempt not to go into Critical Parent mode, in response to Silva's invitation to respond to her hurt, angry Child. By constantly inviting Adult, I was attempting to resist the invitation to rescue. One of the main emphases, I believe, in therapeutic work with people with learning difficulties, is this facilitation of their use of all ego states, so that they become able to function without symbiosis. This is done by:

1 spotting the psychological invitations to symbiosis, and talking about it;
2 spotting the pull to respond in a way that will result in symbiosis, and resisting it, again, bringing the pull to respond in this way out in the open;
3 making interventions which invite the use of unused ego states.

People who are more severely limited in verbal communication will still be offering invitations to symbiosis – all the above applies to non-verbal communications too.

Passivity

There are four styles of passive behaviour which a person may use to establish a symbiotic relationship. All passive behaviours prevent the person from sorting out their life and solving their problems.

The passive behaviours are:

1 withdrawal or doing nothing;
2 over-adaptation;
3 agitation;
4 incapacitation and/or violence.

Withdrawal or doing nothing involves using energy to deny awareness and responses – For example, when John withdraws and goes off to his room when people criticise him, or when Joyce stares into space or buries her head in her hands when approached.

Over-adaptation is figuring out what people think others want of them, and attempting to conform to that expectation. Others are seen as parental figures and are more important than themselves. People who are over-adapting are trying to take responsibility for satisfying the needs of others without checking this out with them.

Thus, Jane often wants a hug, but assumes because she has Down's syndrome that people won't want to hug her. Richard assumes that whenever anyone is angry it's because he's done something wrong.

Agitation involves the use of energy in behaviours which are not productive, such as twitching, pacing, rocking, smoking, talking non-stop and so on. Sometimes just making people aware of it is enough, or more direct confrontation from Parent may be needed. However, at the same time support needs to be given to the person's Child ego state; for example: 'Mary, I really care about you, so stop wringing your hands and hurting yourself. . . !'

incapacitation and/or violence behaviours are a refusal to think and solve problems, and are immediate demands to take over responsibility. The person is really terrified underneath, and these are last-ditch attempts to ward off the imagined disaster. Going sick, going crazy, attacking someone are all in this category of extreme passive behaviours.

These behaviours are escalated from one to the other, from 1 to 4 and it is important to realise that people who are carrying out agitation or incapacitation are *not able to engage Adult* so they need to be brought down to withdrawal or over-adaptation and then asked to think.

We can use the spotting of passive behaviours to help us to enable clients to become active and problem-solving, thereby using more of their capacities, and becoming more independent. Frequently they will have been encouraged to take passive social roles, and learned how to get people to do things for them, think for them, and treat them like people who cannot do things for themselves. We need to spot these invitations to become symbiotic, and constantly invite them to use *all* their ego states, while we use all of ours. Frequently, people will behave in a much less 'mentally handicapped' way once they cease being passive.

Frame of reference and redefining

If a group of different people look out of a window at a stormy sea, they might report what they see in the following way:

'It's a wonderful, wild, magnificent scene!'
'What a horrible, depressing, grey picture!'
'How scary! The sea looks really angry and threatening!'
'I bet its a great day for catching cod down on the beach!'
'Look at the beautiful curling waves and the whirling cloud-shapes'.

Anyone listening might imagine that we are not all seeing the same scene. But the view is the same; what is different is *how* we look.

We call this the *frame of reference*.

Each person perceives the world according to their unique frame of reference. We learned much of it from our parent figures, and therefore maintain our frame of reference by much use of the Parent ego state's definitions, that is, ideas of how we are, others are, and the world is. We may speculate that of the group of people above, one had a parent figure who also feared the sea, one who was thrilled by it, one who saw its beauty, and so on.

The implications for therapeutic work are: that it is important to realise that clients will not have the same frame of reference as us, and that we must bear in mind *their* frame of reference. The more we can understand how their world seems to them, the more we can help them to change. Unless they change their frame of reference, they will only change to a limited extent. When we make the initial change contract, they will be seeking change *within* their frame of reference. As they develop and grow psychologically, their frame of reference will change too, and so their therapeutic goals will change. For example, a client with whom I worked had a very disfiguring congenital condition started off contracting 'to have a best friend'. After some work with his Child ego state (in which he moved from chair to chair between his confident part and his ashamed part), he contracted to have a girl-friend in the romantic sense. When he had established a good romatic relationship with a young woman, he contracted with me to have the confidence to propose to her, which he did. She actually turned him down, but he is now happily married to another, older woman, who actually proposed to him! As he moved through therapy, his view of himself changed, which meant that his frame of reference was different. Thus his goals changed.

However, we need to enable clients to change their frame of reference by first understanding it, then helping them to see how it is not working for them. It is no good just forcing our frame of reference on them without sensitivity. Our role needs to be supportive while they test out reality and modify their frame of reference as a result of this journey through finding out what will work best for them.

Frame of reference and the script

Part of the frame of reference is the *script*. The total frame of reference is vast, and entails all the person's views of everything in the world. Some of these views will ignore, unconsciously, some information which would be relevant to solution of problems. Thus, some aspects of the frame of reference entail *discounting*. The script consists of that part of the frame of reference which involves discounting. Discounts can involve stimuli, problems and options, about self, others or the situation, and can be of various levels. A person who bangs their head against a brick wall when angry is discounting their pain at a very profound level. This may be because at an early age, in response to very tragic situations, they decided it was necessary to cut off the sensation of pain when they were angry. Or for someone who can think quite well, but stops thinking when scared, and reports that they are confused and cannot think, they may have taken an early decision that 'life will be easier if I get someone else to think for me'.

In *Principles of Group Treatment*, Berne defined life scripts as 'an unconscious life plan'. Later, in *What Do You Say after You Say 'Hello'* he developed this definition that a script is 'a life plan made in childhood, reinforced by the parents, justified by subsequent events, and culminating in a chosen alternative'. Our clients found ways to survive which worked for them originally, but which may strait-jacket them in adult life.

In the life of every individual, then, the dramatic life events, the roles that are learned, rehearsed and acted out, are originally determined by a script. This script bears a striking resemblance to a play. Each has a cast of characters, dialogue, acts and scenes, themes and plots, which move towards a final act. The script is a person's ongoing programme for a life drama which dictates where the person is going with his or her life and the paths that will lead there. It is a drama an individual compulsively acts out, though most of it will be carried out outside awareness. Everyone has a script which she or he is following. Some people follow a script that is heroic, or tragic, or like a soap-opera; as children grow up they learn to play parts; as victims, rescuers, persecuters; and then unconsciously seek others to play complementary roles with them (refer back to the section on symbiosis).

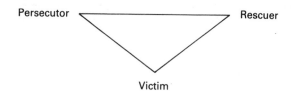

Figure 7.3   *The Karpman Drama Triangle*

Individuals follow scripts, families follow scripts, couples follow scripts. The interplay of these scripts affects the drama of each person's life and of their outline, or their subculture. People with learning difficulties are cast in roles early on. The earlier they are classified as 'different', the earlier this casting will occur. To be born with a Down's syndrome face is to be given a set of responses from others which have embedded in them some obvious and not so obvious messages – for example, injunctions such as 'don't make it', 'don't belong', 'don't grow up', 'don't think', 'don't be close', 'don't feel', 'don't be yourself', and later 'don't be sexual', 'don't be independent' and so on. There may also be the more basic message conveyed of 'don't exist'.

There may also be commands, some of which play a special role in scripting: Be perfect; Be strong; Try hard; Please others; Hurry up. These are called driver messages, because the Child feels a compulsion to follow these commands. She believes she can stay OK as long as she obeys the driver and doesn't go against the injunctions. Everyone also receives a set of permissions; thus, people with learning difficulties may well have received permission to be fun, kind, loyal, musical, good mimics, passive.

In response to all these preverbal (injunctions and permissions) and verbal ('you must' – or driver) messages, the Child makes a *script decision* – that is, decides how to live her life. This is reinforced by the Parent figures, and modified as the Child develops. At the time, it is the best way to survive, but later we all become strait-jacketed by our script, and are unable, while in script, to be autonomous.

Working with scripts

When working with clients' unconscious life plans, I believe the first task is to find out what are ways in which it affects them in the here and now. Thus, for Suzanne her script decision, which was 'I'll deny my own needs and try to please other people', meant that she sat in our sessions trying to get it right for *me*. She would start off very withdrawn, then become over-adapted, as she tried desperately to work out what I wanted from her, and how to please me. One session proceeded like this:

Joanna: What do you want to change today Suzanne?
Suzanne: What do you want me to do? [*smiles*]
Joanna: I want you to tell me how you'd like to be different in an hour's time.
Suzanne: Be different?
Joanna: Be different from how you are now in some way.
Suzanne: Do you want me to be different?
Joanna: No, but you told me that there were some things that you wanted to change about yourself.

Suzanne: Yes, there are.
Joanna: So, what do you want to change today?

Often, the script will be seen working in small and big form; that is, it can be seen in the above interchange with Suzanne, but could also be seen in the fact that she'd agreed to the smallest, darkest room in the group home, and that she would stay up cleaning the kitchen when the others had gone to bed. She cleaned the toilet, she carried the heaviest shopping. In her family she'd got her recognition (strokes) for being helpful, pleasing others, denying herself. I worked with her by giving her recognition (stroking her) for *being*, not for doing. I showed her I liked her come what may, that she was OK by me whatever she did, that she could feel all her feelings, express all her feelings and above all she didn't need to please me to be OK, or for that matter please anyone. She even learned to ask for nurturing from others, though that took a very long time.

I use relaxation, visualisation and other exercises to help people get in touch with their core feelings and needs. While clients are being in script, they are out of touch with reality, because they are discounting vital information about themselves, others and the situation. Any intervention which helps them be in touch with reality is helping them to move out of script, and be free to choose moment by moment what will work for them.

Games and rackets

People keep themselves in script by repetitively setting up negative experiences through their interactions with others such that they hold themselves in script. By inviting other people into set patterns of behaviour which end in a predictable, uncomfortable way (the payoff) someone can reinforce their faulty script beliefs. For example, Dick who has Down's syndrome, used to pick beautiful haughty-looking women without learning difficulties, to go out with him (usually within 2 minutes of acquaintance). They always said no, so he believed he'd never have a girl friend. Once he'd confronted his game, of going for the unattainable in order to get the 'kick me' response he was unconsciously seeking, he started to ask young women he already knew and liked to go out with him. Games are repetitive patterns of behaviour with a concealed motivation towards a negative payoff. They prevent honest, intimate and open relationships between the players. Yet people play them to reinforce their early opinions about self, others and life, and to fulfil their sense of destiny (script).

In therapy, games are an excellent source of therapeutic insight, however, and will enable the therapist and the client to understand how the person's script is being played out. By seeing the alternatives and learning how to relate to others in straightforward ways instead, clients can gradually be helped towards really taking charge of their own lives.

Working with rackets

Like games, rackets are ways of staying in script and not being authentic. Every child discovers that some feelings are prohibited in her family, while others are rewarded. She expresses the prohibited feelings, her needs are not met. She soon becomes skilled at covering over the forbidden feelings, and showing the permitted ones instead. Soon, she works out a set of beliefs and thinking patterns to 'justify' the substituted feelings. Thus, when someone offends Gerald, instead of feeling angry with them, he feels scared, and then ashamed, believing that he is to blame, and that that's because he's 'no good'. In his childhood, anger was not allowed, but it was OK to feel guilty, and anxious. Once Gerald allowed *himself* to feel angry, he became much more potent, and even stood up straighter.

Gerald used two-chair work to discover that he actually felt very angry with the staff of his hostel. He put a staff member on a cushion (in his imagination) and talked to them as if they were in the room. By getting in touch with, and expressing, what he really felt, he unblocked his real feelings of anger and sense of injustice. Now he is on the hostel committee, and is active in the local self-advocacy group.

Summary

Transactional Analysis is a very appropriate way of working therapeutically with people with learning difficulties. It is a respectful model, and therapists work in a contractual way, thereby client and therapist agree the goals together. The theory and techniques are accessible and adaptable, and work towards the client's autonomy and self-empowerment.

The model applies very well to people with profound learning difficulties. Most techniques adapt to non-verbal ways of working. Everyone perceives ulterior levels of transacting, and once clients give up the old scripty ways of behaving, they are often seen as giving up much of the 'mental handicap' too.

My husband, Steve Richards, and I run workshops and act as

consultants for people who work with clients who have learning difficulties, applying Transactional Analysis principles. We work with basic grade staff and managers in day and residential care, and with parents, enabling them to find new ways of keeping themselves and others OK and facilitate real change. Mainly concerned with clients' empowerment, we work with self-advocates in their quest for personal growth and for real influence in planning and monitoring services. Also involved in special education, we work with staff, managers and pupils in setting the scene for young people with learning difficulties as they prepare for adult life.

Parents, too, have gained much from attending our workshops in Transactional Analysis, sometimes working alongside their family members, and sometimes applying it to their own adjustment to their life circumstances.

There are many resources developed in Transactional Analysis, for use with children and adults, individually and in groups. For information about how to explore TA for yourself or your organisations, contact me, Joanna Beazley-Richards, at 2 Quarry View, Whitehall Road, Crowborough, East Sussex TN6 1JT, telephone 0892 655195.

Further reading

Berne, Eric (1964) *Games People Play*. Harmondsworth: Penguin.
Berne, Eric (1966) *Principles of Group Treatment*. New York: Grove Press.
Berne, Eric (1975) *What Do You Say after You Say 'Hello'*. London: Corgi.
Schiff, Jacqui (1970) *All my Children*. New York: Evans.
Stewart, Ian (1989) *Transactional Analysis Counselling in Action*. London: Sage.
Stewart, Ian and Joines, Van (1987) *TA Today*. Nottingham: Lifespace.
James, M. and Jongeward, (1978) *Born to Win*. New York: Cygnet.

8

The Deviancy Career and People with a Mental Handicap

Joan Bicknell and Suzanne Conboy-Hill

The deviancy career – an explanation

Normalisation is a word used widely in services for people with a mental handicap but one aspect of normalisation, the 'deviancy career', has not had the impact that it might have done. Many studies of people with a mental handicap are cross-sectional (Lund, 1985; Corbett, 1979; Reid, 1983), which, while useful in many ways, fail to exhibit the life experiences, life-style and life plan of the individual with a handicap. A longitudinal examination of the lives of such handicapped people (Langness and Levine, 1986) usually reveals stressful life events or psychosocial crises (Brown et al., 1973; Paykel, 1978). These are major happenings that have social and personal significance. They can be classified as entrance or exit in nature (a major addition to the life-style or a reduction respectively) or as negative or positive (a major added stress or a reduction of stress).

There is insufficient evidence to know whether there are more life events or a greater proportion of exit or negative life events for the person with a mental handicap compared with non-handicapped people. However, the risk for those with disability is that the life event will be managed by people in a care-giving role who may be influenced by negative attitudes or negative assumptions about disability. In addition, the person with a handicap is not always consulted by the carer, even though such involvement may be possible. A deviancy career is therefore started when wrong decisions are taken and the psychological or physical deterioration that results in the person with a handicap is seen to justify the original decision.

A useful start to the analysis of life experiences can be made at the anecdotal level to look at some of the short- and long-term sequelae there might be, both good and bad, when major decisions are made in the lives of persons with a mental handicap, and how often inappropriate decisions are based on negative assumptions.

This chapter attempts to fill this gap in our knowledge by examining the issues involved in the deviancy career, looking at the histories of four individuals for whom negative life events and assumptions led to, or almost led to, strategies which would have further deprived or isolated them.

Deviancy begins with assumptions

Whenever a life event or psychosocial crisis occurs in the life of a person with a mental handicap, carers may feel that certain negative outcomes are inevitable: . . . about the newly diagnosed handicapped child, 'He will destroy the family'; about the deaf child, 'She will never lip read so don't bother teaching her'; about the mentally handicapped adult faced with a bereavement, 'He doesn't have a time concept so he won't notice'.

Because of such negative expectations, the experience of the handicapped person in that crisis may be impoverished. They may be shielded from the full range of human emotions that others share on the basis that they cannot understand, that they will be harmed or that they will behave inappropriately. Such a lack of experience of emotions will limit the development of the individual and this in turn may be responded to by further limitations of experience. Some may respond at this stage by a cry for help through a behavioural change, regression or physical illness. All of these pleas for help can once again be mismanaged by a reduction in life experience or freedom and, frequently, by medication. Indeed, these changes may be anticipated by those who believed the original negative expectation and quoted as 'evidence' that the person with a mental handicap must be shielded from the rich tapestry of life. Too many carers in the mental handicap service will be familiar with this dreary set of self-fulfilling prophecies where the lack of sensitive and informed intervention leads to the cry for help that is drowned by medication, constant observation or security.

Conversely, a positive intervention made on the basis of real and not assumed need may often create exciting opportunities for people to become more self-aware and aware of others. Consequently, life becomes richer in experience and individuals become more mature and more able.

This compares with the vicious circle of deprivation outlined by the normalisation philosophy in which a history of 'never have' leads to projections of 'never will', so reducing the need for provision of opportunities and resulting, not surprisingly, in the failure of the handicapped person to develop (see Figure 8.1). Interestingly, this thinking has influenced the development of many

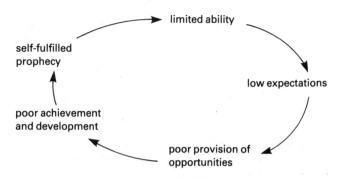

Figure 8.1 *Circle of Deprivation*

disadvantaged groups, resulting in the restriction of educational and social opportunities on the grounds that inherent intellectual flaws in these groups would render such opportunities pointless.

Some stories and their implications

The following stories describe both positive and negative interventions and the impact, or potential impact, upon the individual concerned. It is particularly salutary to recognise that the negative type of intervention usually happens in an environment that apparently lacks stimulation, love and care in the first place although it is worth noting that stigma breeds its own social isolation and desperation and it can be no accident that the more stigmatised the group, the less resources appear to be available to it. As a society, we have tacitly approved the appalling conditions in which disadvantaged people have lived and their carers worked. It should not be surprising that such overwhelming desolation gives rise to emotional barrenness in those required to sustain it.

Q's story

This is a story of early deprivation leading to behavioural problems which elicited increasingly isolating control strategies.

Q was born in Vietnam and suffered gross deprivation as an orphan at the time of the invasion by the Vietcong. Serious infection had almost destroyed his vision and all his hearing. The little vision he had left was finally lost in a valiant attempt in the UK to restore some eyesight. He was 14 years old at the time of the following intervention.

Q was sensorially deprived and this was made worse by his habit of biting his carers. He also injured himself and for both of these behaviours he was heavily sedated until he showed akathisia (pointless, restless movements). No one touched him for fear of being bitten and, to deal with this biting, a helmet was made with a visor which, by its shape, occluded the sense of smell. Small wonder that he became even more seriously disturbed and was excluded from the taxi to the school, then from the school itself, to lead a monotonous life in a single room on the top floor of a house for Vietnamese children – a life devoid of all sensation. He also had gross offensive diarrhoea and failed to grow.

Qs deviancy career could have progressed further, condemning him to a life of isolation, distress and a reputation for challenging behaviour and poor potential, but fortunately the cycle was halted at this point, for his diarrhoea was found to be gluten induced, and a diet solved this problem. The helmet was discarded, medication stopped and he was treated as a sensorially deprived child who had missed early ordinary life experiences. He was brought from his single room and allowed to mix with other children. He was allowed to regress and for most of the day was carried on the hip of the most senior member of staff who was not discouraged by some severe bites. Water play was used a lot with blowing, sucking and feeling games, using a shower, for example. He was fascinated by tactile toys such as those made of soft plastic, and also fern fronds. His pleasure at creating an intermittent light in front of his eyes suggested some residual vision, finally lost by the surgery referred to earlier. Fortunately, the touch of the same toys still gave him pleasure. He grew in height and weight, almost certainly due to adolescence, the control of his gluten-induced diarrhoea and possibly also to the cessation of his deprivation. He began to attend a special needs unit and all his symptoms stopped, although some returned whenever he felt stressed.

This boy lived in a highly deprived environment. At one point he was heavily sedated, wearing a helmet and with the removal of his teeth being considered. He was regarded as dangerous as well as difficult. The sensory deprivation was about to increase unless a few risks were taken. A positive series of interventions with a totally new life-style to which he responded resulted in him becoming a content adolescent of normal height and weight for his age, occupied at all times with activities he liked. He reverted to self-multilation when stressed but not to biting. Q illustrates well the deviancy career and how one negative intervention may lead to another.

J's story

This is an example of how expectations and assumptions almost resulted in a series of negative strategies which would have distressed J and disrupted his family relationships, probably resulting in behavioural difficulties for him and a further loss for his mother.

J was a man of 41 years with severe intellectual limitations, unable to speak and supposedly unable to convey the simplest wish. He lived in a long-stay hospital where the pattern was set years ago, whereby every Sunday both his parents visited him and had tea in the Friends' Centre. This pattern was disrupted by his father's death. His mother failed to mourn, feeling that her sadness would add to J's confusion, but J could not understand why two chairs were wanted instead of three and dragged a third to the table, hitting his mother as he did so. This pattern of behaviour, with mother distressed now by J, continued for four years before anything was done.

A negative intervention was about to occur, that mother would stop her visits and J would be sedated until he could no longer rebel. Fortunately, a positive intervention became possible when a therapist offered to come each Sunday and work with J and his mother. The intervention consisted of pushing away the third chair with the words 'Daddy's gone – he won't come again'. In these sessions mother's tears were seen as a positive sign of her need to mourn and J was encouraged to comfort her. In one session J pulled the chair to the table ten times but the therapist pushed it away with the same words on each occasion. After several Sundays of this intervention, J began to accept that two chairs were sufficient and became adept at comforting his mother. They began to enjoy each other's company and J settled, not looking for the third chair or his father.

The negative intervention suggested at this point in his deviancy career would have been sedation for J and asking his mother not to visit. Both would have impoverished the lives of J and his mother. In addition, his carers would have failed in their responsibility to support his mother and help her to maintain regular and pleasing contact with her son.

A's story

This story shows how failure to recognise the distress underlying extreme behavioural challenges could have caused A further confusion and resulted in a highly isolating and controlling environment for her.

A was a most disturbed girl of 10 years living at home with her mother, father and brother who were devoted to her and under-stood her ways. Her behavioural peculiarities extended through day and night and the entire household routine had evolved to meet those needs. Respite care, overnight stays and 2–3 hours in the daytime or evening were all that was requested by this family, exhausted by the constant screaming, rituals and disturbed behaviour.

Respite care had been refused by all units contacted or tried either because of her reputation or her behaviour while in the unit.

Finally she came to a home that allowed her 'to be' rather than one that expected her 'to do'. This existential approach meant that she was successfully managed although with some difficulty. At night she was restless and was allowed to creep into bed with the member of staff on night call and spend the night there. She awoke in the morning surprised that it was not her mother but at least an acceptable alternative had been found!

An existential approach to the care of children with learning disabilities is hardly ever considered. 'To do' and make progress becomes the catch-phrase of acceptability and one way in which the quality of care is measured. The feeling from those who looked after her, including her parents, was that she had never found herself, that she had never experienced the difference between her inside world and the outside world, nor had she accepted external reality for what it was. Being at this very early stage of development, at the separation of self from non-self, it was hardly appropriate to expect that she would perform for others. Rather, for her peace of mind, A needed a mother figure both during the day and at night.

R's story

In this story, negative strategies arose from one simple failure to recognise a common need. R's behaviours were 'diagnosed' rather than understood and the result was a downward spiral of deprivation and sedation.

R, 10 years old, had multiple and mental handicaps, in particular affecting his ears, eyes and face. He had been abandoned and lived in a children's home where others had less profound handicaps and some had physical handicaps with normal intelligence.

Hard work was done by all of those in contact with him to raise his level of achievement and his deviancy career was destined to be minimal. Then the senior member of staff left. It was presumed R had no concept of time and little of language. After the departure, all the children showed their grief in one way or another and this was expected and accepted by the staff. All, that is, except R, whose behaviour was seen as pathological and unacceptable and not related to mourning in any way. The result was that he was put in a long-stay hospital where he was labelled a behaviour problem and was heavily sedated in a locked ward. The last time he was seen, some years after the event, he was rocking and banging his head against the wall with no awareness of visitors or of those around him.

This was a tragic intervention that should never have happened. His behaviour, at a different level from the others, was still a response to the loss of his carer and would have been time limited and responsive to positive intervention.

There can be no justification for what happened to this child who was making the best of his many handicaps and was misunderstood at the time of his greatest need. The intervention meant that his bereavement response was magnified to encompass the tragedy of his move from all those he knew and loved.

The effects of a deviancy career

The four stories described here show watersheds where the choice between negative and positive interventions can be made, the ease with which negative interventions seem to spring to mind and the vastly different outcomes which might be expected from choosing one or the other.

In discussing the implications of these choices, a number of points can be made. First, there is a tendency to respond to the negative behaviour of disabled people in ways which include withdrawal, isolation, punishment, deceit and simple failure to acknowledge feelings. All of these strategies would be utterly unacceptable if applied to someone without disabilities but are nonetheless frequently offered as reasonable propositions by carers who often have sincerely held affections for their client or relative. Thus, control is imposed rather than structure offered and punitive measures taken to eliminate behaviours instead of rewards being given for behavioural development or attention and comfort provided in response to emotional distress.

The cycle is one of hopelessness, helplessness and desperate attempts at containment. The deviancy career compounds the original disability of the individual and becomes a part of that person's 'personality package' to be responded to as a unit, and measures are taken to control or eliminate anything which moves beyond some boundary of equilibrium. In this world, there can be no distress, excitement, frustration, anger or pain, only behaviour disorders or problems to be eliminated.

Most importantly, the deviancy career combined with stigma and the emotional drives of carers as described by Main (1957) have the power to multiply handicap in a person who was, at the outset, simply disabled. The vicious circle of rationalisation and justification serves to maintain the individual in a dependent and deviant position and is likely to provoke further deviant behaviours as reactions to confusion, frustration and sensory, intellectual or emotional deprivation.

Where positive choices are made, the circle is disrupted and the individual becomes the focus of interventions based on personal development and emotional growth. It should be intuitively obvious that this kind of environment is more likely to encourage healthy, adaptive behaviours and feelings but somehow, where disability is concerned, we seem to find it easier to stack the odds even further against people and then blame them for the results.

Challenging deviancy with positive philosophies and strategies

Fortunately, it has been possible to challenge unhelpful attitudes, and the dramatic progress of many previously undervalued social groups bears witness to the wisdom of breaking into the vicious circle in ways which have become variously known as positive discrimination, normalisation and social-role valorisation, and of which the deviancy career is a mirror image.

Many features of the behaviour of mentally handicapped people, once thought to be located within the individual and arising entirely from the handicapping condition, are now known to be largely located in the systems and practices of institutional organisations which interact with the limitations and disabilities of individuals leading to gross behavioural disturbance including withdrawal.

In 1957, Main wrote of the underlying emotional drives of carers, and pointed out that people who failed to respond to nursing and doctoring by 'being cured' were likely to meet an onslaught of punitive measures disguised as treatment. Main was describing the psychiatric services of the time but it takes little imagination to extend the concept to other 'incurable' groups, including those owning attributes which are *perceived* as undesirable and incurable but which, were it not for the behaviour of others, would have considerably less impact upon the owner's life. As it is, the perception of undesirability and incurability results in a spiral of disadvantages which serves both to punish the individual and, at the same time, allows those doing the perceiving to feel benevolent and tolerant by supporting treatment and facilities, many of which preserve the social status of disadvantaged groups and encourage a culture of dependence and gratitude.

Normalisation, social-role valorisation and positive discrimination offer a way out of this culture, and discussion of the deviancy career provides a graphic illustration of the compounding effects of disadvantage and disability.

However, in the rush towards egalitarianism and 'shared care' (the client with the carer), it is vital to remember that the intrinsic disability is real and has implications for the individual's understanding, behaviour and ability to take responsibility. In this sense, people with a mental handicap are unique, they are not as able as their chronological age would demand, nor is it appropriate to address them at the level of a deduced mental age. A 40 year-old man, functioning at the intellectual or emotional level of a 3 year old, has 40 years' experience of operating at that level, is likely to be street-wise and knowledgeable and probably takes himself to the pub at lunch-time! Nevertheless, his limitations need to be recognised, allowances made and interventions tailored to acknowledge this unique human composite.

It is easy to find fault; we can criticise carers for being unfeeling, professionals for failing to see what is happening and taking steps to correct things, society for stigmatising groups of people then choosing to ignore them, leaving others to get on with the job of 'caring' under difficult conditions. The fact is that all of these elements of the equation are people – us – and we need to understand the motivating factors behind our behaviour, make them explicit and then address them constructively. This process involves the internalisation of the basic assumption that people with learning disabilities have the same rights and feelings as anyone else.

Given this framework, it becomes apparent that respect, dignity and emotional support should be first principles in tackling problems with which our clients may present us. What remains, then, is to devise and define the tools to do the job. Fortunately, many already exist. Normalisation and social-role valorisation (SRV) as philosophies, the Individual Plan system and Gentle Teaching as approaches to personal development, have all contributed to a change in thinking away from knee-jerk reactions to crises and towards the ongoing personal development of individuals.

Normalisation and social-role valorisation

Developed largely by Wolf Wolfensberger in the 1970s, these philosophies were designed to shift attitudes away from the vicious circle of deprivation and negative expectations (see Figure 8.1) and towards at first 'normal' and, later, valued life-styles.

The notion of positive discrimination is inherent in the principles of normalisation and SRV and, gradually, people with a mental handicap have begun to experience life-styles which are much more in accordance with those to which 'ordinary' society might aspire.

The principles of normalisation and SRV are therefore at the root of tackling the problem of the deviancy career and carers will need to start by carefully examining their reasons for recommending particular courses of action. Taking heed of Main's paper, we must all be aware that our own primitive need for dependent and grateful subjects for whom we can care may be driving our actions. Justification in terms of 'handicap' or 'disturbance' is all too easy.

Individual Plan systems

This is a method of putting SRV into operation by individualising needs which are clearly stated, linked to strengths the person already possesses and translated into achievable goals. Outcomes are measured through the use of Opportunity Plans and each person's goals reviewed at regular intervals (see Appendix).

Within this framework, it appears to be much easier for carers to view clients as individuals with thoughts and feelings as well as behaviours, and the punitive cycle of deprivation becomes less accessible. In addition, carers seem much more likely to consider 'talking therapies' for clients as they gain knowledge and understanding and so begin to advocate for emotionally sensitive services where these are appropriate. The system also constitutes a valuable quality assurance tool in that clearly defined needs become equally clear goals which can be measured and related back to the original assessment, so failures in strategy, practice and service can be identified.

Gentle Teaching

Devised by John McGee et al. in the early 1980s, this is described by its proponents as a 'non-aversive method' of creating 'bonded relationships' (McGee, 1990). Using a simple task, a nut and bolt, to provide a focus for the relationship, the teacher uses the strategies IGNORE (unwanted behaviour), REDIRECT (towards the task), REWARD (any sign of cooperation) in the context of a controlled environment. Negative signals such as 'No' or 'Not there' are never used, verbal and social interaction being reserved for reward. The central tenet is one of errorless learning in which the relationship rather than the task is emphasised. The experience of 'driving off' carers and teachers through difficult behaviour becomes much less likely.

This technique tackles the deviancy career head on by removing all negativity from the interaction. In this way, people who have historically alienated carers, permitting them to fall back upon controlling, deprivational strategies, can regain positive social contact and so begin to make personal gains in many other areas.

The implications of attitude change

The implications of properly implementing positive philosophies and methods are massive – truly client-led services require adequate funding and this requires that service providers at all levels explore those issues of dependency, disability, stigma and punishment which have, in the past, constructed such a negative world for our clients. Having done this, they then need to make objective judgements about personal life-styles based upon sensitive evaluation of individual needs, arguing convincingly for funds wherever necessary.

Society itself needs to make some changes, reappraising attitudes to disability which, in the final analysis, allow people to believe that something is satisfactory because 'that's what they're used to' or 'they don't know any better, do they?' The principles of human rights suggest that, if it is not good enough for 'us', then it should not be regarded as good enough for 'them'.

In the meanwhile, those of us working in these services are in a position to make our own changes by modelling dignified interactions with clients, addressing the possibility of emotional roots to problems, offering interventions which are humane and developmental, and arguing at all levels for services in which respect, dignity, value and emotional growth are of paramount importance.

References and further reading

Brown, G.W., Harris, T. and Peto, J. (1973) 'Life events and psychiatric disorder II', *Psychological Medicine*, 3: 159–76.

Corbett, J.A. (1979) 'Psychiatric morbidity and mental retardation', in F.E. James and R.P. Snaith (eds), *Psychiatric Illness and Mental Handicap*. London: Gaskell Press, pp. 11–25.

Langness, L.L. and Levine, H.G. (eds) (1986) *Culture and Retardation. Life Histories of Mildly Mentally Retarded Persons in American Society*. D. Reidel Publishing Company.

Lund, J. (1985) 'The prevalence of psychiatric morbidity in mentally retarded adults', *Acta Psychiatrica Scandinavica*, 72: 563–70.

Main, T. (1957) 'The ailment', in T. Main, *The Ailment and other Psychoanalytic Essays*. London: Free Association Books (2nd edn 1989).

McGee, J. (1990) 'Gentle Teaching – the basic tenet', *Nursing Times* 86 (32) (August 8).

McGee, J. Menolascino, F.J., Hobbs, D.C. and Menousek, P.E. (1987) *Gentle Teaching: A Non-aversive Approach to Helping Persons with Mental Retardation*. New York: Human Sciences Press.

Paykel, E.S. (1978) 'Contribution of life events to the causation of psychiatric illness', *Psychological Medicine*, 8: 245–53.

Reid, A.H. (1983) 'Psychiatry of mental handicap. A review', *Journal of The Royal Society of Medicine*, 76: 587–92.

Wolfensberger, W. (1972) *The Principle of Normalisation in Human Services*. Toronto: National Institute on Mental Retardation.

Appendix

STRENGTHS/NEEDS LIST

NEXT IP MEETING

CLIENT'S NAME: ....   DATE: ....

DATE OF BIRTH: ....   TIME: ....

CLIENT'S KEYWORKER: ....   PLACE: ....

DATE FORM COMPLETED: ....

CLIENT'S NEEDS	CLIENT'S STRENGTHS
(Include anything realistic which will benefit client over next year, e.g. skills client needs to acquire, opportunities for learning, experience, leisure to be made available to client.)	(Include anything which might help meet needs, e.g. existing skills relevant to a skill needed, things client likes or enjoys, people willing to work with client.)

PEOPLE TO BE NOTIFIED OF IP MEEETING:

LONG-TERM NEEDS FOR SERVICES:
(Briefly note any points requiring discussion at IP Meeting.)

Accommodation

Volunteer/Advocate

Education/Training

Personal Counselling

Work

Leisure/Social Activities

Other:

CLIENT .... DATE OF IP MEETING .... NEXT IP (provisionally) ....

NEED	GOALS	ACTION REQUIRED	PERSON RESPONSIBLE	OUTCOME – SUCCESS RATING	FACTORS & COMMENTS TO BE NOTED	RESULTS

OPPORTUNITY/ACTION PLAN

CLIENT ....
KEYWORKER ....
Sheet no. ....

Record *all* attempts at an activity using the key. Add further details/comments about an attempt where you think they might improve the quality of a future IP and any other information you would like to include.

A = achieved without help at all.
R = achieved, but needed reminding.
H = achieved with help or support.
X = unsuccessful, but attempted.
NA = not attempted (give reason why, i.e. client ill, staffing, environment, other).

ACTIVITY/OPPORTUNITY

9

Countertransference with Mentally Handicapped Clients

Neville Symington

At the time when I was conducting a workshop on the psychother-apy of mentally handicapped people at the Tavistock we were all confronted one day with a very shocking piece of knowledge. It was a piece of knowledge that each of us possessed but it had not come to light until one particular session of the workshop. It was that we all treated mentally handicapped people with contempt and that we did not have this contempt towards 'normal' people. I will explain the matter in more detail.

In the workshop we had decided in one term to try and differentiate our psychodynamic technique with mentally handicap-ped people from 'normal' people. Thus, we investigated our manner of interpretation, the nature of the transference in this category of client and the anxiety attending on change. And so the question of countertransference also came under review. It was then that the discovery to which I have alluded was made. On the level of consciousness we had a sympathy towards mentally handicapped people which had in part instigated the formation of the workshop. We had also come to realise the painful isolation in which many mentally handicapped people live. On the level of consciousness, therefore, we were passionately devoted to our work with these people and had a self-righteous self-regard and felt critical towards those colleagues of ours who would only consider people suitable for psychotherapy if they had a university-level IQ.

Our contempt, then, had been below the threshold of awareness. This is how the shocking story of our inner attitudes came about. We first realised that there were certain things which we did with these clients which we did not do with others: for instance, with most clients the procedure was that the receptionist would ring and say that Mr or Mrs So-and-So was in reception and did we want him or her sent up to us. We would say 'Yes' and the person would come up in the lift and make their way to our consulting room. However, when the people we were expecting had a mental handicap we would invariably go to the lift and meet them and bring him or her along to our consulting room. We somehow assumed that it was necessary to do this, but was it? Was our behaviour patronising? Could they find their way from the lift to our consulting room? We decided that they could, and when we put it to the test we found that they were all able to do so. In an attitude that is patronising there is some contempt, so we went on to question ourselves as to whether there was any further contempt in our attitudes. Were there any ways, even subtle, in which we treated these people with less respect? Then one woman in the workshop bravely admitted that she remembered the week before on a Wednesday morning when she was trying to decide how to dress that morning and considered momentarily whom she would be seeing that day. Remembering that 'I was only seeing my mentally handicapped client' she decided to wear the shabby dress. Then someone else said that the previous day he had looked at his watch and saw that it was 2 o'clock so he must go to his consulting room as he had a client; but then, remembering that the client was a person with a mental handicap, he said to himself that he had time to have a quick word with a colleague because 'my client would not mind if I were a few minutes late'. Bit by bit each of us came out with similar confessions. In subtle ways all of us were treating these people with contempt.

When some members of the workshop presented a symposium on psychotherapy with people with a mental handicap at the Annual Conference of the British Psychological Society in 1981 and one member imparted this piece of information the members of the audience were shocked. One person who was eminent in the field said that we were contemptuous towards people with a mental handicap because we were all used to treating sophisticated Hampstead intellectuals. We did not research the matter more widely but observation tells me that this countertransference exists in many carers of people with a mental handicap and not just those members of that Tavistock workshop. I will tell you of just one incident that illustrates the point. I was interviewing a mentally handicapped man at a large mental hospital. A secretary put her head round the door and said, 'Dr, would you like a cup of coffee?' I said, 'Yes please,' and then she looked at my client and said, 'And would you, Len?' and he said 'Yes'. When, however, five minutes later the secretary reappeared she had only one cup of coffee which was for me and she had evidently obliterated Len from her mind altogether. When I brought this to his attention he just shrugged his shoulders with depressed resignation. In what follows I am taking it as a fact that mentally handicapped people are treated with contempt at a level which is below the threshold of awareness. I want to investigate why this is so and what it implies in terms of technique in therapy.

In the animal kingdom the flock of birds attacks and kills the one that is wounded. It is also so with a pack of wolves and many other species. There is, I believe, also an instinct within human beings to kill off the handicapped member. It is deeply shocking when this actually occurs as it did in Nazi Germany. It is however one of the deepest anxieties of people who are handicapped, either physically or mentally. The fundamental existential question of mentally handicapped people is: 'In truth would you prefer to blot out my existence?' On one occasion I was treating a mentally handicapped girl and evidently at the end of a session as she was leaving I folded my arms. When she returned for the next session the one question on her mind was: 'Why had I folded my arms when she was leaving?' Was I relieved to be rid of her? Would I not really prefer it if she was wiped off the face of the earth? In that sensitive novel *Walter* by Peter Cook he describes how Walter's mother decided to push him over the bridge on to the line before an oncoming train but, at the actual moment, she could not bring herself to do it. What the mentally handicapped person is concerned with is not the surface appearance of things but what the therapist feels at the centre of his or her heart. That is why the only matter that the client was concerned about was why I had folded my arms.

Now I want to propose a shocking suggestion. Let us suppose that with that client I *do* want to get rid of her, that I *do* wish she would take a running jump into a lake. Let us provisionally say that that is exactly what I want. I then need to ask myself what would be the reason for it? Is it that I share the instinctual impulse of the animal kingdom to get rid of the damaged member? I could just say 'Yes' but it is not as simple as that. When I told you that all the members of our workshop shared an experience of contempt for mentally handicapped people it left out the fact that we have all sometimes felt a similar feeling towards a *particular* client. I have had clients who get into a frenzy if I am a minute late: I have had clients who show no external sign of minding at all. What was distinctive about the mentally handicapped clients was that the same feelings were experienced towards the whole group by all of us. It was not that we had not experienced such a feeling towards one particular person rather than another but that the mentally handicapped person invariably evoked that contempt. What I am getting to is this. Is it the *mental handicap* itself that evokes this reaction, or a psychological concomitant that always accompanies it? If it is the psychological concomitant then what exactly is it? What is it that provokes contempt? Let me try to describe this psychological attitude.

In my home we once had a woman to stay. As she walked through the door she said, 'Oh, it's so kind of you to have me. I could easily have gone and stayed at a hotel. I know that it must be an awful trouble to you to have me, when you are all so busy.' Then as we showed her up to her bedroom she said, 'Oh dear, I am afraid it troubles my eyes to have a bed facing the light of the window.' We hurriedly said, 'Oh, that's all right, we'll move it for you around against the wall.' Then she said, 'Oh no, don't trouble, I'll do it. I am sorry I don't want to be a nuisance.'

A bit later that day I yawned and she said, 'Oh, I can see that I am a burden to you.' When my wife at table moved her chair to accommodate our guest, 'Oh, I can see it would be far easier if you did not have me here.' When I started to read the newspaper in the sitting-room she said, 'Oh, I can see I must be boring you.'

I think you get the picture of what I am talking about. She focused her attention on every gesture in evidence of her conviction that she was a nuisance and a bother and that we would far prefer to be rid of her. Her focused attention to every gesture of ours and the constant interpretation of it along those lines were exasperating to us and it produced the very desire in us for which she kept such a sharp look out. In other words we all began to wish she would go and the sooner the better, but it was the focused attention that produced this wish in us. To have to be on constant guard against yawning, reading the newspaper, is exasperating in the extreme. It is this focused attention generated by a paranoid motivation which is so tiresome and which made us all wish she would disappear for good. I think we have all met people like this but how should we describe this particular pathology? I wish now to examine it more closely.

This paranoid focus comes out of an omnipotent ego structure. If when I am yawning it is because of this woman guest, if when I read the newspaper it is because of this woman guest, then she feels herself to be very powerful. The thought that I might yawn because I got up too early that morning or that I read the newspaper because there is an interesting item of news I want to know about is an affront to her omnipotence. It actually suggests that she may not be as powerful as she thought. What I am saying is that what I call *paranoid motivation* is generated by the presence in the ego of a powerful god-figure. It is a god-figure who cannot bear to be ignored. I am making the inference that many of the mentally handicapped people whom we were treating were behaving like our unwelcome female guest. It is this paranoid focus that leads to the exasperation and desire to have done with the person once and for all. What I am proposing is that the contempt that we all felt is generated by the omnipotent introject which itself fuels the paranoid focusing and that it is this which generates the contempt and the desire to get rid of. What I am saying, therefore, is that it is not the mental handicap itself that generates this particular countertransference but rather *the emotional tides stirred by the god-figure within*. We might say that this introject tries to arouse the animal reaction.

What happens though is that the reaction is aroused at a subliminal level and then compensated against at the level of interpersonal interchange, so neither is the mentally handicapped person obliterated but nor is he or she encouraged to develop, so remaining stuck. The human is different from the animal in that he or she is offered the opportunity to rise to a level of action higher than the instinctual but the only way of achieving this is through thorough self-scrutiny such as we attempted in the workshop.

What are the reasons for this omnipotent ego structure present within the mentally handicapped people who presented themselves for psychotherapy at our workshop? Underlying it is an ego that is disintegrated. The integration of the ego comes about in normal development when the infant makes emotional contact with the personhood of the mother. When the mother remains a functional object in emotional perception the ego cannot integrate and the mentally handicapped individual's ego stays dysfunctional. The dysfunctional ego is reinforced by society's attitudes. It is rare for mentally handicapped people to have jobs in the work-force. When it comes to offering work to this category of persons the attitudes are as patronising as were the attitudes of the therapists in the Tavistock workshop. That these people are frequently capable of doing jobs in the work-force is very likely. In emergency situations this has been recognised. During the last world war mentally handicapped people were given jobs in the army. To feel useful to the community is ego enhancing and diminishes omnipotence. The long-term rehabilitation of mentally handicapped people requires them to be integrated into the work-force. In the absence of a war every available hand is needed, so too is a revised system of values that gives recognition to the precise capacities that mentally handicapped people are able to contribute. It is outside the scope of this chapter to discuss the ways in which social reorganisation could assist the personality development of this category of persons. However, it is clear that a radical re-evaluation of social goals is necessary. It is my belief that such a reorientation of values would benefit not only those who are mentally handicapped, but also the emotional lives of most of us.

When the members of that Tavistock workshop first became aware of this contempt the immediate reaction of one member was guilt and this transmitted in varying degrees to others. The problem, however, is that guilt cripples and is ineffective. I believe that it was this contempt that existed below the surface of awareness that created the guilt that then made us overcompensate and so go and meet our mentally handicapped clients at the lift. The particular problem about such a guilt is that it creates an infertile cycle. Contempt is stirred up in the therapist, which fashions guilt, which leads to a patronising attitude, and the real problem of this is that it leads to a sterile situation in which no change can take place. This, I believe, is at the heart of the problem: there is a deep-seated aim within the mentally handicapped person to block development. I want first, however, to examine the thesis that a mentally handicapped person subtly stirs up this contempt about which I have been speaking.

The feelings that are below the threshold of consciousness in the therapist are what constitute the countertransference. Those feelings of contempt that I have described were the countertransference of each one of us. At the moment when they become conscious they are available for interpretation and no longer constitute a countertransference. My contention is that this feeling of contempt was stirred up in each one of us by our mentally handicapped clients through a power derived from the omnipotent introject. If we were in touch with our own mental handicap rather than denying it through our own omnipotence then we would not be host to these powerful stirrings. This means that the tendencies in us to be contemptuous towards people damaged or less fortunate than ourselves derives from a mentally handicapped enclave in each one of us that is unbearable. The mentally handicapped person then slips into this ecological niche of our own unbearability. There is comfort there because there is no challenge to development. Thus is created the cycle of contempt–guilt–pity and all further development is stifled. We do not desire development in the person we feel sorry for, or pity.

Something else we discovered in the workshop was this. Many of these clients would be in a hospital, a sheltered workshop, at home with parents or carers without being able to go to school or a job. The therapy would progress well, even quicker than usual, and the point would come when the client was all poised to move from the sheltered position and this would be on the point of happening when there would be a set-back. The client would stop therapy or would behave in an alarming way that would prevent the new step from happening. This happened again and again in our workshop and the feeling in the therapists was one of despondency. We learned two things: that there was a powerful resistance to a developmental step and that such a step was inseparable from severe psychic pain. It was coming up against such a severe pain barrier that usually made these people retreat.

In his classic book on this subject the American psychoanalyst, Pierce Clark (1933), believed that people with a mental handicap are fixated at the foetal level of development and when there is a psychological thrust towards birth it is countered by a violent regressive pull back to the womb. This model makes sense of the experience which we all had in the workshop. The therapist, in order to break out of the infertile cycle, has to help the client face an indescribable amount of pain. The first step on this journey is however the moment when the therapist recognises the contempt. With acknowledgement of it there is hope of growth but without it, there is none.

Reference

Pierce Clark, L. (1933) *The Nature and Treatment of Amentia*. London: Baillière Tindall and Cox.

10

Group Analytic Therapy for People with a Mental Handicap

Sheila Hollins

Introduction

This chapter will explore the possibilities and practicalities of adapting group treatment techniques based on psychoanalytic theory to this client group. A brief review of the literature will be followed by discussion of some theoretical and technical issues. Illustrative clinical examples from work with groups have been selected to show what might actually happen in a group.

Theoretical issues

What is psychoanalytic therapy?
There is a popular misconception that psychoanalytic psychotherapy is primarily an intellectual activity, whereas in reality it is an affective one. In other words it is a process which engages the therapist and the client emotionally. The first task of the therapist is to make an emotional bond which can then be used therapeutically. The main requirement of psychotherapy candidates is that they are capable of making an emotional relationship.

Group analytic therapy developed out of the body of psychoanalytic knowledge, but now has its own theoretical and clinical base. Formal training of group analysts is a lengthy and intensive process involving personal group analytic experience for trainees, and supervision of groupwork by a training analyst for several years. Some relevant experience in a caring profession is required before acceptance for training. Most psychiatrists will have had some supervised group therapy experience as part of psychiatric specialisation, but few will have completed formal group analytic training. This chapter is an introduction to group analytic therapy which should enable practitioners to make and support referrals to appropriately qualified therapists. Initially this involves making a realistic assessment of what one is going to ask of the therapist.

Indications for therapy and therapeutic aims

For any patient or client the main aim of group analytic therapy will be to improve interpersonal relationships. A subsidiary aim will be to enable the individual to accept his or her own limitations. Understanding and reconciling one's own internal and external reality will be part of this and does not need to be at a high intellectual level. In addition, psychotherapy may have more clearly defined goals related, for example, to maturation, or to accepting the loss of a parent. Contraindications for group analytic therapy would include a formal diagnosis of a serious psychiatric disorder where an individual has difficulty with reality testing.

There is a reluctance among some professionals to allow psychiatrists or therapists access to people with a mental handicap, but this has something to do with the inappropriate historical proximity of mental illness and mental handicap services, and perhaps to a desire to protect the client from a traditional medical model of treatment.

Some people are under the impression that mental handicap and mental illness are mutually exclusive, a view which is firmly challenged by Spensley (1985). Emotional disturbance and formal psychiatric disorder have both been shown through population studies to occur more commonly in children and adults who have a mental handicap (Rutter et al., 1974). Anna Freud (1970) wrote of the difficulty in differentiating the organic and emotional causes of symptoms of disturbed psychic function.

Mental handicap itself refers to the combination of the developmental delay and the immaturity of the social adaptation made by the individual. Offer et al. (1984) noted that the severity of the functional disability was directly correlated with the degree of psychological disturbance. In particular they found that when the functional disability was easily noticed by others, the individual's self-image and self-esteem were more impaired. The psychotherapist works to increase the patients' social adaptation and acceptance by society through their own acceptance of themselves.

History of practice

For the 25 years since 1965 very few relevant papers written in English could be traced. Several papers described work with groups of adolescents or adults living in institutional care (for example, Cogan et al., 1966; Miezio, 1967; Slivkin and Bernstein, 1968; Pantlin, 1985) but few references to out-patient groupwork (Hollins and Evered, 1990). Some papers described work with groups of parents (Smith et al., 1976). A number of papers discussed the pros and cons of a psychotherapeutic approach (for example, Stavrakaki and Klein, 1986; Matson, 1984; Coffman and Harris, 1980; Woody et al., 1966) and the use of play, music or drama therapy or techniques such as role-play (Weinstock, 1979). However, from the paucity of the literature and the tone of the discussion therein, it is clear there has been very little confidence in the past in the use of group analytic approaches with people who have a mental handicap. There is no research evidence that group analytic therapy is not effective but the authors of published case reports are modest in their claims, although enthusiastic and optimistic about the value of their work. Stavrakaki and Klein (1986) warn against the risk of dilution of the skills of the therapist through overlap with more informal patient meetings, educational or experimental groups. They argue that the aim of group therapy in this field should focus clearly upon the need to comprehend and alter disordered personality functioning, and thus to improve communication and social interaction at large in society. Given that social style and temperament contribute more to adjustment as an adult than intellectual levels, such aims are valuable.

Technical considerations in working with groups

Confidentiality Beginning work with people who have developmental intellectual handicaps such that they require special services to lead an ordinary life, raises the problem of the therapist's relationship with the care-givers. When we think of the traditional psychoanalytic model of therapist and patient or patients, we think very much of intimate relationships which are bound by the confidentiality of the treatment setting.

Of course the institutionalised life led by many people with mental handicap is far from ordinary, and to offer treatment to people living in long-stay hospital wards provokes considerable curiosity. It is very rare in such a setting that anything is totally private, and explanations about the reasons for the desired privacy are readily misunderstood. If therapy is such an important part of the treatment programme, why are the carers being excluded from it? The more the maintenance of privacy is insisted upon, the more suspicious and uncooperative the carers may become. In addition the therapist(s) may be party to information about the client between sessions with pressure exerted on them to take up day-to-day issues in the therapy. Similar problems can be expected in work with adults who still live with their family of origin. For the parents of an adult 'child' who functions in many ways like a 4 or 5 year old, there is little they do not already know about them, and they will expect to know the details of anything new which happens.

The Child Psychiatry model of someone working with the person who has a mental handicap, and someone else working with the parents, with an occasional meeting together, may be appropriate. The confidentiality of both therapeutic alliances must be respected, and the effect of the involvement of the care-givers on the therapeutic process borne in mind.

The members of the group will also be invited to respect the 'secrets' and insights which are shared in the group. Clearly understanding about this cannot be guaranteed, but it is possible to work towards a mutual respect for each other.

Other boundaries of space and time   It is essential to identify a 'safe' place for therapy which will not be booked for different activities, or invaded during a session. There may need to be a waiting-room, or access to the group room during the gathering time, so there is minimal interaction with people who are not involved in the group process before the session. The time of each session should be regular, and observed absolutely. Therapists will set an example by arriving and leaving on time, and such careful observance of time boundaries helps group members to learn that they cannot manipulate the therapists to give more or less of their time than was contracted for.

Deciding on the type of group   Groups can be run in a residential or work setting such as a hospital ward or hostel or day centre with a group of people who already share some part of their daily lives. Alternatively a 'stranger' or out-patient group may be organised by bringing together individual referrals from different sources. In practice the latter type of group may contain fewer 'strangers' than might be customary with a different client group. People with mental handicap have several possible points of contact with other potential group members. They may have been to school together, or met at a respite facility, at a day centre or dance. Groups may be closed, accepting no new members after the sessions have got under way, or open, allowing new members to join when a vacancy occurs. The duration may be fixed in advance although open-ended groups are also a possibility.

Recruiting and preparing the members   Some initial 'getting to know' each client is essential, with each potential member having a chance to decide for themselves whether they wish to join. Carers, whether informal or formal, should meet with the therapist to clarify the appropriate distance they might need to maintain during the life of the group. As already mentioned it is probably advisable for carers to have a third party such as a social worker or community mental handicap team staff member with whom to liaise about day-to-day matters. Even at this early stage the therapists are advised to discuss their assessments with a supervisor, and to seek regular supervision. At the point of joining the group some members will realise they are not motivated or interested, and will fail to attend again.

Group therapy – a clinical illustration

Since 1981, when I began my first group with this client group, I have been involved either directly as a therapist in a group or as a supervisor for psychiatric trainees running groups. The clinical work described in this chapter has not been written up elsewhere and largely derives from a group which met from 1983 to 1986. A more recent group has been written up for a specialist readership (Hollins and Evered, 1990).

An open group for adults with mental handicap was held weekly in a group room in a district general hospital for three years, each session lasting for an hour. The members were selected roughly according to the following criteria, which are similar to criteria used by Miezio (1967). Their symptoms were predominantly neurotic, and their level of intellectual handicap moderate, with the ability to speak retained although speech defects were common. They were all able to relate to their peers in some way. The membership changed slowly over time with only one of the original members still in the group at the end. However, the six members who were present at the end had been attending regularly for an average time of a year. There were two therapists, one male and one female, both experienced psychiatrists and both with previous supervised experience in group analytic therapy. The male therapist changed twice but the female therapist remained constant. All the clients were expected to have a social worker or keyworker from the Community Mental Handicap Team to limit the responsibility therapists could otherwise feel for members' daily problems.

The last six members will be described briefly and some of the important themes explored. D was 17 when he joined the group. He lived with his mother, stepfather and one of his three other siblings. He had had no regular daily activities outside his home since the age of 15, and did not participate in domestic activities at home. He had serious problems trying to achieve some separation from his mother and did not have a clear individual identity.

K was in his late 30s and lived with his mother who had recently retired and was in poor health. He was holding down a gardening job with difficulty when he joined the group, but had decided to retire on grounds of ill-health by the end of the group.

C was in his mid-20s when he joined and was planning to move from a social services hostel into a bedsit on his own – a move he achieved during the second year of the group. He was somewhat garrulous and often did not 'hear' what was being said, or fell asleep, to the annoyance of other group members. He was determined to be successfully independent, and it was a long while before he 'admitted' to visiting his parents every Sunday for lunch.

B was 28 and apparently living in her own council flat in the same neighbourhood as her mother. She suffered severe bouts of anxiety and tearfulness, and in due course it came to light she was living at her mother's flat and only occasionally going to her own flat to sleep. She was having relationship problems with a neighbour who also had learning difficulties and attended the same social education centre.

J was 19 and had lived in residential care since her early teens when her mother died. Her father visited her about once a year and she had developed a rich fantasy life to compensate for her painful feelings of abandonment. She used a manic defence as a thin disguise for her depression. J was one of only two members who had to be escorted to the group, and the escorts were unreliable, constantly changing and obviously having no idea of the nature of the treatment and the need for confidentiality. Although time boundaries were adhered to strictly it was not unusual for a new escort to walk in before the end and to stand and wait for the group to finish. Needless to say the escort would be asked to wait outside until 'time', but these few occasions showed the change which took place in J after the intrusion, as she reverted to the 'giggly little girl' known in the hostel, her depression once again hidden.

M was 21 and lived with his mother. He was hoping to find work and blamed his poorly controlled epilepsy for his lack of success. If he failed to attend, the group would worry about him as on occasions he had turned up straight from Casualty with stitches in his head. He had no regular day care, giving the impression that he thought himself more able than the people at the social education centre. It gradually emerged that he saw himself to be as handicapped as J – the other member of the group with a speech defect like himself.

Group process and content

At first all the group members seemed so preoccupied with their own experience of pain and inadequacy that it was difficult for them to allow any space for other people's hurt to be expressed. They ignored each other, and then felt rejected in turn when they were ignored. They vied for the therapist's attention and different members attached themselves to one or other therapist, being particularly annoyed if 'their' therapist was not present. Some brought inappropriate requests for practical help outside the group which the therapists encouraged them to refer back to their keyworkers. Even some of the keyworkers would phone between sessions wanting details of progress or to know about issues of concern to their client. The therapists sometimes experienced profound feelings of boredom leading to difficulty staying awake. It became clear that these feelings were putting us in touch with some of the pain for our clients of being damaged, and some of our own pain and intolerance of their disability. These feelings were usefully shared with the group. As other authors have suggested (Menolascino et al., 1986), the problem of the idealisation of the therapist(s) and of an individual's care-takers could be addressed, the group members could give up their expectation of being 'cured' and the therapists could drop the burden of being expected to 'cure' the members' handicaps. It began to be possible to be happy despite having a mental handicap. Slowly the group became a group as interest and concern for each other developed.

Themes such as loss and separation from home and family, of dependence and independence, and trusting and not trusting other people predominated. One group session was videotaped and the recording played back to the members. D, while watching the replay, said, 'I'm really proud of myself, I'm not just a dimwit, I'm caring and thoughtful'. Like Harry, the man Symington (1981) described in his paper on individual psychotherapy, D had an internalised maternal fantasy that he was inadequate, helpless and unintelligent. What price would his reassessment of himself be in his relationship with his mother? Certainly her ambivalence about his attendance increased, and undermined the therapy, with hospital admission eventually being arranged by his family and keyworker.

A theme to which C returned time and again was that of the insincerity of 'normal' people who welcomed him one day and rejected him the next. Towards the end of the group, C became very quiet, and eventually owned up to the sad insight he had gained that his idealised image of other people was false. His disappointment was real but he accepted it, and felt better able to face life on his own without the group's help.

The group process resembled that described by Miezioi (1967) of an initial phase of rejection, a middle phase of conditional acceptance and a terminal phase of sharing. The outcome for many of the group members included diminished egocentricity, enhanced self-esteem and improved awareness of other people.

Discussion

Group analytic therapy is effective but is not an easy option for the therapists. There seem to be some similarities with the work which has been documented with severely deprived children (Boston, 1979; Britton, 1978; Henry, 1974). Such therapists have needed ongoing support and supervision from colleagues to enable them to contain the feelings of despair and anger projected by their patients. Supervision groups and staff support groups are necessary. Of course not all people with mental handicap will, or indeed should, present themselves for group therapy, but a willingness on behalf of the clinical or social work team to consider this as a treatment option will enable more people to have the opportunity.

The future

Decisions about life-styles of people with mental handicap may be made more for administrative convenience than to reflect the genuine choice of the individual concerned. Advice to respect friendship rather than geographical ties in the process of deinstitutionalisation may be difficult to implement for other reasons too. Many people living in large groups in hospital wards will have successfully defended against close relationships for a large part of their lives. Being moved into domestic sized homes with some of the same people may provoke different stresses and strains which upset previous tolerance patterns. The intimacy of small group living demands skills in relationship building among support staff (Menolascino, 1989).

In 1989 the British government published a White Paper on Community Care called *Caring for People*, which provided a framework for the care of vulnerable people into the next century under the leadership of social service departments. In addition, from April 1991 the National Health Service and Community Care Act required each district health authority to assess the health and social care needs of every patient before discharging them into the community. This includes people discharged from mental hospitals. The paper stressed that community health services should enable people with disabilities to live in their own homes as long as possible. Specialist health care including community psychiatric care has increased gradually since the 1971 White Paper: *Better Services for the Mentally Handicapped*. The role of the psychiatrist has evolved over this period so that two distinct functions are emerging – both quite different from the role of the medical superintendent of a mental hospital (Bicknell, 1983). Both of these functions require psychotherapeutic skills, and group skills are particularly valuable.

First, there is a developmental role for the psychiatrist. This includes an understanding of the emotional and social development of disabled people in the context of their family or carers, teachers and peers. We know that psychological distress, low self-esteem and depression are much more common in young people with physical disability (with or without learning difficulty) (Offer et al., 1984; Rutter et al., 1974). We know that problem behaviour which challenges the resources of carers is much increased in people with mental handicap. The psychiatrist can use psychotherapeutic skills with groups of carers (parent groups, staff support groups) and with client groups as discussed earlier in this chapter.

There is a danger that in reorganising services and emphasising the residential, occupational and leisure needs of people with mental handicap, that their developmental emotional needs may be overlooked. However perfect the physical environment and the practical support offered, there will always be a need for skilled help for some people to achieve emotional and behavioural maturity. Other chapters in this book address a wide range of therapeutic options which are appropriate.

The second role of the psychiatrist is more akin to that of the general adult psychiatrist. Mental illness does present as a second or dual diagnosis in many people with mental handicap. Estimates vary between 16 per cent and 50 per cent (Lund, 1985; Menolascino, 1989), depending on the population studied – whether institutionalised or not. Diagnosing mental illness and understanding the effect of such an illness on a person with complex learning and social difficulties requires specialist expertise in all the staff involved. Neither a training in mental handicap nor in mental illness is sufficient on its own, but joint training or experience is essential. If in-patient admission for assessment and treatment becomes necessary, the whole range of treatment options should be available. In particular, emphasis must be placed on relationship building within the unit, with regular group meetings being an integral part of the treatment setting. Because of the inherent difficulties in coping with transition experienced by most people with mental handicap there must be an overlap between the two roles described; one of which is firmly planted in the community health services as part of a multidisciplinary specialist health care team and the other within the acute psychiatric service.

Conclusion

In a fundamental reorganisation of services in which the lead responsibility for this client group is being transferred from health authorities to local authorities, it will be important to retain relevant specialist expertise. Mechanisms must be built in to continue to bring such expertise into the settings where people live and work so that emotional needs can be met in a preventive way rather than by expensive hospital admission at a point of crisis and breakdown. Group approaches to treatment are an economical way of working and require little more than an accessible and comfortable room with enough chairs for the members, and a guarantee of no outside interruptions and supervision for the therapists.

References

Bicknell, J. (1983) 'Inaugural Lecture: The psychopathology of handicap', *British Journal of Medical Psychology*, 56: 167–78.

Boston, M. (1979) 'Interim notes on a study of psychotherapy with severely deprived children', *Child Abuse and Neglect*, 3: 539–46.

Britton, R.S. (1978) 'The deprived child', *The Practitioner*, 221: 373–8.

Coffman, Thomas L. and Harris, Malcolm C. (1980) 'Transition shock and adjustments of mentally retarded persons', *Mental Retardation*, 18 (1): 3–7.

Cogan, F., Monson, L. and Bruggeman, W. (1966) 'Concurrent group and individual treatment of the mentally retarded', *Corrective Psychiatry and Journal of Social Therapy*, 12 (5): 404–9.

Freud, A. (1970) 'The symptomatology of childhood', *Psychoanalytic Study of Child*, 25: 19–41.

Henry, G. (1974) 'Doubly deprived', *Journal of Child Psychotherapy*, 3 (4): 15–23.

HMSO (1971) *Better Services for the Mentally Handicapped* (Government White Paper). London.

HMSO (1989) *Caring for People* (Government White Paper). London.

Hollins, S. and Evered, C. (1990) 'Group process and content: the challenge of mental handicap', *Group Analysis*, 23 (1).

Lund, J. (1985) 'The prevalence of psychiatric morbidity in mentally retarded adults', *Acta Psychiatrica Scandinavica*, 72: 563–70.

Matson, Johnny L. (1984) 'Psychotherapy with persons who are mentally retarded', *Mental Retardation*, 22 (4): 170–5.

Menolascino, F.J., Gilson, S.F. and Levitas, A.S. (1986) 'Issues in the treatment of mentally retarded patients in the community mental health system', *Community Mental Health Journal*, 22 (4).

Menolascino, F.J. (1989) 'Model services for the treatment/management of the mentally retarded and mentally ill', *Community Mental Health Journal*, 25 (2).

Miezioi, Stanley (1967) 'Group therapy with mentally retarded adolescents in institutional settings', *International Journal of Group Psychotherapy*, 17 (3): 321–7.

Offer, D., Ostrov, E. and Howard, K.I. (1984) 'Body image, self perception and chronic illness in adolescents', in R.W. Blum (ed.), *Chronic Illness and Disabilities in Childhood and Adolescence*. Orlando, FL: Grune & Stratton.

Pantlin, A.W. (1985) 'Group-analytic psychotherapy with mentally handicapped patients', *Group Analysis*, 18 (1): 44–53.

Rutter, M., Tizard, J., Yule, P., Graham, P. and Whitmore, K. (1974) 'Isle of Wight studies', *Psychological Medicine*, 6: 313–32.

Smith, E., McKinnon, R. and Kessler, J.W. (1976) 'Psychotherapy with Mentally Retarded Children', *Psychoanalytic Study of the Child*, 31: 493–514.

Slivkin, Stanley E. and Bernstein, Norman R. (1968) 'Goal-directed group psychotherapy for retarded adolescents', *American Journal of Psychotherapy*, 22 (1): 35–45.

Spensley, S. (1985) 'Mentally ill or mentally handicapped? A longitudinal study of severe learning disorder', *Psychoanalytic Psychotherapy*, 11 (3): 55–70.

Stavrakaki, O. and Klein J. (1986) 'Psychotherapies with the mentally retarded', *Psychiatric Clinics of North America*, 9 (4).

Symington, Neville (1981) 'The psychotherapy of a subnormal patient', *British Journal of Medical Psychology*, 54: 187–99.

Weinstock, A. (1979) 'Group treatment of characteriologically damaged developmentally disabled adolescents in a residential treatment center', *International Journal of Group Psychotherapy*, 29 (3): 369–81.

Woody, R.H. and Billy, J.J. (1966) 'Counselling and psychotherapy for the mentally retarded: a survey of opinions and practices', *Mental Retardation*, December: 20–3.

11

Grief, Loss and People with Learning Disabilities

Suzanne Conboy-Hill

Introduction

Throughout this book, many concepts are discussed which have a bearing on the perceptions, understanding and treatment of people with a learning disability. The deviancy career describes how an initial label tends to set in motion a pattern of increasingly negative interventions in response to increasingly negative behaviours, resulting in a downward spiral of distress, frustration, control and containment (Bicknell and Conboy-Hill, Chapter 8). The notion of contempt in which people are offered unnecessary allowances or receive benign but demeaning compliments (Symington, Chapter 9) indicates the presence of underlying value judgements based on our feelings about the owner of a particular label. Our apparent attempts at denial of the disability through the constant shifting of terms (Szivos and Griffiths, Chapter 5), as if changing the language will change the feelings people have about disability or, better still, get rid of the problem altogether. And the tendency to place and maintain people in a subordinate, childlike role (Beazley-Richards, Chapter 7) in which compliance, gratitude and constant good humour are the indices of clients' adjustment. These concepts describe not new behaviours in carers and therapists but new ways of understanding some of the old behaviours in terms of fundamental emotional drives.

In this chapter we are discussing the experience of grief and loss. In recent years Freud, Bowlby, Kubler-Ross, Hinton and Murray-Parkes have all made significant contributions to the understanding of grief and many organisations have sprung up to support people experiencing loss of various kinds. However, it is only in very recent times that any attempt has been made to recognise or understand the implications of loss for people with learning disabilities, whether that loss be of close friends or family, staff members, jobs or routines, and it is unclear why this should be. However, there appear to be two major possibilities.

First, there are Western attitudes to death and dying which militate against open discussion of these life events. In our society, death, grief, disability and other notions of imperfection are generally regarded as taboo subjects. We prefer to avoid confrontation with these issues as much as possible and use euphemisms wherever some sort of discussion becomes necessary. Thus, we talk of 'passing on', 'gone to sleep', 'pushing up the daisies' and so on in order to avoid saying that someone has died. Second, there are our attitudes to disability, particularly where mental handicap is concerned, which conveniently allow us to practise denial strategies by rationalising them in terms of the other person's supposed level of understanding or emotional functioning.

It might be argued also that denial of emotional functioning in disabled people has been a central factor in our ability to see as satisfactory the sorts of life-styles such people have been required to live. In other words, failure to recognise the impact of loss on people with learning disability arises directly from our need to see such people as lacking in effective emotional apparatus, thereby justifying unacceptably barren life-styles. This conveniently feeds into our own need to avoid discussion of pain and grief and so the cycle of ignorance and inaction has been perpetuated.

What has it been like for clients?

Generally, speaking, the kind of interventions offered to people with learning disabilities have been medication or modification. Where behaviour has been identified as troublesome, the person has been either sedated or trained out of it, often without reference to any possible emotional cause, perhaps because of the issues described earlier. Indeed, behaviour modification in its purest form was designed to take no account of internal, non-observable factors, focusing entirely on the recordable facts of stimulus, response, reinforcement.

Clearly, the omission of reference to internal events such as thoughts and feelings is a major one and it would be easy to criticise those who practised, and perhaps still practise, in that way. However, we need to remember that all of us are influenced by prevailing ideologies to some extent, and the one which promoted medication and modification did so in a climate where staff often worked in dreadful conditions with large numbers of 'patients' – sometimes 80 to a ward staffed by two people, and with little thanks from a society which would prefer to believe that mentally handicapped people do not exist, let alone have feelings about how they want to live.

This climate is slowly changing and, in many parts of the world, including Britain and America, the principles of normalisation have facilitated the development of a more humane approach and resulted in the closure of many large institutions in favour of a life in the community. However, attitude change is a slow process and Crick (1988) has observed that clients are often 'treated' behaviourally or with drugs following a bereavement and that newly bereaved people are often forced to move house and day care within days of a death.

My own experience is of clients being 'diagnosed' as behaviour disordered following multiple deaths in the ward; being told that their relative has 'gone away'; being excluded from family mourning rituals; being denied knowledge of the death of friends but also being on the hospital 'body gang' which operated at night to remove a dead resident from the ward to the morgue.

These data suggest that the experience of death for clients is likely to be exacerbated by misinformation, exclusion, the bizarre practices of institutions and the stereotyped views and attitudes of others which arise from labelling effects.

Normalisation and grief

Oswin (1981) applied the principles of normalisation to grief, noting that people with learning disabilities had: 'the same stages of grief as anyone else, the right to grieve as individuals, the same right to consideration, the right to have special help for particular difficulties'. Clearly, Crick's (and my own) observations suggest that there is some way to go in establishing these rights. The reasons for this are no doubt complex and interdependent but are probably rooted, as discussed earlier, in prevailing attitudes to death and in stereotyped beliefs about the capacity of children and 'the mentally handicapped' to understand death.

The first logically leads to the development of sophisticated strategies for dealing with death without open discussion and the second lends itself readily to the denial process so that carers can leave the matter well alone 'in the client's best interests'. However, it is probably valid to ask about the level of understanding which might be required to appreciate death or loss and to benefit from counselling.

Cognitive development and grief

Bihm and Elliott (1982) and Sternlicht (1980) showed that concepts of death in their subject population of mentally handicapped adults related quite strongly to Piagetian levels of cognitive development in that those who had reached the level of concrete operations had more realistic ideas about death than those who remained at the pre-operational stage. However, this does not appear to mean that people whose developmental levels may be below this are unable to perceive and be distressed by loss. The literature now contains numerous case reports discussing the responses of people of very varied levels of ability to the loss of friends, relatives and pets (for example, Brandt and Bower, 1975; Bradford, 1984; Thurm, 1989; Kloeppel and Hollins, 1989; Kitching, 1987; Mansdorf and Ben-David, 1986). The reactions themselves are also highly variable and often take the form of regressed or aggressive behaviour.

It seems possible, then, to say that people with learning disabilities are likely both to perceive and respond to the experience of loss, that their perception is likely to vary with level of cognitive development, and that the behavioural manifestation of the emotional response to loss may be 'atypical' in terms of what we might expect from generic literature on grief which is derived from studies of people with average cognitive functioning. Emerson (1977) observed that about 50 per cent of people referred with difficult behaviour of new onset had experienced a significant loss in recent times and in my own work, grief has been significantly associated with a range of behavioural problems, including voluntary mutism, self-injury, anorexia, loss of continence skills and aggression.

Help, support and therapy

So how about therapy? Is it necessary? What approach is most useful and can people benefit from it? The answers to these questions are undoubtedly highly individual, both to the client and to the therapist. What I would say, however, is, first, that negative changes in behaviour following a loss suggest that the loss is significant and that the client is distressed; and second, that this distress may not require formal therapy any more often than it does for people without mental handicaps but that acknowledgement, sensitive listening and support may be vital to the person's adjustment to the loss.

Given this framework, 'level of understanding' becomes an issue to address when deciding on the type of support or therapy rather than whether or not this should be offered at all. As regards counselling, it should always be the case that the counsellor finds out what the client understands and believes about something and uses this to move forward. There can be no difference for clients with learning disabilities but one is perhaps brought more sharply up against this principle as the numbers of shared assumptions based (often spuriously) on ideas of a roughly common life structure begin to reduce. Work which shows that even very young children have some construct of death and that this can be used to tell them the truth and help them through their feelings provides a rationale for proposing counselling-type activities. Similarly, studies showing that children are often more distressed by the avoidance behaviour, misinformation and deceitfulness of adults under these circumstances than by the loss itself underlines the need for a more honest, accepting approach from staff or carers.

In summary, then, carers need first of all to be able to acknowledge that losses of various sorts are likely to have an emotional impact upon clients. Second, they need to be able to note changes in behaviour which might be indicative of distress in response to a loss. And third, they need to have developed skills towards differentiating between normal and abnormal grief, offering support for the former and seeking specialised help for the latter.

Helping staff identify and cope with a client's grief

Therapists, carers and referrals
So how can people – clients, carers and therapists – overcome the prejudices, defences and other barriers to effective communication and support? There are probably two main points of contact, and, like the chicken and the egg, which comes first is a matter for debate. Carers are the people working most directly and intensively with clients and it is they who know the person best, detect change and frame any referral for help. Therapists, psychiatrists, psychologists, nurses and social workers are, on the other hand, the professionals to whom clients are referred and so are in a position to influence the range of reasons for referral and the interpretations which might be placed upon someone's behaviour.

In the past it has been ideologically expedient to frame behaviours in terms of the label and so nurses got into the habit of referring 'behaviour disorders' while psychiatrists and psychologists responded in kind, each in their own tradition.

Today's new breed of carer, community based, un-uniformed, often untouched by medical and psychological institutional practices, has perhaps a greater tendency to empathise with clients and so seems inclined to consider the explanatory value of feelings at the same level as any other factor. Today's therapists, then, need to be in a position to accept emotionally based interpretations and offer, according to their own professional model of practice, an appropriate investigative approach in which these interpretations have a place.

Psychologists and research

Psychologists in particular are behavioural scientists and so are ideally placed to consider *psychological* constructs of death, dying and grief, the role of cognitive functioning in the understanding of death and the facilitation of the grieving process. To date the contribution of psychologists to these areas has been at a level one might describe as discrete, most contributions coming from psychiatrists and social workers whose theoretical perspective may be quite different.

Workshop training

One way I have found of tackling the metaphorical chicken-and-egg problem has been to run workshops for carers designed to introduce the idea that loss impacts upon clients, facilitate an understanding of our reasons for avoiding this and then provide guidelines for a process called active listening (Egan, 1982). By this, carers are enabled to support clients through the normal grieving process.

These workshops began in Bromley Health Authority where I cut my psychological teeth, and have developed since, partly through the Lisa Sainsbury Foundation and partly through Brighton Health Authority. The teaching is based on my own practical experience plus a synthesis of useful concepts drawn from cognitive psychology, essays in bereavement and grief by such as Kubler-Ross, Hinton and Murray-Parkes, counselling techniques (see Murgatroyd, 1985) and grief therapy (for example, Worden, 1983). It is as yet naive, simple and primitive but, if it seems to help, that matters more for the moment than how it helps. However, this too will need to be addressed in due course so that the approach will develop and become more comfortably based in a sound theoretical understanding of the processes involved.

Premisses of active listening

So what are the premisses and components of the active listening approach? The first premiss is that active listening has its roots in counselling in that it uses silence, touch, reflection, questioning and empathy in order to facilitate clients' understanding of and progression through their distress. As such, it makes explicit a central tenet of counselling, that of checking assumptions, which is perhaps not emphasised enough under ordinary circumstances but may be one of the major factors to have excluded the use of counselling with our clients.

In my view, checking assumptions and understanding between two people is a fundamental part of the counselling process. Unfortunately counselling, like many of the 'talking therapies', has been largely a middle-class option so that a good many assumptions about life-style, background, culture, attitudes and even the counselling relationship have not routinely been checked and so have seemed to drop out of the repertoire.

People with learning disabilities are perceived, often correctly, as having so little in common with therapists in terms of life experience that people seem to believe either that counselling would be a useless exercise or that some highly specialised technique is necessary. I would argue that neither is strictly true. Therapists need to do here what we should be doing with all our clients, mentally handicapped or not, and that is checking out fundamental assumptions. This premiss leads to my first articulated guideline which goes as follows:

> Find out what the person understands and believes and use this to tell the truth and help them move forward.

The second premiss is that, while the basic active listening procedure is sound and applicable, there is often a need for fine tuning and knob twiddling to get it right for people whose major defining disability is one of cognitive processing.

Special problems of counselling mentally handicapped people

Complexity of cognitive ability

While we can all be said to have gaps in our intellectual functioning here and there, generally speaking most people have the cognitive apparatus which appears to be necessary to facilitate emotional processing of various sorts. Grief has been described as having stages (Kubler-Ross, 1981) and these have cognitive labels such as denial or acceptance, or involve cognitive constructs such as guilt, defensive blaming, rationalising and so on. Where the cognitive machinery is less sophisticated, clearly there is likely to be difficulty making sense of feelings and this problem must be addressed.

Emotional vocabulary

Similarly, many people with learning disabilities have an impoverished emotional vocabulary, perhaps due to our tendency to concretise our communication with them but perhaps in part due to the level of abstraction required to triangulate upon the meaning of words such as 'hurt', 'frustrated', 'angry' and so on. Many people I know use one word to describe a range of feelings; one chap was 'annoyed' about everything from the bus being late to being lifted by the police for attacking his father. Another described most of his outbursts as 'not very nice' and applied the same label to the provoking agent even though these ranged from dinner being ten minutes late to putting his hand through a window and needing stitches. This often means that, before much in the way of counselling, active listening or therapy can be done, many people need to learn a vocabulary to describe their feelings.

Attention span

Attentional factors can also be a problem. Somewhere deep in our collective psyche is an expectation that therapy sessions last 50 minutes and, while some therapists may be able to achieve this with some clients, I have found it to be the exception rather than the rule. This is sometimes because people are unable or unused to focusing on anything for any length of time, sometimes because of a natural wish to avoid the pain of attending and sometimes because of other (to that person) more significant demands.

For these situations, among others, I have developed the 'Quit While You're Winning' principle. I make an attempt to estimate a person's ability usefully to engage in the session and aim to curtail it just before the point of aversion is reached. This has implications for the 'counselling clock', the proportions of which have to be adapted to sessions ranging from one hour to five minutes.

Summarising the problems and minimising the difficulties

For staff, I summarise these considerations in the following way:

1. Learning disability – this constitutes a whole range of thinking, reasoning differences, and not just IQ.
2. Poor ability to attend or focus for any length of time.
3. Poor or limited understanding of death, dying or grief.
4. Poor ability to express emotion.
5. Limited verbal skills.
6. Limited abstract ability.
7. Limited experience of normal reactions to loss, death or grief.

8. A tendency for others to interpret distress as a behaviour disorder.

However, everyone is different, few people will arrive complete with all the disadvantages listed and there are things that we can do to minimise the problems. We can:

1. Begin by recognising that people with mental handicap can experience grief.
2. Look out for changes in behaviour which might indicate distress.
3. Listen to find out what the person makes of their situation.
4. Repeat ideas often so the individual is encouraged to learn the new situation.
5. Keep ideas simple and concrete where necessary.
6. Teach an emotional vocabulary.
7. Quit while we're winning.

Putting ideas into practice

The next step in the process is to put these ideas into operation. For therapists already skilled in their own methodology it is a matter of adjustment and the understanding that mental handicap does not translate as 'inaccessible', 'incomprehensible' or 'different species' but boils down to a set of variations on a theme whose major feature is intellectual limitation.

For untrained carers who may have a central role in supporting someone through a quite normal grief reaction, the situation is different. If they have come to accept the reality of grief as an experience clients may have, they then need to be able to distinguish normal from abnormal grief and to facilitate the first while knowing to refer on for the second. For this reason it is helpful to examine the pattern of normal grief as described by people working with non-learning disabled clients so that a framework can be provided within which changes in behaviour might be understood. For instance, if you know that withdrawal, anger, memory or attention problems, hallucinations, searching and regression are normal responses to grief in 'ordinary' people, it may be easier to understand a reversion to incontinence, uncharacteristic aggression, aimless wandering, refusal to cooperate, or loss of interest in activities in someone who is unable to understand or communicate their feelings of loss.

I developed a QRST system for active listening, find it helpful and offer it to staff, again with no apologies for its naive simplicity. QRST simply stands for:

Questions – ask, don't tell.

Repetition and rehearsal – help the person remember by repeating the information in different ways and accepting their rehearsal of correct information.

Silence – listen rather than talk.
Supply – words to describe emotion.

Time – allocate sufficient uninterrupted time.
Touch – use this instead of empty platitudes.

Problems for therapists and carers offering support

Clients' expectations

Clearly there is nothing at all magical or special about the concepts outlined here and so there should be nothing special or magical about offering support to clients grieving over a loss. Nevertheless it can not be said to be the easiest of encounters. Expectations are often crushed under the boot of pragmatism – having arrived with my grief therapy package to talk to a client whose friend had died and expecting to launch into my QRST routine, I was stopped in my tracks by the query 'Can I have his dinner then?' On reflection, this was no different from our own expectations of gain after the will is read but was less disguised by social veneer.

Privacy and safety

A further discovery that I have made, along with those about clients not knowing 'the rules' of counselling and sometimes not believing that what I do with them constitutes a proper job at all, is the sad fact that the loss of institutional settings has led also to the loss of quiet sanctuaries in which to see people. Community workers are rarely accorded their own offices because, managers rationalise, they are supposed to be out in the community. The community, on the other hand, rarely has provision for private interviews, let alone counselling or psychotherapy in which security and safety with the therapist are paramount. Thus, I have variously, and unsatisfactorily, carried out such sessions in bedrooms, empty cafeterias, the manager's office (much to the trepidation of the client) and, on one miserable occasion, in a large sports equipment cupboard.

I succumbed to these constraints feeling that, if I did not, my clients would not be offered a service and that, to complain would somehow label me as status conscious. In time, however, I have come to realise that, whether my own status was compromised or not, that of my clients certainly was and so I try to ensure that reasonable provision is made before embarking upon a series of sessions. This remains a problem which does not appear to have an easy solution.

Nevertheless I learned ssomething of importance during this process which was that I myself could be responsible for the safety and security of my client quite independently of the circumstances under which we were operating.

I learned how to deal with interruptions without removing eye contact from my client or losing the thread of what each of us had been saying. Sometimes it was necessary to maintain that thread while physically evicting an uninvited participant. And occasionally, warring factions would burst on to the scene, necessitating prompt and decisive action in order to avoid an even greater dust up in an even more confined space.

The techniques involved in dealing with these situations are simple and available to anyone willing to practise, which means that staff working in small group homes, nurses working on large wards and therapists working in less than ideal community facilities can employ them to make the best of the available time and space. They are as follows:

Assertiveness – particularly in dealing with staff who interrupt.

Use of an adult-to-adult mode – to ensure that clients feel respected and of central importance despite the interruption.

Eye contact – to indicate that the client is still 'on' and the interrupter is 'off'.

Gesture – to show that you are aware of the interrupter but would, respectfully, like them to leave.

Tone of voice – firm, clear, well modulated to keep the client calm and avoid them feeling responsible for your anger at being interrupted and to encourage the interrupter to remain calm and, hopefully, leave.

Clear instructions – to let both parties know what is going on – 'Jack and I are busy now, we will be out at. . . .'

Not cutting short a client's time because of an interruption – this seems to promote clients' confidence in your ability to take control where necessary and so promotes feelings of safety.

Maintaining the thread and feeding it back immediately after an interruption – 'I said that . . . and you were telling me that . . . can you go on from there?'

Like the checking of assumptions, it seems to me that these techniques should underpin any professional practitioner's style but they are of immense value to people working in environments where counselling interactions are not a central part of the job and where the setting is not geared to such interactions. Trained practitioners therefore have a clear role in facilitating the development of these skills in the people who need them so that clients can be supported through their grief by the people closest to them at the time when they need that support most.

Examples of grief counselling encounters

I would like to illustrate some of these ideas now with a few practical examples. These are not case-studies and, as with much real-life work, they tend to reflect rather less theoretical model than serendipitous opportunism.

In each case behavioural disturbance was the reason for referral although grief had been recognised as the cause for one person. The model used was one of guided mourning in which the individual is taken in stages through an acknowledgement of the loss and their feelings about this, towards emotional expression and eventual resolution whereby thoughts of the lost person may be sad but not debilitating and the client can begin to centre their world around new relationships and activities.

For my clients, this has broken down into a series of sessions which focus first on identifying the loss, establishing its reality and discovering what the person understands by this. Then we move on to the identification of emotions, the labelling of these and the use of words or behaviours such as crying to express them. Finally we begin to look back on the good things the two people shared in order to establish a framework for suggesting that there can be more good things in the future and the lost person would not want the client to feel bad for ever. The time scale involved depends very much upon knowledge, understanding, vocabulary and, of course, the significance of the loss. So far, however, the task has simply been to get the person on the right road for normal grieving and to support carers while they do this. Grief therapy as such has not yet been necessary.

Another point to note, obvious to therapists but perhaps not so obvious to untrained carers, is never to make assumptions about the quality of the relationship the client had with the lost person. Many people I have met have quite ambivalent feelings about parents or siblings, seeing them as responsible for 'putting me away'. Others have idealised their carers, perhaps for the same reason or because, living at home, there is no way of dealing with the dependency, helplessness and uselessness often engendered by such a relationship. The underlying hatred and resentment is often transparent but the client is unable to acknowledge this and so is likely to have great difficulty with grieving. In awareness of these possibilities, I never assume that relationships were straightforward even if the person is described as 'my friend' or 'wonderful – the best mother you could ever want', and I warn carers to avoid inadvertent judgements by asking questions or using non-verbal communication rather than jumping in with 'I expect you loved your mum didn't you?' or 'John was a really good friend to you, everyone will miss him'.

Ginny

Ginny was in her late 20s and lived in a large institution where she had been for some years. Her sister, also mentally handicapped, lived in another institution and there was little family contact. Ginny had been anorexic in the past and had become mute. Her mouth was often a tight white line across her face, her knuckles were clenched and white and she had bad skin, greasy hair and an institutional appearance.

The referral was made by Trainers in the special Moving On facility which Ginny attended in preparation for moving to a hostel in the community. They were concerned that she had failed to turn up for a week or so and, on checking with her ward, had discovered that she had been debarred as punishment for her behaviour, which had been to wreck her bed space, tipping the lot out of the window. Consequently, my brief was to address this behavioural outburst and ameliorate it so that Ginny could continue her preparation.

Interviewing the nursing staff provided descriptions of Ginny as a 'good girl', 'very quiet', 'no trouble' and doing little of any import around the ward. No special relationships were noted and no special circumstances identified which could have precipitated her behaviour.

It was the Trainers, talking to another resident of the ward, who discovered that three people there had died within a short space of time and that one of these had been Ginny's best friend. No one had discussed this with her, she had not been to the funeral – indeed no one knew if there had been one – and her 'behaviour disorder' occurred just weeks after these events.

With some reservations in view of her elective muteness, I decided to offer Ginny counselling for what I hypothesised to be her grief. Everything was against us – no reliable room, a noisy corridor with noisy co-occupants, dingy furniture and tight-lipped suspicious stares from Ginny who looked more like a cornered shrew than a grieving person grateful for someone to talk to.

Looking through Ginny's notes, I had speculated that her anorexia, mutism and occasional violent outbursts in the context of an otherwise highly controlled, exceptionally quiet demeanour were expressions of her increasing anger and frustration at the life she was leading and abandonment by her family. Certainly these behaviours were punishing both to herself and to others and so it seemed likely that anger and rejection would be the prevailing emotions in this relationship. I would need to establish some degree of trust and to offer a way of understanding her feelings without becoming a source of comfort myself because I too would leave her as soon as the job was done.

I had not, at that stage, developed my QRST approach but nevertheless used all of those techniques. Questioning soon revealed through nods from Ginny that she was aware of the deaths on her ward and that no one had talked to any of the remaining residents about them. When I probed her understanding of emotions, Ginny looked sharply interested as I described how it might feel to be angry or upset about something and what this might make some people do. She nodded a few times during this part of the work and occasionally whispered something which I was unable to hear.

My first attempts to use touch were rejected by Ginny who pulled her hand away quickly and refused to have anything more to do with me that day. Interestingly, more out of desperation than planning, I chose then to sit in silence rather than end the session and this seemed to confuse Ginny who, in retrospect, had probably never been in a close one-to-one situation with someone who was making no demands on her whatsoever but was still paying her attention. Ginny was pressured into speaking her first words to me, 'Go now?' She left but returned on time the next week.

Subsequent sessions developed the emotional labelling and attempted to let Ginny know that her feelings were quite normal. She needed no repetition and was not volunteering any rehearsal so these techniques were redundant. Touch, however, became more acceptable to Ginny who spotted my hair brush and indicated that she would like to brush my hair with it. I accepted and asked her to bring her brush next time so that I could do the same. She did and this led to her being able to accept massage of her extremely tense neck muscles, a technique which we were able to pass on to staff.

Ginny gradually relaxed with me and liaison with staff enabled us to set up a visit to her friend's grave. She did, however, go through a phase of rejecting me, popping her head around the door and hissing something through clenched teeth. I presumed that I had touched upon a defence that was being reconstructed or re-evaluated and that, if I stayed where I was for the time I had said I would be there, Ginny would return. Sometimes she did not but she always acknowledged my presence at the next session either by hissing at me as before or by coming in.

Ginny now lives in a community house, having moved on from the hostel. She is still relatively silent and still has angry outbursts but her appearance had improved dramatically the last time I saw her and she was ordering a meal for herself at the centre restaurant.

Bobby

Bobby was a young man of about 19 who lived in a large social services hostel and had quite close contact with his parents whom he visited every other weekend. He too was relatively non-verbal through choice and, when his father died, seemed to have little reaction. A few weeks later, however, Bobby began to spend a lot of time in his room, to be rejecting of staff and to be incontinent of urine. Staff very perceptively related this to his loss, pointing out that he used to go home for the weekend every fortnight and now could not because his mother, frail and unwell, was now in a home. Presumably sufficient weekends had gone by for Bobby to realise the truth of his father's death or the reality of its implications, and any hope or fantasy he may have had that the funeral was a social occasion and about something else had been destroyed. Significantly, Bobby had lost a close relative and a habitual life pattern at the same time.

With Bobby, therapy or guided mourning was simply an adjunct to staff support. I talked to the staff about grief and loss, supported their belief that this was the cause of Bobby's change in behaviour and let them know that not only was it quite normal but that they could do much more than I could to help him through it.

With the help of some hand-outs, Bobby's keyworker took on the role of supporter, offering time, comfort and affection to Bobby, especially at weekends, and I took Bobby through the guided mourning process.

By this time I had set out the QRST procedure and found it provided me with a series of starting-points in what otherwise seemed to be an unpromising situation. Bobby not only chose not to speak but was also rather less able than Ginny had been and his ability to understand or remember what had happened was questionable. It was possible that the memory of the event *per se* had faded but that the emotional reaction to it had not and was being revived each time a weekend went by without going home.

Against my better judgement, we held our sessions in Bobby's bedroom, there being nowhere else which could guarantee privacy. I began by asking Bobby if he knew why I was there, he shook his head and so I said that I had heard that his Dad had died and that he was upset. Bobby's head dropped and I took this to mean either that I had connected with his feelings or that he thought he was going to be told off for behaving badly. I decided to pre-empt the latter by commenting that people get upset sometimes when someone dies and that sometimes they want to be on their own or they get cross with other people. Each of these pieces of information was delivered in a single unit with grammatical and syntactical simplicity so that I could check on Bobby's reception at each stage. Sometimes Bobby would raise his eyes to mine, the expression in them ranging from puzzlement to distress, each of which was dealt with appropriately.

Through this process it became as clear as seemed possible that Bobby needed confirmation that his father had died and that this was why he could not go home any more. He also needed to visit his mother and to receive physical comfort for his distress.

Bobby's keyworker was able to respond to these needs and shortly afterwards, reported that Bobby had said to her 'Hole in the ground. Box', which she took to be a request from Bobby for confirmation of his father's death. We had discussed his possible need for rehearsal and so confirmation was given and Bobby was allowed to repeat this phrase whenever he wished.

In the mean time I was able to take Bobby on to describing his feelings, again by labelling them myself and using touch whenever his expression appeared to be one of distress. Eventually, at the beginning of one session, Bobby brought out a very old photograph of a man, a woman and a small boy. I asked him who that was and he pointed to himself. The man and woman, he confirmed by nodding, were his parents. This was a holiday snap and seemed to be a cue to talk about past memories in a more positive light, and so we did, and Bobby smiled.

At about the same time, Bobby's keyworker reported that he was accepting people more, spending less time in his room and was rarely wet. She had arranged some visits to his mother who, it transpired, was resident in a home only yards from the hostel, and some other relatives had been contacted who might be able to take Bobby to their home some weekends. I stopped going to see Bobby when he frequently appeared to be too gainfully occupied to do more than cast me a glance in passing.

Bobby's keyworker continued to offer support and comfort until Bobby began to shrug this off in his more normal way in favour of interesting things to do rather than solitude.

Edna

Edna was in her late 60s or early 70s. Her exact age was unclear because her birth certificate had been lost and the hospital where she had lived since she was 14 years old had given her the nominal birthday of 1 April.

At this late stage Edna had moved from the hospital to a large hostel divided into flats. Her history was one of increasing frustration and desperate attempts to visit her family, all of which were denied, and eventually Edna ended up in a locked ward with a reputation for being a 'wildcat' – hysterical and unpredictable.

At the hostel, Edna appeared to be an extremely anxious, rather obsessional woman who was articulate and extremely concerned about pleasing staff. She had known most of the residents for many years and when one of them, Joe, became ill with cancer, everyone worried about how the rest, especially Edna, would handle this.

It transpired also that many of the staff were anxious about how they themselves would cope. For a good few members of staff, this would be the first death they had ever experienced and for most, the first in which they had professional involvement.

Joe was quite clear that he had no wish to go into hospital and so it became increasingly likely that he would die at home. This confronted all of us[1] with the necessity to act in order to support both the staff and the residents. Joe, for his part, refused all attempts to discuss his condition and relaxed into the role of a demanding, crotchety old man with great ease, snapping his fingers for 'roll-ups' and making loud demands from his room for drinks, biscuits and other facilities which both staff and residents jumped to!

Our good fortune was that we were in the catchment area of St Christopher's Hospice and contact with them proved to be of great value. Their home care team regarded the staff and residents as Joe's family and offered support during his time at home. For our part, we were able to help the hospice staff relate to Joe when he did have to be an in-patient for a short time.

In the meantime, I set up training sessions for staff aimed at helping them to explore their own feelings in preparation for the necessity of dealing with residents' questions, anxieties and insecurities. The hostel was new; would residents think that anyone who came there died? Would they blame the staff or think they killed Joe? Would they ignore the whole event, leaving the staff feeling frustrated and helpless?

Strenuous efforts were put into getting the whole business 'right'. Hospital protocol about death procedures still applied and had to be negotiated, a funeral had to be arranged and family invited, a vicar had to be sought and no one knew how this request would be received.

In the end we got it three-quarters right. Joe died in St Christopher's but he was not alone. All the staff and residents had been prepared and were told gently, the funeral was arranged, and family, staff and residents left together from the hostel, returning there afterwards for sherry, sandwiches and tea.

Contrary to some expectations, none of the residents behaved as though this was a party despite the fact that none of them had been to a funeral before and that the refreshments looked a lot like the ones they had come to expect from social occasions at the hostel. What went wrong was our own briefing of the vicar who referred to Joe's workmates, which no one understood, his role as head of the family, which he never had, and how his colleagues would miss him.

The service was too rushed and too brief for our residents, many of whom were physically slow, which meant that getting in and out of the chapel became a somewhat undignified procedure. Many, not surprisingly, were a little slow to catch on to what this was all about and there was no room for explanations or translations at the time. Ten minutes may not be sufficient when you know what to expect and are geared up to it. When the situation is completley out of your experience, it takes longer to adjust to the mood and ambiance. Consequently, Joe had no ambiance at his funeral, just a lot of shuffling, some inappropriate remarks and the ungainly exit of a bunch of rather confused people. Staff were angry and hurt and the residents no doubt picked this up. We resolved to do better next time.

However, this story started with Edna and it was Edna's response sometime after the funeral that led to my further involvement. She had become more anxious and obsessional and seemed very frightened about something. Talking to Edna revealed that she had a sketchy but firm belief in God. She was a Catholic but had been going to a Church of England service and also helping out at the church from time to time.

This discussion was initiated by Edna's sudden query, apropos of nothing, as to whether Joe had gone to heaven or not. As an atheist, this was tricky ground for me so I fell back on the old 'Why do you ask?' routine. It transpired that she knew Joe had been what she described as a 'wicked old devil' and it worried her that he might have gone to hell because of this. A few more judicious questions established that she thought God might forgive bad temperedness and crotchety behaviour, particularly when someone was ill, and that was all that Joe had really been guilty of.

I thought this might be the crux of the matter but no, there was something else. I asked Edna 'Is there someone else you think might go to hell for being wicked?' After much beating about the bush, the real issue emerged and it was about Catholicism versus other religions. Edna thought that helping out and going to a Church of England church constituted such wickedness that she would not be let into heaven and desperately needed reassurance that this was not the case.

Under these circumstances, I have a firm principle which is that I will not deny what a client believes, neither will I pretend to be able to answer theological questions with conviction. I compromised by saying that many people hold the view that religion is like a staircase and you go up it to the landing. Because there are lots of religions, there must be lots of staircases but there is only one landing and that is where heaven is. This explanation, offered to Edna, meant that being a Catholic and going to a Church of England church could not be wicked because they were both staircases to the same heaven, which was where God was. Edna was happy with this but I was not. The staff of the hostel helped me out by tracking down a sympathetic clergyman who was able to answer Edna's questions helpfully and with conviction, so alleviating much of her anxiety.

Final comments

These stories are not accounts of perfect interventions; they represent an evolution of ideas, thoughts and processes which will continue and of which this chapter and this book are a part. To address these issues fully there needs to be proper recognition of the feelings of mentally handicapped people and resources put into the provision of training and support for carers, professionals and therapists. Access to ordinary counselling and support services would be ideal but as yet, the practitioners within these services are not geared to our clients' needs and the services themselves are often not free.

Death and loss are the only predictable features of life and yet little attention is paid to their impact upon our clients. Life in the community is going to bring these issues into sharp focus because the reality can no longer be hidden behind anonymous institutional procedures. Carers are often young, emotionally close to clients and lack the support that the older institutions provided in the form of large staff groups, schools of nursing, tutors, ward managers and the psychiatrist in the office down the corridor. Thus, they and, through them, the clients, are vulnerable.

As we begin to view and treat clients as people with feelings, we will need to confront our own difficulties in communicating distressing information to people we have previously felt conveniently able to deny that information.

Note

1 I include myself because I had quite strong ties with the hostel at that time although staff may feel that I was less 'us' than 'them' and certainly they were responsible for many of the innovations with which I also associate myself through the use of 'we'.

References and further reading

Backer, B., Hannon, N. and Russell, N. (1982) *Death and Dying – Individuals and Institutions*. Chichester: Wiley Medical.

Bihm, E. and Elliott, L. (1982) 'Conceptions of death in mentally retarded persons', *Journal of Psychology*, 111: 205–10.

Bradford, J. (1984) 'Life after death', *Mental Handicap Bulletin*, 34, 6–7 May: 64/8.

Brandt, E. and Bower, P. (1975) 'Johnny's bird is dead and gone', *Canada's Mental Health*, 23 (2): 19–20.

Crick, L. (1988) 'Facing grief', *Nursing Times*, 84 (28): 61–3.

DesNoyers Hurley, A. and Hurley, F. (1986) 'Counselling and psychotherapy with mentally retarded clients', *Psychiatric Aspects of Mental Retardation Reviews*, 5 (5): 22–6.

Egan, G. (1982) *The Skilled Helper: Model, Skills and Methods for Effective Helping*, 2nd edn. Monterey, CA: Brooks/Cole.

Emerson, P. (1977) 'Covert grief reactions in mentally retarded clients', *Mental Retardation*, 15 (6): 44–5.

Hinton, J. (1967) *Dying*. Harmondsworth: Pelican.

Hollins, S. and Grimer, M. (1988) *Going Somewhere*. London: SPCK.

Jones, E., Farina, A., Hastorf, A., Markus, H., Miller, D. and Scott, R. (1984) *Social Stigma – The Psychology of Marked Relationships*. Freeman.

Kennedy, J. (1989), 'Bereavement and the person with a mental handicap', *Nursing Standard*, 4 (6): 36–8.

Kitching, N. (1987) 'Helping people with mental handicaps cope with bereavement', *Mental Handicap*, 15 June: 60–3.

Kloeppel, D. and Hollins, S. (1989) 'Double handicap: mental retardation and death in the family', *Death Studies*, 13: 31–8.

Kubler-Ross, E. (1981) *Living with Death and Dying*. London: Souvenir Press.

Langer, E. (1983) *The Psychology of Control*. London: Sage.

McLoughlin, I. (1986) 'Bereavement in the mentally handicapped', *Mental Handicap Bulletin*, 64–7; also in *British Journal of Hospital Medicine*, Oct.: 256–60.

Mansdorf, I. and Ben-David, N. (1986) 'Operant and cognitive intervention to restore effective functioning following a death in the family', *Journal of Behaviour Therapy and Experimental Psychiatry*, 17 (3): 193–6.

Murgatroyd, S. (1985) *Counselling and Helping*. London: Methuen/BPS.

Murray-Parkes, C. (1972) *Bereavement – Studies of Grief in Adult Life*. Harmondsworth: Pelican.

Nelson, N. (1983) 'The mentally retarded: treatment problems and solutions in social casework', *Journal of Contemporary Social Work*, January: 45–8.

Oswin, M. (1981) *Bereavement and Mentally Handicapped People*. London: Kings Fund Report.

Oswin, M. (1990) 'Grief that does not speak', *Search*, 4 (Winter).

Owens, G. and Naylor, F. (1989) *Living while Dying*. Wellingborough: Thorsons Publishing Group.

Sternlicht, M. (1980) 'The concept of death in preoperational retarded children', *Journal of Genetic Psychology*, 137: 157–64.

Strachan, J. (1981) 'Reactions to bereavement', *Journal of British Institute of Mental Handicap*, 9: 20.

Thirm, A. (1989) *Nursing Times*, 85 (32): 66–8.

Worden, J.W. (1983) *Grief Counselling and Grief Therapy*. London: Tavistock Publications.

12

Sharing Memories: The Role of Reminiscence in Managing Transition

Helen Fensome

Introduction

Reminiscence is the act of recalling memories of past events, though as Merriam (1980) has pointed out, there is little consensus on what exactly constitutes reminiscing. This activity is undertaken by different people at various times in their lives, to different extents in a variety of ways, with a variety of goals or motives and a range of consequences or outcomes.

Much of the clinical work described in the literature concerns groupwork with elderly clients. The group provides a structured forum for sharing memories and in addition to whatever benefits the reminiscence itself affords, people may establish or develop relationships with other group members.

Below is an account of such a group run for people with a mental handicap. In contrast to the literature which is mainly about elderly people who have been admitted to institutions later in life, the work below was with people who had lived in an institution for almost all of their lives until very recently and were then resettled in a hostel in the community.

Resettlement of long-stay clients

One of the basic tenets of the philosophy behind resettlement is that managing the transition from hospital to community is not simply a case of getting people out of hospital; it is necessary to continue to manage the change. There is a vast literature on the benefits of community care, reviewed for example in Shepherd (1984), with occasional warnings such as that by Bennett and Morris (1983) that although there is much guidance on what *not* to do in order to avoid institutionalisation of clients and staff, there is little or no guidance on how to provide good alternative, community-based care.

These two points together lead to the (usually implicit) injunction to those who provide community care to provide continuing care for clients who come out of institutions, which gives them a very different experience from what they had in those institutions, but without giving specific guidelines on how to achieve this.

Second, an important thrust behind the move to community care comes from the principles of the philosophy of normalisation (for example, Wolfensberger, 1972). Normalisation is a set of principles directly generated from a particular ideology. The staff in the hostel where the clients lived were all given training in the principles of normalisation when they started working there, and all espoused a high level of commitment to the philosophy. Normalisation and old-style hospital care are incompatible in terms of their ruling ideology.

Fried (1963) noted that involuntary resettlement is often accompanied by symptoms of grief including depression, angry feelings and a tendency to idealise the lost place. Parkes (1972) also made explicit comparisons between the reactions to the loss of loved ones or body parts and reactions to involuntary residential relocation. Such signs were evident in the clients in the hostel: they expressed sadness, dissatisfaction, desire to return to the hospital and idealisation of the hospital.

Neugarten (1968) found that in non-handicapped groups, older people tended to be particularly vulnerable to adverse effects of relocation and indeed in the hostel it was the older residents who were voicing the most problems.

Romer and Heller (1983) found that an important source of support for relocated residents came from their peers. They said that there was considerable evidence that peer relationships played a critical role in successful adjustment of mentally handicapped adults in community settings. The clients in this hostel had not been 'moved on' with their existing friends, but were grouped according to level of need for staff support.

Heller (1982) summarised much of the literature on community adjustment in this group of clients, and noted that a very important factor in the degree of success of the adjustment made depends on the characteristics of the staff. He included a study by Coffman and Harris (1980) which found that the emotional reactions of mentally handicapped clients to transition difficulties are the same as for 'normal' people (i.e. depression, anger, hostility, nostalgia), but that these symptoms are often inadequately recognised in them. Thus, if clients are dependent on staff, the staff members' sensitivity and reactions bear on the quality of adjustment of the clients.

Reminiscence therapy

Reminiscence is an activity which can be observed in many elderly people. According to Coleman's (1986) account of changing attitudes towards reminiscence, in the late 1950s and early 1960s it was seen very negatively because it was felt to be associated with the withdrawal of the person into themselves, away from the 'real' world.

Butler's (1963) seminal paper on the 'life review' process led to (or reflected) a change in practice and attitudes towards reminiscence: his proposal was that it was necessary for the individual to undergo a process of life review in order to come to terms with life as they had lived it. There has been considerable effort put into defining and distinguishing the concepts of reminiscence and life review. Butler saw the two as different in that the life review process *involved* reminiscing but was not synonymous with it. Life review was that type of reminiscence in which the past was actively evaluated, and conflict was necessary for resolution to occur.

Thus, in the 1950s and 1960s there seem to have been general prevailing attitudes about the value of reminiscing, and research studies at that time were aimed at measuring the effects of reminiscence in groups of elderly people. McMahon and Rhudick (1964), for example, found that good adjustment in later life correlated positively with the amount of reminiscing done by people.

Overall the studies did not, however, produce unequivocal results: some suggested that reminiscence was a useful or beneficial activity in later life while others did not. Recent reviews of the empirical literature (for example, Thornton and Brotchie, 1987) all emphasise the uncertain status of reminiscence.

In reviewing the literature on life review reminiscence, Molinari and Reichlin (1985) called for a closer correspondence between clinical and research work. They made the point that research and clinical work have been running separate courses such that experimental studies have been aiming to define the parameters of reminiscence and clinicians have been concerned with promoting this therapeutic process with the elderly. Molinari and Reichlin called for the two lines to come closer together as the experimental data must be collected before definitive statements can be made about the clinical importance of reminiscence for the elderly.

In conclusion, clinical and experimental studies in the literature have failed as yet to come up with any consistent findings about the value of reminiscence for elderly people. This may be simply because the value of the activity varies from one person to another (and perhaps from one period of the individual's life to another). Following this line of thought, some authors have attempted typological descriptions of attitudes to reminiscence in the elderly (for example, McMahon and Rhudick, 1964) of the sort attempted for general styles of adaptation to aging (for example, Neugarten, 1968). For the time being, though, it can only be concluded that particular individuals may or may not benefit from reminiscing about their past life or from undergoing a process of life review.

Account of a reminiscence group for elderly mentally handicapped clients living in the community

The groupwork was carried out in a day centre for people with a mental handicap. All the clients came from a hostel in the community. I set up the group because when I began to work as a psychologist in this hostel I became aware of considerable unhappiness among the older residents about their move from the hospital they had lived in for many years. I was impressed by the strength of feeling of the clients about the hospital and how widespread that feeling was among the people living in the hostel.

The hostel (which consisted of three flats – two on the ground floor and one on the first floor) had opened 18 months before and 24 clients had been moved there. Clients were placed primarily on the basis of their level of need for support, and the hostel provided a high staff-to-client ratio, with 24 hour staffing. Because this was the main criterion for placement, many pairs of close friends had been placed separately, sometimes at great distance from each other, and often without informing people where their closest friend(s) now lived. Because it provided high-support living, many of the clients in the two ground-floor flats were elderly (8 out of 16 were over 60 years old). Many of them had lived in the hospital since early childhood and hence since the 1910s and 1920s.

Senior support staff were trained nurses and had previously worked in large institutions for some time. More junior support staff were younger and without any formal training. Both groups showed commitment to their roles in caring in the community and enthusiasm about the work they were doing. They ran an Individual Planning (IP) system with keyworkers and seemed keen to incorporate requests of the clients into their IP plans. The staff showed an apparent lack of awareness of clients' unhappiness about leaving the hospital, but this seemed to be an isolated 'blind spot'.

Thus, it seemed that there was a considerable need relating to the past within the hostel. This was being experienced by clients as unhappiness and sadness. For some reason this need was not being met or responded to by the staff at present. This need was not confined to a single client, but was being expressed by several, which raised the possibility of running a group of some sort with those clients.

Planning and setting up the group

In order to set up a feasible group which would have the support of the staff working with these clients, I began with some preliminary enquiries. I wanted to get an idea of why staff might not be responding positively to this expressed need of the clients, and needed to check whether the hostel manager would support my idea of running a group. I also needed to assess the feasibility of running a group in terms of the practicalities and whether staff time would be given to getting clients to the day centre.

To meet these aims I began by talking to one of the two Trainers in the hostel, who himself had had considerable involvement in preparing clients for their move from the hospital to their community home. He said that it was difficult to address the strength of feeling clients were expressing about many things, particularly the hospital, and pointed out that it was not possible to have much one-to-one contact with clients in the flats because of the physical layout of the flat (sitting-room, shared bedrooms) and the demands on staff time. He remarked that to the staff, the hospital was a vile and disgusting place, so it was very hard to talk about it in a positive way.

I then had a meeting with the manager of the hostel and discussed with him the idea of holding a group for people to come and discuss their feelings about the hospital within the context of a reminisc-ence-style group. He was very positive about the idea and promised his support for it. He undertook to ensure that staff time and transport would be available to take the clients to the day centre at a regular time each week.

Once I had had the idea approved by the manager I met with both Trainers, as they would be the staff involved in bringing clients to the centre. They were extremely interested in the idea of the group and asked if they could take part in the group too. They expressed a desire to learn something about setting up and running such groups.

Aims of running the group

I had a number of specific aims in setting up and running the group. The first was to bring members of the group together to share common memories and feelings and to develop group cohesiveness. Second, I wished to validate the members' sense of loss and acknowledge their difficult feelings. Third, I aimed to help them to start to come to terms with the loss so that they could invest more energy in their new life in the hostel. In addition, the group provided a way of instigating staff training with the Trainers in the hostel on how to run discussion-based groups with clients. The group therefore had a two-fold function of providing something for clients and providing the possibility for the Trainers to learn something about running discussion-based groups.

I arranged eight sessions at a fixed time every week, each of one and a quarter hours' duration. I met with the two Trainers to plan the overall structure of the group, and we planned the first session. At this meeting we discussed who to invite and decided on those people over 60, because we felt that otherwise the group would be too diverse in terms of their past experiences. As they knew the clients quite well, the Trainers invited individually each person in the flat over 60. Of the eight in this age group, five said they would like to attend. In addition, I explained to the Trainers that we would need to meet together for half an hour a week to discuss progress and difficulties as they arose, and plan future sessions.

I collected materials I could find to aid in the reminiscence process: a film which had been made about their hospital, and about its history and current closure. I also came across the manuscript of the life story of a man (AW) who had lived in that same hospital, which he had written as his memoirs shortly before be died.

The five people who said they would like to attend were all men. Alfred, aged 88, had lived in the hospital since early childhood and when asked why he originally went there said, 'I've no idea'. Alfred had a very good memory and a lively mind. He now had a lot of difficulty hearing, so we had to speak very loudly, and also had considerable problems with his eyesight. Apart from his sensory difficulties he did not seem to have any problems understanding what was said, and his level of handicap was presumably mild.

Herbert, age 84, was the most verbal and easy to understand. He was slightly physically disabled as he had a club foot. He had a very good memory and he too had been sent to the hospital as a small boy. He said that he was admitted when his father died, because his mother was not able to cope with both him and his brother. Again, he seemed to have no problems in understanding what anyone said and his handicap was difficult to see.

George, aged 86, was quite difficult to understand: he did not enunciate his consonants very clearly, but Herbert had known him for a long time and when others found it difficult to understand what George said, Herbert sometimes explained what George was saying. He had a good memory. He too seemed to have a very mild level of handicap and said he first went to the hospital as a 'babe in arms' when his parents both died.

Wilfred, aged 81, had a marked physical handicap such that he had considerable problems with motor control and coordination. This meant that his speech was rather limited and very difficult to understand, and he tended to communicate instead using sign language. He had a good memory and a very sharp sense of humour. When asked why he went to the hospital originally he said he did not know.

Bob, aged 65, had Down's syndrome and seemed to have more difficulty than the others in understanding what people said in the group. He was quite difficult to understand because his articulation was very unclear. He had a different set of memories from the others, and was generally preoccupied with the death of his best friend a year before.

Brief account of the group
As well as the materials I had for the group's use, at the first meeting George brought with him, without prompting, his photo albums which contained many pictures of life in the hospital. In future sessions all of the other members brought their photos in turn. Herbert had for a long time kept a diary of entertainments in the hospital which he brought to show us.

In the first session we began with a general discussion of people's memories of the hospital. Among George's photos were several of the farm at the hospital, which led to us talking about the jobs people had done there. George had worked on the farm, Wilf worked in the tailor's, Alf worked in the kitchen and bakery, Bob had done domestic work on his ward and Herbert had worked in the Brush shop. People described how different the hospital had been then, when numerous trades were practised and there were lots of workshops. The discussion raised memories of how much things had changed there since the early part of the century. Group members could remember much of their early time there and these early memories often came up in the course of this and other meetings.

For the second session Herbert brought his photos, some of which were very old and showed residents and staff in old-fashioned clothes and uniforms. I read out parts of AW's life story, which included a lot of information about how things used to be, including daily routines on the wards. Herbert pointed out that all the wards were different, so that everyone had slightly different accounts of daily events. People in particular remembered mealtimes, getting up and going to bed routines. Wilf said that on his ward, if you did not get up in time a member of staff would throw cold water over you. George said that on his ward, if you stayed in bed the staff would pull the bedclothes off you. Someone pointed out that life in the hostel was very different, which people felt was good, but also that there was less discipline.

After the second session I asked the group if they would like to visit the hospital in one of our scheduled times, to see how the closure was progressing. They were very keen to do this and expressed great interest in the idea, and George said very proudly that it would mean that he could show me and the Trainers where he had worked. I therefore wrote to the chief nursing officer asking if we could visit and especially if we could see the now closed parts of the hospital. I felt that it was important that members should see the reality of the closure to aid in the process of coming to terms with losing it, rather than visiting those parts which still functioned.

In the next session we talked about social events which took place in the evenings and at weekends. Alf told us about football and cricket games on Saturdays in which he and George took part. Bob said he preferred not to play because he felt it was dangerous. Wilf remembered watching the games. On Mondays a film was shown in the main hall for all the patients. These were often Westerns and were enjoyed by many people. On Fridays there was often a dance with a brass band which everyone enjoyed. On Sundays everyone had to go to church, which was something they did not have to do at the hostel, and George was pleased about this as he had never liked going. We talked about special occasions like Christmas, Easter and Harvest time. In the summer there were fêtes with processions which many people dressed up for. Also there were particular special occasions such as the Coronation of the Queen, for which there was a huge celebration. We went on to talk about how social events were different in the hostel: they were enjoyable, but people missed the sense of the whole hospital coming together to share a big celebration.

During the fourth session we watched a film about the hospital and this reminded people of memories they had of places pictured in the film. Herbert brought the old diaries he had kept, in which he had recorded all the air raids over the area during the war, with the time they started and how long they lasted. He also had a record of the films that had been shown each week in the main hall. In this session people began to talk of how they had both happy and sad memories of the hospital. We discussed how it can be sad to remember things from the past, when remembering unpleasant things or thinking about things which were happy but which don't happen any more. Alf had a lot of memories about awful things he had witnessed and told us about some of them.

The night before the fifth session Alf died. We talked about him in the group and felt that we would all miss him very much, particularly the friends who had known him a long time. As we were only a small group all the members were very important and we felt we would miss his contributions as he had lots of memories of the hospital from a long way back. Alf's death reminded Bob of his close friend who had died, and Bob talked of how he missed him a great deal as they used to do so much together. Bob had lots of happy memories of their times together and told us about some of these.

We talked for a while about things which were sad to remember from the past, and unpleasant features of the hospital. Wilf recalled the wards being extremely cold in the days before central heating and George explained how they used to have a fire in the middle of the ward as the only source of heat. We went on to talking about what people remembered from when they first went to live in the hospital. None of them liked it at first, though George said he was too young to remember his early days there. In those days the wards were all locked, so you were locked in and then let out at certain times to go to school. As Herbert said, it took a while to get used to the place, but when he did he began to enjoy it. He felt that the same might be true of moving to their present home and that they might take a while to get used to it there, but that they would probably come to like it with time. In fact Wilf said he already did like it, as did George. Herbert and Bob, however, were not so sure, although there were some things they liked about their new life-styles.

We used the sixth session to visit the hospital. We made a day of it and first went out for lunch to a pub near the hospital. Then we drove round all the grounds and visited the farm, where George went to see some of the animals and say hello to the people he used to work with there. As we drove round Herbert pointed out the place where people who ran away from the hospital used to hide as they went over the wall to get out. George remembered hiding there himself once when he ran away.

We went up to the main corridor of the hospital which was now mainly boarded off and almost deserted. A woman who still worked there came out of her office to see who we were as she said it was unusual now to see anyone around as there were only 180 people left in the whole hospital. This was a shock to people in the group as they remembered the corridor as being absolutely full of people rushing from one place to another. We bumped into a few people whom Herbert, George, Bob and Wilf had known, who still lived there. They said how quiet it was now and how the final plans had been made for the last people to leave. As we drove out of the hospital gates at the end of our visit, everyone turned and waved goodbye to the hospital, which was about to be closed for good. On the drive home, George remarked that Alfred would have been as shocked as they all were to see how much the place had changed since they had left.

The following week we discussed the visit and how it had felt to see such changes in the place. George said he missed the animals, but now knew what would be happening to them once the hospital closed. People described other changes that had happened in the past in the hospital, such as how when war broke out all the male staff were called up to fight, so the wards had to be left unlocked. Herbert, George and Wilf all remembered this as a good move, but Bob couldn't remember that time. When the staff came back from the war the hospital started to employ domestic staff for the first time, which meant the end of their jobs for many people. For instance, Wilf no longer had a job of cleaning the main hall. This change made a big difference to the life of the hospital and George said that from then on the domestic staff did all the work while the patients sat down the whole time. When we asked if this was boring he laughed and said no, as he had gone over to the farm in all his extra spare time.

In our final meeting people expressed regret that the meetings had come to an end and said they had found them interesting and enjoyable. Wilf, Bob, George and Herbert had enjoyed talking about their experiences, and the Trainers and I had enjoyed learning about life in the hospital over the last 70 years. We talked generally about moving on from one place to another, and the advantages and disadvantages of moving. Bob said he would be moving to a different flat in the hostel the following week, which he was very much looking forward to. Moving home was something we had all experienced at one time or another, so we all had thoughts on the good and bad things of leaving one place and starting life in another. We agreed that the longer you live somewhere, the harder it can be to get used to the new place, but felt that this usually happens with time.

Changes over the course of the group
The group became a very cohesive unit, such that by the end, the vast majority of the communication was between group members while early on it was almost all between a group member and myself or one of the Trainers.

The attitudes of people towards the hospital had changed considerably. It was now no longer idealised and clients expressed the thought that although it had been sad to leave, perhaps it had been the right time to move on.

In the hostel, the group members recounted the story of their visit to the hospital to other residents, and the Trainers remarked that they had shown pride in knowing something of their old home and in being able to pass on the information to fellow ex-residents. Thus, they had gained experience which they themselves valued, and which they saw as of value to other residents in the hostel.

An unexpected function of the group emerged following Alfred's death. The group served as a place where people could talk about their sadness at his death, and where they could have time to think about him, and keep his memory alive in a particular way. He was often mentioned in the sessions following his death, and so his presence remained throughout the course of the group. An example was George's saying what he thought Alfred would have felt had he been there to see the hospital with us.

The two Trainers felt they had learned a lot about running discussion-based groups, and were interested in being involved in similar work in the future. We discussed the ending of the group and the Trainers decided to arrange social activities for the members of the group appropriate to their age (for example, Music Hall evenings held locally). Thus, a spin-off from the groupwork was an awareness in the Trainers of the differing needs of elderly clients.

Five months after the end of the group I spoke to one of the Trainers by phone. He said that one outing had been arranged for the elderly clients and had gone very well. He was soon leaving and the other Trainer was planning a future outing. He said that the group members sometimes talked about the group and the hospital, both with affection, and still had reservations about the hostel. Other elderly clients who had moved to the hostel were unhappy at the move, but the Trainer said that as he was leaving, it was unlikely that another group would be started for some time. The other Trainer wanted to set up another group when she had more time.

Comments

One practical problem which arose was that Robert was much younger than the others: he was 65 while the rest were in their 80s. This was a consequence of our inviting everyone over 60, and was something I would prefer to avoid in future. It meant that although he shared memories of the hospital, he had very different memories of his time there. As a result we had to be careful to include him in the discussion by linking what others were saying with what he remembered. I felt there was a danger of him feeling isolated in the group, particularly as he apparently had a more marked learning difficulty. Nevertheless he attended and joined in with enthusiasm, and when I discussed the issue with the Trainers they agreed that it was a difficulty, but said he always asked on Tuesdays whether the group would be happening that day and was always the first to get ready to go to it.

My measures of change were based on observing group process and content and inferring change from that. I did not take particular measures of people's mood or level of adjustment to their new home before and after, and in retrospect this would have been useful in evaluating the intervention.

Proactive work of this sort requires the professional to be active and take the initiative throughout the intervention. The morning after Alf died one of the Trainers phoned to tell me of his death, and said that he assumed that the group would no longer take place that day. I said this was something we needed to think about, and had an impromptu meeting with the Trainers. After we had thought about it we agreed that the group should go ahead, but that we should make clear to members that if they did not want to attend that day there was no obligation for them to do so. Although the work was shared, I felt that responsibility for focusing thinking about the group fell upon me and that I had to bear in mind throughout the dual purpose of providing a group for the clients and training for the staff. In the example given here, that meant that it would have been inappropriate for me simply to have announced that the group would take place that day, and that it was necessary for me to work with the Trainers in helping them to come to a decision based on thoughtful reflection of the needs of the members that day.

Future directions and research

The outcome of this small group suggests that group reminiscence work may be usefully undertaken with clients who have a mental handicap. Change seemed to have taken place in the members' attitudes to their long-term home and hence their past lives. In addition, however, there were two further outcomes which, with this client group, may be particularly worthy of note. Those are, first, that the group had begun to communicate with each other more about their memories and hence they were beginning to get some of the peer support identified by Romer and Heller (1983) as being very important. Second, staff working with the client group (and not only with the members of this group) had developed a greater awareness of the needs and interests of elderly clients and were beginning to act on this awareness by arranging outings appropriate for the older clients.

Rather than claiming enormous success in this piece of work and expressing an urgency to introduce it in other settings where possible, I feel it is more appropriate to entertain this approach as a possible way of working with this client group when circumstances and needs expressed by clients would seem to indicate it.

Given the move into the community from the large hospitals there is at present an aging population of ex-hospital residents who have somewhat different life experiences from those people who have lived in hospital for a relatively short time or who have never done so. In the coming years this group will dwindle in size as the older people die, but for the time being they represent an important and sizeable group of people with particular needs. Interventions such as reminiscence-based work with this group, centred on their past life in the particular hospital they lived in, may be a very valuable way of helping them with some of the many problems faced generally by elderly people, and with some of the specific problems this group face as a consequence of having moved out of their long-term home in what might seem rather bewildering circumstances, to a very new and different and possibly bewildering environment.

In terms of the needs for future research, the review papers cited earlier spell out what is needed in terms of clinical and experimental work, and the coming together of the two. There is still a lack of empirical evidence on the effectiveness of reminiscence groups: experimental studies have tended to focus on refining the definition of the term while clinical accounts of groups have tended to stress their potential benefits rather than attempting to assess objectively how useful the groups are. What is called for in the literature now is a linking of the experimental and clinical work to set up more impartial, but clinically relevant studies to do just this. So far the research which has been carried out has not included groups of people with a mental handicap, but if reminiscence work were used more clinically with this group, then there would be the potential to contribute to the field of reminiscence and life review research. Perhaps the onus should be on professionals working in mental handicap to broaden their work and research to include reminiscence therapy, rather than being on researchers into reminiscence processes to extend their studies to include people with a mental handicap.

The closure of the large hospitals is much more than a simple resettlement operation. The philosophy surrounding it essentially concerns providing a better quality of life to people with a mental handicap or mental health problems. As one of the central tenets of the philosophy is about valuing people as individuals, reminiscence work has much to offer beyond easing the transition from hospital to community.

As a technique which relies on the individual as the expert on their own unique history it offers a means of working with someone which can promote their sense of identity and enhance their self-esteem and self-awareness. Further, it may help the individual to develop or consolidate their sense of life-long development, from past to present and into the future. It must be remembered, though, that any assessment for reminiscence work should be an assessment tailored to the needs of the individual: as noted in the introduction, reminiscence is not a panacea for unhappiness in later life.

References

Bennett, D. and Morris, I. (1983) 'Deinstitutionalisation in the UK', *International Journal of Mental Health*, 11: 5.

Butler, R.N. (1963) 'The life review: an interpretation of reminiscence in the aged', *Psychiatry*, 26: 65–75.

Coffman, T.L. and Harris, M.C. (1980) 'Transition shock and adjustment of mentally retarded persons', *Mental Retardation*, 18: 3.

Coleman, P.G. (1986) *Aging and Reminiscence Processes. Social and Clinical Implications*. Wiley: Chichester.

Fried, M. (1963) 'Grieving for a lost home', in L.J. Duhl (ed.), *The Urban Condition*. New York: Basic Books.

Heller, T. (1982) 'The effects of involuntary residential relocation: a review', *American Journal of Community Psychology*, 10: 471.

McMahon, A.W. and Rhudick, P.J. (1964) 'Reminiscing: adaptational significance in the aged', *Archives of General Psychiatry*, 10: 203–8.

Merriam, S. (1980) 'The concept and function of reminiscence: a review of the research', *The Gerontologist*, 20: 604–9.

Molinari, V. and Reichlin, R.E. (1985) 'Life review reminiscence in the elderly: a review of the literature', *International Journal of Aging and Human Development*, 20: 81–92.

Neugarten, B.L. (1968) *Middle Age and Aging*. Chicago, IL: University of Chicago Press.

Parkes, M. (1972) 'Components of the reaction to loss of limb, spouse or home', *Journal of Psychosomatic Research*, 16: 343.

Romer, D. and Heller, T. (1983) 'Social adaptation of mentally retarded adults in community settings', *Applied Research in Mental Retardation*, 4: 303.

Shepherd, G. (1984) *Institutional Care and Rehabilitation*. New York: Longmans.

Thornton, S. and Brotchie, J. (1987) 'Reminiscence: a critical review of the empirical literature', *British Journal of Clinical Psychology*, 26: 93–111.

Wolfensberger, W. (1972) *The Principles of Normalisation in Human Services*. Toronto: NTMR.

13

Working with Staff around Sexuality and Power

Hilary Brown

Staff are constantly confronted by their own feelings and conflicts in the work they do with the people they care for. Whether they are taking a grown man to the toilet for the first time or helping to make a judgement about whether a particular relationship is positive or exploitative, they are bound to draw on their unconscious as well as conscious experience, on their private world as well as their public or professional knowledge. They, alongside their managers and advisers, may seek to deny the impact of their own behaviour on the intimate experience of the people they are caring for. Services have traditionally distorted the sexuality of people with learning difficulties by desexualising them (as in calling them boys and girls, or lads and lasses) or by emphasising their sex (as in males and females) and acting to suppress sexual behaviour through segregation, withholding information or punitive responses. These strategies diminish people with learning difficulties, damaging their self-esteem and their value in the eyes of others.

In this chapter I want to discuss the implications for staff of dealing with sexual issues in their work with service users and the support they should be offered. Over the past ten years services have begun to articulate, through guidelines and policies, the response which they want staff to make to the sexuality of people with learning difficulties. Yet these guidelines have omitted as much as they reveal – they do not accurately reflect the sexual issues which staff have to deal with but the 'acceptable' and 'speakable' face of those issues. Nonetheless, the first guidelines (Hounslow, 1982) broke a powerful taboo, acknowledging as they did that employing agencies have a responsibility to set boundaries around the behaviour of their staff and around the decisions which they were having to make. As community services develop the range of options open to people with learning difficulties, the potential for both positive and detrimental sexual contacts increases but staff still receive little support beyond these embryonic policy frameworks whose status, mirroring their own, is often ambivalent.

Defining terms

'Psychotherapeutic' tends to mean different things to different people and I think it important to define the way in which I shall be using the term. This is particularly so given that I would not advocate psychotherapeutic ways of working to the exclusion of other kinds of interventions and I do not want to polarise 'soft', 'emotional', 'supportive', psychotherapeutic approaches and 'hard', 'scientific', 'controlling' behavioural ones, when both, used appropriately, can be helpful and respectful. I want, however, to locate a psychodynamic understanding of sexuality as one crucial dimension in training, management and treatment models, and I base this assertion on the belief that despite our 'adult' opinions, values and attitudes towards our own sexuality and that of others, we are disproportionately influenced by early learning which remains out of our awareness, so that our actions are motivated by impulses which we do not understand and seem not to be able to change or control. Psychotherapeutic approaches are therefore those which help people to make conscious attitudes and values, which influence their behaviour, but of which they are not aware. Making these explicit is the first step towards thinking about the sexuality of service users in a consistent and supportive way.

Sexuality is a multifaceted aspect of our personalities and experience. It is not something which can be put in a compartment and divorced from our upbringing, from the way our bodies have been and are used or treated, from our beliefs, from our experience with those who are more powerful than ourselves or those over whom we exercise power. It involves 'the interplay of an amazing variety of physical needs and desires in both men and women, needs and desires combining the longings, fears and humiliations, self love and self loathing we have experienced or imagined in our intimate contacts with others throughout a lifetime' (Segal, 1989: 141).

A narrow and rigid definition plays into the hands of those who would prefer to see the people they are caring for as being too handicapped or too childlike or too disturbed or too isolated to have sexual issues which deserve to be addressed. It also leads to hopelessness if the only 'sexuality' which is respected or acknowledged is heterosexual intercourse and that is not a viable option for a particular person at a particular time. Recognising distinct strands within an open-ended concept of sexuality enables support to be tailored to individuals at different times of their lives, no matter how severe their difficulties. Thus, I define sexuality in relation to:

– one's *body*, including other bodily functions, body image, sensual

pleasure, experience of pain or punishment, disabilities, movement, fitness, nakedness, ageing, illness;
- one's *gender*, including identification with or rejection of role
  models, differential experience of parenting and being parented,
  social expectations and stereotypes, gendered rules and standards
  of behaviour and dress, differential economic status and power
  (any or all of which may be sanctioned according to one's class,
  religious, cultural or ethnic group);
- one's *relationships*, including friendships and sexual partnerships,
  chosen and enforced contacts, love, anger, tenderness and abuse,
  comparisons of self with others, power and powerlessness.

Holding all of these dimensions in mind helps us to balance our
interventions and to consider people as whole people whose
physical, social and emotional needs are intertwined and inseparable.

In all of these dimensions adults with learning difficulties may
have experienced dislocation and distress. Parents who have
children with visible handicaps describe a kind of mourning as they
struggle to make sense of what has happened. They may feel
confused, depressed or isolated. These feelings are bound to affect
the experience of bonding, the quality of sensual and tactile
relationship the parents establish with their child. Ambivalent
feelings may be near the surface as issues of survival are faced and
surmounted (see Mannoni, 1972). Control and enjoyment of bodily
functions may have been delayed or frustrating and for some people
remain so. Moreover, medical complications may result in hospita-
lisation and early separations for the baby and mother. Sensory
handicaps may also get in the way of intimacy. Later, as the child
begins to identify with the same-sex parent or other role models,
they may receive double messages which exclude them explicitly or
implicitly from speculations about their adult options. Furthermore,
their relationships with peers may always be mediated by parents or
carers and their social networks fragile.

Thus, in approaching the sexuality of people with learning
difficulties we have continually to juggle between acknowledging
the 'ordinariness' of their issues and taking into account the
'extraordinary' problems they have had to face at different stages of
their lives and the consequences of these for them in adulthood.
Sometimes this can be very painful, as, for example, in facing up to
the subculture which existed in institutions. John, a young man who
recently moved through a hospital closure programme, sometimes
publicly replays the 'tape' of what happened on his ward: 'Stop
wanking Watkins . . . put it away . . . you've got a big one . . .

what have you been up to then?' – and so it goes on.

Confronting the brutality and barrenness of many people's lives may help staff to approach such behaviour with respect and sympathy rather than with punitive attitudes or an assumption that people with learning difficulties inherently act abnormally. It is more helpful to understand their sexual behaviour,

> . . . not as a diluted approximation of normal psychosexual adjustment in younger children, but as purposive behaviours learned according to unique experiences of the retarded person. . . . These include the extremely unnatural stimuli available to him in institutional settings, as well as the motivational and emotional consequences of inadequate learning and family experiences in the community. . . . Viewed from this perspective, the sexual adjustment of mentally handicapped persons is at least as normal for their environment as is the sexual adjustment of non handicapped populations.
>
> (Rosen, 1972: 99–100)

To avoid such awareness staff may collude by maintaining taboo areas which they believe are too awful to raise; these areas of painful silence, 'danger zones that had to be avoided at all costs' (Miller, 1984: 180), do not enable adults with learning difficulties to acknowledge the strength of their feelings. Carers would prefer to act on the assumption that the handicapped person is unaware of the discrepancies between her or his own life and those of others. But they may find comparisons with siblings almost unbearable (see Szivos, 1989), or feel strongly about not being able to find a sexual partner or the probability of not having children of their own. Without support, staff may not be able to acknowledge that they are responsible for the extent to which people with handicaps are able to speak out about things which are important to them, or to appreciate the alienating effect of their cheerful act on someone who is struggling to come to terms with their felt differentness.

Attitudes towards people with learning difficulties

Differentness, and the stigma which attaches to it, is central to the concept of Normalisation, which is a prominent component of training for all levels of staff. *But staff are taught about it as if it were something outside of themselves.* Historically people with learning difficulties have been cast in roles which limit and distort their sexual lives and feelings (see Craft and Craft, 1985). Wolfensberger (1972), in his early formulations of the Normalisation Principle, taught people to take notice of this imagery and sensitised professionals to what they were saying unconsciously about the people on whose behalf they were supposed to be acting. He noted the images which consigned people with learning difficulties to less than human status, which portrayed them as inert like vegetables or bestial like farmyard animals. A history of people with learning difficulties (see Ryan and Thomas, 1980) shows how such imagery has interfaced with different attempts to understand the place of people who are visibly different in society. This has varied from the 'holy innocent' of the eighteenth century to the more menacing notions enshrined in the eugenic movement's legislation early this century: notions which are still influential in determining the way services structure their response to the sexuality of the people in their care.

On the surface, service workers speak to their good intentions but the reality consistently betrays them. Like a Freudian slip, the hidden agenda leaks out expressing 'what we do not consciously take responsibility for meaning' (Rich, 1976: 202). The rigid policing of the language we use about people with disabilities is a response to this – not only a way of denying difference or a genuine commitment to listening to service users as we would all hope. It reflects the way each of us on occasion has to 'police' our own cruel streak which might otherwise escape through humour, sarcasm or contempt. Training staff to recognise other people's insensitivity and the distortions of systems and institutions which shape the lives of people with disabilities, is one step, but helping them to acknowledge, accept, *but not act on* their own ambivalence is a separate task.

Rather than encouraging people to disown such imagery they can be encouraged to explore their own first recollections of people with visible handicaps: how did they make sense of differentness, how were they told to behave towards people with handicaps, what place did people with disabilities have in their lives? No matter how 'ideologically' sound we become in adulthood it is inevitable that we also carry around frightening and disturbing images from childhood. We may have suppressed knowledge of cousins or neighbours whom we have simply 'forgotten' because we were not able to integrate them into our own worlds or activities. Owning that some of this damaging legacy belongs to us all is an alternative to locating it in history, or outside of our particular network or service system. It allows us to take responsibility without blaming others.

A further way in which people with learning difficulties are devalued is by being linked with and spoken to as children. Despite the exhortation to ensure that people are treated in age appropriate ways, faced with caring for dependent adults, staff will tend to fall back on the earliest and most powerful models they have of dealing with dependence, that is of their own parents or care-takers. Such a model was observed by Morris (1969) in her seminal work on institutions and noted as a mixed blessing in that it underpinned close and interested relationships but ones in which both the impact of favouritism and authority were unchecked. Exploring this tendency with staff helps to make explicit the critical ways in which they are not free to act as parents to the people they care for and to bring to the surface the extent to which they are drawing on their experience of being parented as well as their everyday experience as parents to their own children. It may help them to learn ways of being powerful and authoritative on behalf of, rather than in relation to, the people in their care.

Staff vs parents

Working *with* parents also challenges staff and can draw them into unhelpful dynamics and competition. Young staff in particular are likely to be in the process of breaking away from their own parents and may express their personal rebellion by championing the person with learning difficulties against the seeming overprotection of their parents. The fact that parents are always described as *over*protective rather than just protective provides evidence for this polarisation. It is as if staff are able to 'project' some of the distress and frustration they experience at work on to the parents who carry the long-term responsibility for their son's or daughter's ongoing dependence. (Dependence may be what young staff particularly do not want to acknowledge.) Professional carers make up the rules whereby a short-term intervention is valued more highly than a lifetime's care. This imbalance leads people to discount the significance of sexual issues as occasions for sadness, disappointment and grief.

If repressiveness, caution, disappointment and sadness can all be located with parents, staff can maintain an image of themselves, and for themselves, which is clear-headed and rational, positive and optimistic. They may shy away from anything messy or unpleasant, from the possibility of exploitation or the experience of loneliness. Helping staff to unravel this triangular dynamic is an important step towards unhooking them from a combative approach to parents and from their unsolicited rebellion on the client's behalf towards a position from which they can advocate on behalf of people with learning difficulties *and* their families and achieve the best compromises that can be worked out for both of them (see Brown, 1987).

Theoretical perspectives on sexual development

In so far as we experience our sexuality as if it were an essential and unchanging part of our personality, as something 'natural' and something we 'are' rather than some ways we have learned to behave, it is difficult to be detached or analytical about the influences which have shaped our own or others' sexual feelings or behaviours. Despite Freud's commitment to 'drive' theory, his early observations about developing sexuality do not conflict with a behaviourist view of sexual behaviour as learned and contingent (see also Chodorow, 1978). He observed the ways in which children gain mastery of and take pleasure in a succession of bodily functions, from sucking to defecating and then on to masturbation and genital activity. Studies confirm the importance of early childhood bonding to later sexual behaviours, so many of the outward elements are the same, the holding, sucking and biting, caressing, smells and closeness. Subjectively people report a loss of self, longing and return to a pre-verbal state of intensity.

'There are thus good reasons why a child sucking at his mother's breast has become the prototype of every relation of love. The finding of an (sexual) object is in fact a refinding of it' (Freud, 1905: 145); and, 'This satisfaction must have been previously experienced in order to have left behind a need for its repetition' (ibid.: 101).

Freud described the focusing of sexualised feelings arising from prolonged pleasure or relief from pain or tension and the more or less accidental association of certain objects or parts of the body which later act as triggers or fetishes to stimulate sexual activity. He concluded that 'a person's final sexual attitude is not decided until after puberty and is the result of a number of factors . . . some are of a constitutional nature but others are accidental' (ibid.: 57). Feminist writers have tended to abandon 'the idea that individuals have any "true" sexual "nature" which exists prior to social intervention and is then shaped by society. There is no "essence" of a person's sexuality which could naturally belong to her or be intrinsic to an individual' (Ruehl, 1983: 215).

However, what is learned is not only a response to the external environment but is somehow incorporated into a whole repertoire of fantasy and imagination as these experiences are taken in during infancy. Winnicott and Klein drew attention to the anxiety experienced as a result of the child's 'largely unconscious imaginative elaboration of the actual experiences . . . including experiences of the outside world and especially of the child's own bodily functions and feelings' (Davis and Wallbridge, 1981: 35). Ucer (undated) observed two kinds of fantasies:

creative fantasy may start in inspirational moments that are deeply rooted in unconscious factors. However such fantasy is then elaborated systematically and is translated into a realistic program of action. Daydream fantasy, however, is a refuge for wishes which cannot be fulfilled and . . . tends to diminish the motivation for psychological and biological maturation.

Fantasy, which because of its early origins can be entrenched and intractable, can therefore act as a trigger to sexual behaviour and is in turn activated by certain bodily states. Behaviours can seem to be without precursors to an outsider but are linked to what is going on in the person's imaginings. Fantasies have to be taken seriously as a potential rehearsal of actual sexual behaviour because,

> Sex offending is not usually a spontaneous event. The offender will have a pattern of behaviour that begins with fantasy, often reinforced through masturbation and ending in some form of attack. Even when the motive of the attack is to 'put down' or degrade and humiliate the victim, I have found that men will fantasise past events or anticipate future attacks. With indecent exposure and indecent assaults the reinforcing through fantasy/masturbation is very strong.
>
> (Thompson and Back, 1987: 10)

Such arbitrariness confronts people who have been told that sexual orientation and behaviour are issues of morality and natural instinct rather than a haphazard learning process, which is often incomplete, frustrating and, for people who find learning difficult, treacherous. If staff are dealing with particularly difficult or threatening behaviours, knowledge about sexual development may help them both to unhook from a blaming attitude towards the client and to protect themselves and others from harm. The embarrassment and rigidity which many people are left with for much of their lives around sexual issues is an outcome of a process of teaching and learning which is always conducted in a relationship in which one person is immensely more powerful than the other, in which shame is a frequent source of feedback and praise or encouragement often missing. As such, people tend to learn what not to do rather than what works for them.

Freud also, before he recoiled from the accounts he was hearing of the sexual abuse of children within families, described how sexual learning took place on different levels, in that during any encounter we learn as both 'subject' and 'object'. In other words, we learn what a particular activity feels like and by watching, how to do it. So if a person is brought up in a respectful way they learn what it feels like to be respected and they can see from the other person 'how to respect someone'. This notion has been popularised within Transactional Analysis in the idea of separate ego states – the Parent which internalises and reproduces the messages received from authority figures, while the Child records and replays direct experiences and feelings. If, however, the behaviour which people have been subjected to is traumatic and their feelings too painful to bear, they will cut themselves off from their experience. Identifying with the person who is in control is one way of switching off feelings which are too disturbing to be acknowledged. The victim of abuse may thus learn to abuse others, that is 'to deal with his/her own victimisation by a process of identifying with the aggressor' (Vizard and Tranter, 1988: 69).

There is evidence of a high rate of sexual abuse among convicted child molestors although this should not be regarded as a simple cause and effect relationship (see also Groth and Burgess, 1979). Staff should, however, consider the possibility of abuse if a service user begins to abuse others and also be encouraged to seek help themselves if they feel able to disclose and receive support for abuse they may have suffered personally. Alice Miller works from the premiss that if people can be helped to articulate their own experience of pain or abuse they will be freed from the compulsion to act out the oppressor's behaviour. She sees such actions as the 'child' in the person trying to tell their story, a story which would not have been credited or believed if it had been told in words when the person was young.

Staff motivation

Staff in services for people with learning difficulties come into the caring professions for a whole variety of reasons. Being low-status work it attracts people who are not able to get better conditions, people whose stress at work is exacerbated by low pay, debt, bad housing and shift work. In some parts of the country the old mental handicap hospital was the major employer in a small town or village and generations of the same family may have worked there. Other people come into the service because they identify with people who are not being valued, they wish to 'walk in the shoes of the oppressed'. If they are able to base their actions on these feelings they may bring particular sensitivity and dedication to the work of caring, a determination to respect people as they want to be respected themselves, an ability to detect practices and interactions which demean or diminish people. It may also be, however, that they are drawn into caring for people with learning difficulties because they can feel powerful in that role. Instead of remembering what it felt like to be vulnerable they may instead be drawn to work in a field where, as staff, they are not likely to be made vulnerable again, where they can be in control. In this case, staff are likely to become more rigid when their power is challenged, to grip on to the authoritarian responses which they learned from observation and to wipe out the potential to identify with the people who are on the receiving end of their oppressive behaviour.

Staff training and support

These issues need to be addressed in both training and supervision if the staff member is to be helped to create new opportunities for people with learning difficulties and to act in a respectful way towards them. Experiential learning, such as that pioneered by the Family Planning Association (see Dixon, 1986), or the British Institute of Mental Handicap, offers an opportunity for staff to relate the issues they face at work to their personal beliefs, experiences and struggles. Such training must be conducted in a way which respects the right of every individual to confidentiality and to privacy. Skilled facilitation is necessary. Warm-up exercises should precede work which is personal and people should be offered a clear rationale and explicit permission to share only those things they feel comfortable with, given the time available and the make-up of the group.

It is particularly important if one is working with a whole staff team that people are not asked to share personal issues outside chosen pairs or small groups. Hierarchies affect the appropriateness of sharing. There may be sexual relationships, harassment or tensions within the work group. Moreover it should always be emphasised that the purpose of these activities is not personal therapy or support, but the task of developing positive sexual options for people with learning difficulties. Drawing such boundaries is important for everyone and is a good model for people who need to learn to keep their own needs separate from the needs of the people they are working with.

Rather than teaching about sexual development, or even worse the sexual development of these 'other' people who happen to have learning difficulties, the emphasis should be on helping staff to identify what influences have impinged on them and relate these insights to the lives of the people with whom they are working. Sharing their ideas in the whole group will help people to identify the common experiences they have but also to recognise the distinct lack of support and validation which has been the experience of many people with learning difficulties. Most adults will have experienced abusive or intrusive sexual encounters at some time in their lives, from which they can learn how to protect and support people with learning difficulties. Together they can explore situations in which people with learning difficulties have found themselves and consider what the service did and should have done to prevent the abusive incident and to respond to their distress. Such training opportunities allow staff to use what they already know about how to support people integrating their understanding into work about proper procedures and safeguards.

Because of the tendency for staff to distance themselves from the feelings and concerns expressed by parents, role-play can be a powerful way of learning about their position. Rehearsing, for example, the consultation process around setting up a sex education programme (usually too little, too late!) or a crisis intervention involving their son or daughter can be useful. Working in mixed groups of parents and staff can also be powerful, and swopping roles gives both 'sides' an opportunity to explore the constraints, attitudes and feelings of the other. Discussions, role-plays and exercises should not be regarded as ends in themselves but as part of a process which includes acquisition of knowledge about sexual development and the issues which arise for people with learning difficulties, together with skills in counselling, educational and behavioural interventions. Nonetheless, they act as a powerful reference point and motivator of change.

Identification and boundaries

Many of the most powerful training exercises rely on a process of identification where staff are asked to put themselves in touch with how they would feel if they were in their clients' shoes. But staff also need to be able to separate themselves from their clients and to maintain appropriate boundaries. It is as if they need to learn from the subjective experience of being on the receiving end of care but then leave this experience behind in order to transfer what they have learned into the way they carry out their role as carer, with all its responsibility for managing and initiating interactions and opportunities in someone else's interests. Sometimes carers and staff find this process so uncomfortable that they stay 'alongside' the person they are caring for in a way which blurs the boundaries and disguises the real difference in power which exists between them. This is not done cruelly but out of a kind of over-concern or over-identification. It may lead, for example, to a situation where a person is being offered a choice that they cannot actually make, in the name of an equality which they do not have. In sexual matters such confusion can be used to imagine real and informed consent where the power imbalance between the two parties has rendered someone liable to undue persuasion or manipulation.

Some writers have questioned whether normalisation would be better reflected if non-handicapped people were to consider people with learning difficulties as potential partners. Williams (1988) challenges the view that relationships between handicapped and non-handicapped partners should automatically be framed in terms of exploitation. In reviewing a book on sexuality and people with mental handicaps, he comments.

> Non handicapped people are assumed throughout to be in the role of professional advisers – never as friends, companions or lovers. It seems a long way off that such a book as this will include a chapter on 'How I fell in love with a person with learning difficulties' or 'My marriage to a person with a mental handicap'.

> (Williams, 1988)

More recently David Brandon remarks that

> Recent history provides plenty of examples of staff and people with learning difficulties going to bed together. Hospitals were often isolated and staff poorly paid, unappreciated and lonely. If it became known it usually meant instant dismissal. My talks with consumers indicate that sexual relationships occurred considerably more often than staff dismissals; a blind eye was turned and, in many cases, genuine pleasure and affection were involved.

> (Brandon 1989)

He goes on to express the concern that moving away from 'stiff necked professionalism' may leave people without support in facing up to 'deeply disturbing problems' which may accompany this change in role. It is important that adults with learning difficulties are not unthinkingly subsumed under the expertise of those working with children who have been sexually abused but there can be parallels which should be heeded. Bentovim and Boston (1988: 17) argue that

> What characterises the relationships of the adult to a child is the authority to demand a particular response and to expect compliance. If the demand is a sexual one then this becomes the sexual abuse of that authority. . . . In this context the sexual use of a child, whatever the justification, is an abuse of dependency and authority.

By definition many people with handicaps are dependent on their carers and live in a culture where compliance is expected if not insisted upon. The use or abuse of sexuality in such relationships presents dynamics similar to those of the child in his or her family. Rose (1983) points to 'the human tendency to invoke love at moments when we want to disguise transactions involving power'. In services as in families, it is difficult to disentangle them.

Blurred boundaries lead to confusion on several fronts. First, they remove a protective shield which enables someone to act as an intimate carer. Doctors, who are legitimated to carry out intimate examinations do so with the most stringent of rules about sexual relationships. Work on social networks and care giving (see Grant, 1986) shows that people who need personal care tend to rely on a particular female relative (usually mother, wife or eldest and/or unmarried daughter) and that if this is not feasible they would prefer to be cared for by an unknown professional. In short, people do not want their neighbours or friends to take them to the toilet; for them to do so would be to disrupt the acceptable social distance which needs to be maintained in order for these ordinary relationships to be sustainable. For many people with learning difficulties the reality is that they need professional care-givers to perform these intimate tasks in order to free them to make contacts which are unstigmatised in the community at large.

Moreover, far from enhancing the self-esteem of the person with a disability, such confusion about boundaries may undermine her or his competence in choosing appropriate and available partners, perpetuating a situation in which

> Most persons with developmental handicaps are inadvertently taught to differentially value their relationships with non handicapped people more than their relationships with other persons with handicaps. They are not taught that individuals with developmental handicaps are also valued persons with whom a caring and sharing relationship could be developed and who may be the only accessible, potential partners.
>
> (Griffiths et al., 1989: 18)

The authors go on to comment, in the context of work with people with learning difficulties who have been referred because of sexual problems, that this confusion often leads to their clients having crushes on film or TV stars, care-givers or members of their family, and occasionally choosing children as potential partners, which causes particular anxiety and distress.

Increasingly we are seeing that staff who are able to think clearly about their role are in a better position to support people with learning difficulties in making new and varied contacts within the wider community, in seeking independent advocates, in making leisure and work opportunities a possibility, rather than in trying to be all things to all people themselves and, when they leave, which they inevitably do, leaving the person as isolated as they were before (see Brown, 1987). This tends to cut across some of the recent discussion about 'professionalisation' (see, for example, Tyne, 1989) which suggests that professional 'status' acts only to allow staff groups to distance themselves from people with disabilities and to organise things in a self-serving way. I would assert that there is a protective function which is performed by such distancing which acts in the interests of people who are exposed to others in ways which give those others power over their bodies or affairs.

Selection of staff

Because staff have to deal with sexual issues at work they need support to help them both identify with the people to whom they owe a duty of care and to detach themselves enough to maintain clear boundaries. In interviews it may be possible to explore with applicants whether they are able to use their own experience as the basis of respectful relationships with service users – asking, for example: 'Have you ever been in a situation where someone made you feel stupid. Can you tell us what that person did? What could you learn from that about how you might support people with learning difficulties in this job?'; or 'in this job you will have to help people with learning difficulties with personal tasks like toiletting. What would you want to tell your carer if ever you were in the position of needing help like that?'; or 'in this job you will need to support people in their relationships and counsel them about appropriate sexual behaviour. How were you given sex education or guidance? Was there anyone who helped you whom you could learn from now you are going to take on that role?'

It may also be possible to pick up very rigid patterns, parental tones, shoulds and oughts, and most importantly an inability to articulate subjective views which might indicate that the person has buried difficult feelings. Non-verbal cues, clothes and body language may on the other hand indicate sexualised behaviour when it is not appropriate and uncertainty about the role of care-giver, especially where the carer is young, or seems to be bringing a personal rather than a professional 'set' to the interview.

The following questions may help the applicant to explore boundaries and confront their expectations:

Do you foresee any difficulties in being a keyworker for the men (aged 50) who live in this house given that you are much younger than them? How do you think you could help them to act appropriately towards you remembering that they have not had much experience of relating to women in the hospital where they lived until recently?

You seem a 'motherly' (or 'fatherly') sort of person from the answers you have given. What are some of the differences between the way you have brought up your children and the way you would relate to the people here?

You say you want to be 'friends' with the people in the house. Can you think of any situations in which you might have to be unpopular to act in the best interests of the people who live here?

Addressing underlying issues in an interview situation is difficult and should be thought about carefully in advance of the interview. Qualities which are sought should be spelt out on a personal specification and particular attention should be given to Equal Opportunities issues and different expectations which arise out of class or culture. Nonetheless, I believe that we do have a right to specify and explore the personal experience which staff bring to their jobs and if this is done in a respectful way, and explicitly, I think it will lead to less discrimination. For example, people who are discriminated against on the grounds of sexual orientation may fulfil these criteria when they are spelt out but at present be subjected to unexplored and unstated prejudice when they apply for care jobs.

Conclusion

Because staff deal intimately with people who are dependent on them they are bound to be drawn back to their own experience of being dependent. To be effective, training and staff support needs to do more than offer a coherent model of how people *should* be treated. Staff must be offered protected space in which they can recall and explore the vast uncharted knowledge they already carry within themselves. Then they may be free to take from it ways of working with people which they know from experience were facilitative and respectful and reject (although this may be difficult) behaviours which caused distress, shame or embarrassment.

Acknowledgement

I should like to thank Anne Craft particularly for her comments during the writing of this chapter and for her continued collaboration and support.

References

Bentovim, A. and Boston, P. (1988) 'Sexual abuse – basic issues – characteristics of children and families', in A. Bentovim, A. Elton, J. Hildebrand, M. Tranter and E. Vizard (eds), *Child Sexual Abuse within the Family*. London: John Wright.

Brandon, D. (1989) 'Can we breach the protective barriers of sexuality?', *Community Living*, April.

Brown, H. (1987) 'Working with parents', in A. Craft (ed.), *Mental Handicap and Sexuality – Issues and Perspectives*. Tunbridge Wells: Costello, pp. 158–76.

Brown, H. with Brown, V. (1988) *Building Social Networks*. Video-assisted training pack in the 'Bringing People Back Home' series. Bexhill: South East Thames Regional Health Authority.

Chodorow, N. (1978) *The Reproduction of Mothering*. Berkeley: University of California Press.

Craft, A. and Craft, M. (1985) *Sex and the Mentally Handicapped* (revised edition). London: Routledge and Kegan Paul.

Davis and Wallbridge (1981) *Boundary and Space: An Introduction to the Work of D.W. Winnicott*. Harmondsworth: Penguin.

Dixon, H. (1986) *Options for Change*. London: FPA.

Freud, S. (1905/1977) *On Sexuality*. Harmondsworth: Pelican Freud Library, Penguin.

Grant, G. (1986) 'The structure of care networks in families with mentally handicapped adult dependants', in P. Gutridge (ed.), *Social Work in Action in the 1980s*. Bangor, Gwynedd: Occasional Paper No. 4, Department of Social Theory and Institutions, University College of North Wales.

Griffiths, D., Quinsey, V. and Hingsburger, D. (1989) *Changing Inappropriate Sexual Behaviour – A Community Based Approach for Persons with Developmental Disabilities*. New Jersey: Brooke.

Groth, A.N. and Burgess, A.W. (1979) 'Sexual trauma in the life histories of rapists and child molesters', *Victimology: An International Journal*, 4 (1): 10–16.

Hounslow 1982 Guidelines for Staff on Sexuality and People with Mental Handicaps.

Mannoni, M. (1972) *The Backward Child and His Mother*. New York: Pantheon Books.

Miller, A. (1984) *Thou Shalt Not Be Aware*. London: Pluto Press.

Morris, P. (1969) *Put Away: A Sociological Study of Institutions for the Mentally Handicapped*. London: Routledge and Kegan Paul.

Rich, A. (1976) *Of Woman Born*. New York: W.W. Norton.

Rose, P. (1983) *Parallel Lives – Five Victorian Marriages*. Harmondsworth: Penguin.

Rosen, M. (1972) 'Psychosexual adjustment of the mentally handicapped', in M.S. Bass and M. Gelof (eds), *Sexual Rights and Responsibilities of the Mentally Retarded*. Proceedings of the Conference of American Association on Mental Deficiency. Region IX.

Ruehl, S. (1983) 'Sexual theory and practice: another double standard', in S. Cartledge and J. Ryan (eds), *Sex and Love: New Thoughts on Old Contradictions*. Harmondsworth: Penguin.

Ryan, J. and Thomas, F. (1980) *The Politics of Mental Handicap*. Harmondsworth: Penguin.

Segal, L. (1989) 'Lessons from the past', in E. Carter and S. Watney (eds), *Taking Liberties: Aids and Cultural Politics*. London: Serpents Tail.

Szivos, S. (1989) 'Self esteem among young adults with learning difficulties'. Unpublished doctoral dissertation, University of Exeter.

Thompson, M. and Back, T. (1987) 'Counselling sessions for sexual offenders prove successful', *Social Work Today*, 15 June.

Tyne, A. (1989) 'Normalisation: the next steps', *Community Living*, July.

Ucer, E. (undated) 'Sexual fantasies in institutionalised retardates'. Unpublished paper, United Cerebral Palsy Association, USA.

Vizard, E. and Tranter, M. (1988) 'Recognition and assessment of child sexual abuse', in A. Bentovim, A. Elton, J. Hildebrand, M. Tranter and E. Vizard (eds), *Child Sexual Abuse within the Family*. London: John Wright.

Williams, P. (1988) 'Review of *Mental Handicap and Sexuality*, edited by A. Craft', *British Journal of Mental Subnormality*, 34 (1): 66.

Wolfensberger, W. (1972) *The Principles of Normalisation in Human Services*. Toronto: NTMR.

14

Demystifying Traditional Approaches to Counselling and Psychotherapy

Alexis Waitman
(with François Reynolds)

Introduction

The debate is no longer about *whether* people are entitled to services, but rather *how* their needs can best be met in ways that validate them as individuals while offering equality of opportunities. Such thinking is more likely now than ever before to be reflected in changing public attitudes and in the noticeable shift in demand being placed on service-providing agencies. Traditionally, services have not been structured to respond to the needs of people with disabilities, nor to their families and carers; such services as have been provided have been inherently bureaucratic, designed more to meet the needs of the organisation providing them, than those of the people to whom they were grudgingly and ungraciously given. Various service initiatives have recently been introduced in an attempt to widen the sphere of services and approaches available. Care Management is one, brokerage another, and, as Szivos (1989) so clearly describes, advocacy is yet another. Doubtless, more will appear as people enter community settings in ever-increasing numbers and new organisations flourish as a changing public sector rises up to meet the demands.

Among these demands will be that of increased access to what have become known as the 'talking therapies'. Along with the rights and responsibilities of community living come the demands and stresses of everyday human existence. One of the ways of dealing with these, widely available to ordinary people, is the choice of accessing one (or more) of these therapeutic interventions which range in depth from active listening techniques through to the deeper more analytical approaches used by some psychotherapists (for example, Sinason, Stokes, Hollins). Most of us use community resources to meet our daily living needs and satisfy our wants and desires. This in turn helps feed our sense of self-esteem, and establish a personal sense of identity as a valued individual within a secure and stable environment. This we accept as a basic human right.

This is not generally true for people with disabilities, especially if the disability is of a mental handicap or psychiatric nature. Sometimes, their needs are specifically related to their disability and these may overwhelm or even dominate their experience of life as a whole. However, just as with the non-handicapped population, some people with a learning disability have need, at some time, for the special kind of relationship that good counselling or psychotherapy can offer.

Like us, people with disabilities are sometimes prone to having been damaged spiritually, emotionally, physically or psychologically, by a system that did not care or understand or perhaps a family that was simply not able to cope, and which was therefore forced into making a difficult, but inevitable decision. The result, however, has often been one of overwhelming trauma, whose manifestation caused yet further mistreatment, misunderstanding or even abuse. Such has been the history of many people who carry the label of 'mental handicap'.

It is all too easy to 'wrap up' or, in modern terminology 'package' such a person in the all-encompassing label of a 'special need'. Consequently, such a life is inevitably one that is described and therefore experienced in a segregated and essentially different way because people are defined by their disabilities, rather than their accomplishments or competencies. They are then forced to lead handicapped and, ultimately, handicapping lives, for it is we, not they, who provide the stigma and the hindrance, albeit often unwittingly.

This chapter seeks to construct a framework for establishing not only an empowered consumer group, but also to offer carers and staff a similar feeling of self-worth. Such feelings and attitudes can lead, in the long term, to the complete disappearance of devalued collectives and, more vitally, to many if not all of the devaluing traditional tasks that were a part of those settings. Empowerment of this kind brings about, as I hope to indicate, an opening up of more creative ways of working with people, but will also bring with it new challenges – not least because so many of the well-established 'safe' professional ways of working will become redundant. There will be increasing contrasts and conflicts between traditional patterns of service delivery and availability, and those that are likely to be demanded by a newly empowered and vociferous user-group.

The client group as a whole has suffered (and I use the word advisedly) at the hands of misguided staff; overly powerful medical consultants, ignorant policy-makers and a fearful general public. Because of all this negativism, the kind of traditional interaction between staff and clients was not of an empowering nature, for no one in such a service felt valued, and it is this that lies at the root of empowerment.

Similarly, where therapeutic approaches *were* applied, these were generally of the invasive drug therapy or behavioural type because it was for a long time felt that where there was no emotional response or intellectual capacity, such an intervention would take effect at a stimulus–response external control level only. And, of course, in many cases this proved to be highly effective in controlling or 'shaping' unwanted behaviour. However, what it did not do was to offer insight, for either party, into the nature or cause of the behaviour, so no growth or development occurred. Such treatments were designed to meet the needs of the service, where control of aggression and 'acceptable street behaviour' became bywords for care in the community. The needs of the people involved were secondary and often completely overlooked.

Where 'people-centred' approaches were attempted these, too, were second rate. Why waste scarce resources on a client group who were clearly not going to get better, and who, given that the majority form an elderly and service-demanding majority, will not benefit to any appreciable extent? A direct result of this kind of flawed but not uncommon thinking was the 'three-day counselling course'. This was a device introduced in order to deal with those 'more able' (more able than what was never more than imprecisely defined) clients who might be able to take advantage of such attention; the method was to select the 'more able' staff (again, definition was imprecise and selection arbitrary) and *send* them on a three-day 'counselling' course. Rarely were staff effectively or professionally trained: expectations of instant expertise were dictated by service expediency. My own feelings about such misguided actions are that they serve only to reinforce a set of already well-entrenched negatives about the people on the receiving end.

I believe it to be professionally unethical to treat any individual in this way, and it is tantamount to an abuse of both personal and professional aspects of life. There is little that is more professionally abusive than a person who reacts on an entirely intuitive level, presenting as an amateur with talent. This, it seems to me, is playing power games for 'who gets the treatment'. It does nobody any good, and holds the potential for great harm, in addition to denying the benefits and intrinsic value of therapy and counselling.

So we can already begin to see how, by being treated in ways consisting of deprivation, denial, rejection and a particularly insidious form of institutionalised oppression, both service users and service providers have felt marginalised and trivialised. There are not always answers – living with ambiguity and uncertainty is often the reality. However, by raising issues and offering alternatives, and where appropriate, by suggesting ways forward, I hope to have stimulated an ongoing professional debate that will offer positive outcomes for like-minded people living and working in the field of learning disabilities.

The costs and benefits of traditional approaches

What has been missing is not skill, talent or expertise. Rather, the lack has been around a reticence to allow creativity, flexibility, adaptability and innovatory ways of working with people with learning difficulties to occur naturally. This has been due in part to a lack of resources: where scarcity exists, creativity is often stifled. However, this is not the whole answer. Conventional training, especially in psychiatry and psychology, often insists on a strictly theoretical application in practice. It is an unusual psychiatrist who views a person with a mental handicap as a 'suitable case for treatment' if we are considering a 'talking' therapeutic intervention. Psychologists, too, have often been guilty of favouring the more behavioural approaches because of their perceived effectiveness over a short time-scale, for 'problem behaviours'. This chapter will be a journey of demystification on which some of the myths and pretentiousness of traditional approaches to counselling and therapy will be pushed aside, creating a space for people with learning difficulties.

There is, it is being argued, a need to accept the benefits of conventional approaches where these have proven to be successful *for the client*. Acceptance is also sought for the notion that there are severe limitations to a strictly applied traditional intervention, which by definition means non-application for vast numbers of people in need. I seek, therefore, to 'open the door' for a clutch of flexible, readily adaptable models of therapeutic contact which are already proving to be effective agents of personal growth and development for people with learning difficulties.

It is not only service users who are denied access in these traditional ways: staff, and carers too, are invalidated when it comes to 'therapy'. On offer here are models which, unlike the 'three-day counsellor', will enable people charged with the increasingly challenging roles of caring in the community, tools and techniques that provide available alternatives. That is not to say that training is not an essential element in all of this. It is. Effective, user-friendly, easily accessible and well-designed staff training, with professional supervision and ongoing additions which seek to increase relevant competencies, are an essential prerequisite to any model offering personal growth and development.

Perhaps it is also important to acknowledge, in our excitement at being at the crossroads of the great discovery, that what we do *can* change lives – that counselling and psychotherapy can, like any other power-tool, be abused and therefore manifest themselves not as healing processes but rather the reverse. In the past, people have been tyrannised and humiliated by therapeutic interventions that were misguided or mismanaged. This can be especially so in groupwork (although as Hollins' work illustrates (see chapter 10), an alternative model is available), and particularly where people with often severe psychiatric problems are included as group members (because this is cost- and time-effective) alongside people with various kinds of learning disability: boundaries become blurred, feelings run very high, and without extremely skilful handling, damage results. Furniture can be repaired or replaced. People are not so easily mended.

Peter Lomas (1987: 91) has said that 'people will most likely disclose themselves fully when in an environment where they feel free to do so; that is, when they feel that they will not be condemned, ridiculed, exploited or punished . . .'. The therapist who coerces is not searching for the truth but believes it is already found, and intends to force it upon the recipient by means that themselves may not be truthful.

It would seem that there is an incipient danger in any therapeutic approach, which is why it is important that, whatever approach is used, whether 'traditional' or alternative, the practice be professionally and soundly supervised. In this way, boundaries on abusive practice are identifiable and damage is less likely to occur.

Nikolas Rose (1986: 91) goes much further, making what is, in effect, a profound criticism of the psychotherapeutic process, in what he calls 'the professional annexation of ordinary human experiences'. These therapies of normality, he states, transpose the difficulties inherent in living on to a different psychological register – they become not intractable features of desire and frustration, but malfunctions of the psychological apparatus that are remediable through the operation of particular techniques. The self is thus opened up, a new continent for exploration by the 'entrepreneurs of the psyche', who offer us an image of a life of maximised intellectual, commercial, sexual or personal fulfilment and assure us that we can achieve it with the assistance of the technicians of subjectivity. Thus, he is saying, a whole host of mind-tricksters is created, selling their wares, and in so doing creating a new and alluring service industry. At a time when entrepreneurship is a highly regarded skill, and when services are literally 'up for grabs' and prices are far from fixed, it would be a foolish person who did not take heed of such a warning voice. There will, it seems in future be even more vulnerable people on whom the vultures may prey – and only some will be service users.

Introducing some alternative approaches

This part of the chapter has been written with the collaboration of François Reynolds, a friend and colleague who has for many years been practising alternative approaches to counselling and to educational provision. Trained both in traditional mainstream educational practice, as well as in Neuro-Linguistic Programming (NLP) and Educational Kinesiology (EK), François shares the belief that people can be enabled to take greater control of their lives.

In order to introduce the idea of an alternative way of offering services to people with learning disabilities, we are going to focus on three approaches in particular: NLP and EK, while also making reference to the concept of Gentle Teaching (McGee et al., 1987).

What has so often been missing, it seems to us, is a clear, simple explanation and understanding of the thinking process. That is not to say that conventional teaching does not have value – simply that there are instances when the premises on which conventional teaching are based – success, achievement, competition, ambition – are neither appropriate nor desirable for the people with whom we work. Clearly, there exists a vast amount of knowledge about the brain and its functions. What is being offered here, however, is a model that places the outer and inner interaction of all the five senses, plus language and overt behaviour, at the heart of the thinking/feeling process.

Traditionally, in work with people with learning disabilities, the area of *feelings* has neither been fully addressed, nor sufficiently acknowledged. Why this has been so, and how it has been allowed to condition approaches to this work, are not important here. What we wish to offer is a model that could easily be made available to anyone with an interest in using it, and, more importantly, with an interest in working with people in a developmental way.

If we reduce this notion to its simplest form, and examine it from an evolutionary standpoint, we might ask what it is that distinguishes a human being from a plant or an animal. Language, and the capacity to be reflective, are the traits that are generally regarded as separating us from the plant or animal world. The contention here is that a human being operates from that 'vegetative' or 'animal' level only, by using language without the additional quality of reflection. In this mode, humans are simply in the relationship of verbal reaction or interaction: there is no extension that shifts the interaction on to a higher plane of responsive and reflective engagement.

Through a recognition of these two modes of human response, we can begin to understand *how*, by using a powerful combination of congruent behaviour and language, it is possible for effective communication to occur, which will in turn release positive, creative and effective forces. This process is, in itself, healing.

Range of human interaction	Attitude, behaviour, and language	Life force released
from Apathy to Complacency	Non-interactive	Material and Vegetative forces
from Antagonism to Competition	Reactive	Animal forces
from Cooperation to Closeness	Responsive and Reflective	Human forces
from Harmony to Oneness	Altruistically Responsive and Reflective	Finer Human forces

Figure 14.1　*Simplified version of the 'life-force' model of communication*

The Life Force Model (see Figure 14.1) rests on the premiss that a deeper level of communication can only occur in an environment where *response* is allowed to take precedence over *reaction* – i.e. where a person feels safe and is enabled to utilise all their own internal power to produce the responses that will communicate their feelings. The model presupposes that human beings have evolved from matter, through the plant and animal stages to a state of 'humanness' and it is as humans that we intrinsically contain these forces or energies. The right combination of these forces is both necessary and beneficial for life and for meaningful interaction to occur. Congruency of language and behaviour extends the range of human interaction which is itself vital for growth, and both frees up the flow and restores the balance of these forces.

In order to acquire the skills of congruent language and behaviour, training in the field of NLP is necessary. NLP is a combination of existing psychological theories presented in a form that make them accessible to a wide range of professionals, largely by emphasising the practical application of the theory involved. Most eminent among the theorists are Carl Rogers, Virginia Satir, Fritz Perls and Milton Erikson. Many people, including those in therapeutic practice, do not yet possess the skills of congruent language and behaviour. It is our contention, furthermore, that traditional forms of education and training do not give sufficient consideration to this need. This, in turn, creates a limiting factor to personal growth and development. And if this is the result for people who learn to teach, then it is plain to see that the people they then make professional contact with will be subjected to similar patterns of inflexibility and rigorous application of theory. How many of us found traditional school-room teaching anathema to our creative spirit? How many did not discover until well into adolescence or adulthood that there are many ways to learn, and many styles of teaching? The element of congruence is usually missing, and the understanding of the importance of our senses in this process is frequently denied. The results are disaffected adults, and, for people with learning disabilities, a total missing-out of the learning process – because the system was not sympathetic to their needs or to their abilities, which remained largely undiscovered.

'Gentle Teaching'

Let us look, then, at the first of these new alternatives: Gentle Teaching. As with so many new approaches, Gentle Teaching found its way into the world of people with learning disabilities through work originally developed in the USA. Making similar assumptions about traditional learning to those outlined above, the tenets of Gentle Teaching encourage staff to challenge their practice and to think in new ways about the people they have chosen to work with. By reassessing the value bases, teachers (used here in its broadest application) are able to move towards the adoption of techniques and styles that are both humanising and liberating. The inherent message of gentle teaching is that there is goodness and value in human relationships, and that relationships built on the assumptions that increase presence and participation (two of the five principles of Normalisation) lead to increased personal growth and development. Gentle Teaching tells us that punishment not only dehumanises the punisher, but leads to a cycle of submission and domination in those on whom it is practised. By adopting a more liberating approach, warmth, closeness and tolerance are likely to ensue. Thus, it might be said, the *forces* of tolerance, understanding and acceptance are freed.

For a relationship to have mutual benefit, it must be based on equality. In relationships with people with learning disabilities, especially in the formative period, there is often an imbalance: we tend in these instances to give but not to receive, thereby creating participation without respect or permission, and giving reward when it is neither expected nor appreciated (see Symington, Chapter 9). In this way, savage feelings may be aroused, releasing strong forces of insecurity. However, as the relationship develops, and greater mutual respect and understanding emerges, the inequality diminishes and we can begin to enjoy the use of teaching strategies which facilitate mutual liberation.

The central purpose of gentle teaching is to use *reward* both as a means and as an end in itself. In traditional methods, the learner is often distanced; in this form, he or she is involved in a relationship of interdependence. A pivotal component is the notion of *redirection*, which follows on from an action that has been ignored. *Reward* is the outcome, the stabiliser, and it can take any appropriate form. The redirection moves the learner away from undesirable action towards the rewarding interaction.

In a five-year study of a Gentle Teaching programme linked with the University of Nebraska, McGee et al., 1987, looked at outcomes for 73 handicapped persons with behavioural problems. The study examined the instances of self-injurious behaviour before the intervention and divided this into categories of high, medium and low; its intensity prior to discharge, and its incidence five years later. More than 86 per cent of referrals entered treatment within the high incidence category. *None* displayed this level on discharge or at any time up to five years later. An exceptionally high 72.6 per cent exhibited no self-injurious behaviour up to five years later.

Neuro-Linguistic Programming

The second empowerment model we wish to introduce is Neuro-Linguistic Programming. NLP acknowledges the internal/external sensory capacity and language as being at the core of the thinking/feeling process. A greater understanding of human subjective experience is available through a study of NLP. Early investigators set about the task of analysing the language, behaviour and subjective experience of people who were universally regarded as being 'excellent' in the fields of therapy and communication. Their behaviour and practice were 'modelled', and the results of the research produced specific detail about language and behaviour that was common to them all. This work has since been constructed into a series of approaches with a broad range of application, each of which facilitates the movement from reactive to responsive communication – as expressed in the 'life-force' model (Figure 14.1).

NLP offers techniques for understanding and modelling our own success. In this way, value for others is also created. So too is a range of extremely effective tools for education in general, and counselling/therapy in particular. NLP is based on the premiss that we use our senses to explore the world – to 'map' it. The world represents an infinity of possible sense impressions and each of us perceives only a very small part – the part we do perceive is further filtered by our own unique experiences which are in turn a function of our culture, language, beliefs, values, interests and assumptions. As O'Connor and Seymour state, 'Everyone lives in their unique reality built from their sense impressions and individual experiences of life, and we act on the basis of what we perceive: our model of the world' (O'Connor and Seymour, 1989: 23). Thus, for work with people with learning disabilities to have meaning for the receiver, it is necessary for the giver to use language forms and constructs that make sense to, and engage with, the other.

Perhaps the most important part of NLP training is the concept known as 'sensory acuity'. This involves developing a heightened awareness of perceptions – noticing things not previously noticed. So far as communicating with people with learning disabilities is concerned, this means paying extra attention to the small but crucial signs that indicate the level of response. When thinking (i.e. communicating internally), a heightened awareness of internal images, sounds and feelings is possible. You need to be able to see, hear, feel what is happening in order to offer a choice of responses. As in all good therapy or counselling, 'outcomes' are important. In NLP terms, if the destination is unknown, the journey will be difficult. To sum up. If you always do what you've always done you'll always get what you've always got. (A selected book list of introductory texts is given at the end of the chapter.)

Educational Kinesiology
Other models which also assist this process now exist, one of which is Educational Kinesiology (EK). Whereas NLP works through language, EK works through bodily response, for example, 'muscle-testing'. Through a technique that tests the relative strength/ weakness of indicator muscles, it is possible to determine brain/ear/ eye dominance patterns. These patterns, in turn, determine input into the sensory system, and the consequent mental processing. Some dominance patterns are far more constructive than others, and are directly related to the flow of communication. EK balancing exercises can restore a state of equilibrium and integration to the thinking/feeling/communicating process, and, in a way similar to that described above, can be used to transform reactive energies

into responsive energies which had been present previously, but were submerged, or locked in. The releasing abilities of NLP and EK enable these positive forces to be released: what follows can be the opening up, often for the first time, of abilities and competencies that had been lying dormant and unidentified.

Before entering into a discussion on how these skills can be acquired by therapists, counsellors and other committed workers in the field, we would like to introduce an example of one of these innovative techniques. For instance, if a client uses 'feeling' as opposed to visual or auditory words or expressions, for example 'The way I'm feeling' or 'It feels like this to me', then in order to maintain the most effective verbal contact the therapist will need to respond with phrases that reciprocate this: 'That feels good to me' or 'Yes, I feel that you are right'. This is utilising basic NLP skills in an everyday way that facilitates communication and allows good rapport to be built. This case history may serve to demonstrate.

Case history: Mary   Mary, now 20, had been classified as needing special care when she was a child. She had learning and communication problems and had attended a special boarding school for most of her teenage years. On her first visit, her eyes were fixed, she seemed timid, even a little tearful, blocked and unable to communicate. It seemed that she was not really hearing what was being said. This was because she was mentally processing almost entirely through her feelings. Her ears were not taking in anything because her eyes were so fixed on my facial expression (NLP observations) so I started to smile at her, slowed down my pace and all my mental and feeling processes and started speaking to her very softly and slowly using feeling words (NLP responses).

I showed her how to do a few brain-balancing exercises from Educational Kinesiology, which help the energetic relationship between the hemispheres, and we had fun with them together. I also used these as a means to get into a 'feeling' contact with her. To my surprise she was able to do them straight away. All this had an immediate effect and a gentle rapport started to grow between us. Within this feeling of closeness she started talking to me hesitantly about the problems of her life and about how nobody ever understood her, and about the mundane work she had to do. She was very coherent and there seemed to be a mismatch with her original assessment.

I gave her specific EK exercises for listening and speaking to do between each visit and helped her to justify what was important for *her* in *her* life. All the time I stayed in close rapport and maintained a responsive and reflective flowing conversation with her.

Within a period of three months and just a few visits, she became much more articulate and able to express her views, feelings and *needs*. Those caring for her were very surprised by this sudden change and realised she need reassessment. She is now in a sheltered flat, and has a real job at a hairdressers. She is positive, perky and has a new hair-style.

Mary's mother is a fast thinker and speaker and processes almost entirely visually and verbally (NLP distinctions). To her, Mary was always 'so slow' even as a baby, so she did most of her thinking, speaking and decision-making for her and 'talked at' her. So their communication was mainly one way or at best *reactive*, when either one or the other was upset. So Mary had no early experience at 'responsive' communication – 'conversation'. However, she took everything in.

Mary may have been wrongly assessed, because she gave the impression from her slowness and lack of coherence that she had special needs and required special care. However, let us consider what her first 20 years of life might have been like, if she had been assessed from the NLP viewpoint and given appropriate coordinating exercises from EK and early training in responsive communication.

With me she experienced perhaps for the first time a truly positive and satisfying interaction and the flow of positive life forces which were released. I taught her how to adjust to the responses of those around her. This was vitally important, because most of them were anchored to 'talking *at* her'. I wonder how many other handicapped people are suffering from this lack of 'conversing', how many more may have inadvertently been wrongly assessed?

It is not only our intention to offer tools and techniques for therapists or professional counsellors: we are anxious that these skills, as described, become readily available to frontier staff, in very kind of agency. We wish also to be clear about the kinds of potential clients for whom these interventions are designed, for they are *all* available to people without speech, or people who have elected to remain silent. In fact NLP and EK, as well as Gentle Teaching, when applied sensitively, and over a sufficient time scale, can be highly effective in eliciting speech where it had been withdrawn through a damaged sense of self.

'Value' as a factor in the enabling process

When Wolfensberger (1972) introduced the concept of normalisation to, it has to be said, a largely sceptical and unaccepting world, he knew he was entering uncharted territory in the sense that human rights, dignity and respect for people with learning disabilities were neither understood nor welcomed. As with most innovative and daring concepts, Wolfensberger's work has been adapted, modified and extended, not least by its originator who, by developing the model to encompass the notion of Social-Role Valorisation, recognised that herein lay the heart of the matter. Valued people performing valued roles in the same environments as everyone else was not only desirable, it was something to be actively sought. For 20 years now, people have been working to bring about not only service changes, but attitude changes too.

Similarly, the work of Jean Vanier (see Williams, 1986) seeks to offer a model that empowers rather than one which devalues. Through a careful analysis of the social attitudes that serve to reinforce the negativity and impoverishment of people's lives (see Figure 14.2), he proposes a model that offers a learning and enriching approach through acceptance of people for the richness and variety they hold within them, rather than a circle of deprivation and rejection, which simply reinforces the negative values previously attached to learning-disabled people. This model of enrichment (see Figure 14.2) akin to Wolfenberger's in its theoretical and philosophical stance, is yet another way of offering staff, carers, policy-makers and service-users alike, a way of 'being in the world' that empowers individuals, without cost to others – save the shedding of potentially destructive attitudes.

THE LIFE EXPERIENCES OF PEOPLE WITH LONG-TERM DISABILITIES

These are all outcomes that can arise as a result of society's behaviour towards people with handicaps. Think of a person with a disability that you know and go through that person's life history and their life experiences to see to what extent some of these things have happened. Jean Vanier calls these the 'wounds' of handicapped people.

REJECTION:
by family, by services or community facilities.

PHYSICAL SEGREGATION:
services that segregate the person from ordinary communities.

ISOLATION FROM SOCIALLY VALUED PEOPLE:
spending most of the time in the company of other people who are also disabled and who have been rejected socially.

LACK OF ROOTS:
living in services dislocated from local communities, or moved between different services that reduce people retaining a sense of place or community.

LACK OF RELATIONSHIPS:
living with, or spending time with, other people who find it difficult to make relationships, or people they have not chosen to live with and do not particularly wish to make relationships.

INSECURITY:
living in situations of poor physical security, where they may be subject to interference from others, or where their property may be broken or stolen.

LACK OF FREEDOM AND CONTROL:
having things done without being consulted or even informed. Generally having little control over their lives, and having freedom severely curtailed.

POVERTY:
being materially poor, with few resources to buy, and therefore having little control over the help they need. Not being seen as a valued consumer.

LACK OF EXPERIENCE AND OPPORTUNITY:
being overprotected and not having key experiences of opportunities that have important aspects of development.

ATTRIBUTION OF NEGATIVE CHARACTERISTICS BY ASSOCIATION:
confusions in the public mind that people with learning difficulties are also mentally ill, that people are also prone to violence.

SYMBOLIC MARKINGS:
The symbols and images that surround people with disabilities, such as large hospital buildings, signs saying 'handicapped children' outside a training centre (with a special school next door). Residential homes that don't look like any house that most of us would recognise.

ILL-TREATMENT:
the risk of physical ill-treatment, excessive use of drugs or restraint.

AWARENESS OF BEING A BURDEN TO OTHERS:
the experience of being spoken of by others in negative terms, or as a problem or a nuisance.

HAVING ONE'S LIFE WASTED:
the awareness of some people that they have been denied opportunities to make a contribution to ordinary society, either through activities or relationships.

Figure 14.2 *Jean Vanier's model*

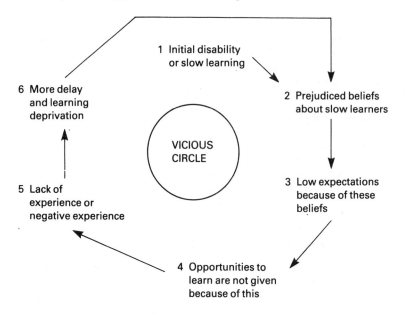

Figure 14.3   *The negative learning circle*

By removing the scars that Vanier describes as 'wounds', possibilities are opened up for advancement and enrichment that are both exciting and achievable:

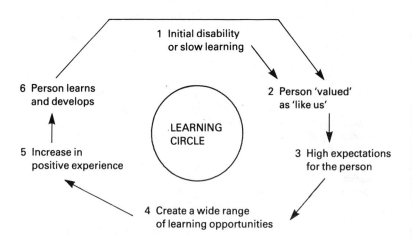

Figure 14.4   *The positive learning circle*

Sensitive training is necessary in the area of sexuality and personal relationships. It should be designed to raise the awareness of staff to the fact that learning-disabled people not only share the same range of emotional expression as the rest of us possess, but need also to be able to discover and test this out wherever possible, and in a safe environment. In this way, the basic skills of counselling can be applied by care staff and others in the 'front line' so that service-users begin to feel both valued and equally treated. In this way, by modelling, offering to mentally handicapped members of the community those privileges usually available to others, we are *valuing* them, and it is this attitude which has been historically lacking in our dealings with people with learning difficulties.

Implications for staff training and development

A renewed commitment to developing and maintaining quality community care services will involve major reorganisation of the way in which staff are recruited, trained and supervised. A model for such a revamped service might want to incorporate some or all of the following components:

1 Communication skills and assertion training and the autonomy necessary to work with service-users and carers to ensure consistency and openness so that work is carried out in the person's best interests – not those of the service.
2 High-quality, regular supervision from a qualified, experienced person who will be able to offer to staff a high level of support, guidance and, where appropriate, practice indications.
3 A reliable communication system for recording as well as for reaching other parts of the organisation, including senior management. Accessibility will be increasingly important for efficient service delivery.
4 The knowledge that they themselves are valued – manifested in good pay and conditions, a clearly defined career stucture and a visible, monitored equal opportunities policy.
5 Opportunities for professional training and other forms of advancement such as courses in NLP and EK and self-development including exchange visits to other establishments in the UK and abroad, where practice is observable.
6 Time for and space during a working week for thinking, introspection, reading and growth, so that they are better able to meet the needs of the people with whom they work.
7 Access to and availability of research papers, journals and other

items of interest, and development in the world of learning disabilities.

8   Praise and genuine appreciation for the work that they do.

Conclusion

Clearly, there will be implications for services and individuals who choose to adopt and introduce these new ways of working: growth and development are rarely cost-less exercises. However, if the commitment to a real life in the community exists – a life that has value and meaning for the individual concerned and for those who enter her or his network of contacts, then training for and commitment to the people who anchor these services is not too high a price to pay. We owe it to ourselves, as well as to the people with whom we work, to make this investment in the future. A future that we shall all share, all enjoy and play a part in, together.

For staff, knowing, feeling and understanding the world from the other's point of view, or being able to share their perception of the world, is a prerequisite to breaking down the barriers of resistance, rejection and denial that serve to prevent growth and cause mutual distress. The 'cognitive map' that is constructed when two people share images and constructs enable them to relate because they can communicate with genuine rapport. Both people *feel* a sense of achievement and bonding, which further reinforces the relationship. By adopting a more free-ranging and innovative approach to counselling and therapy, as we have attempted to describe in this chapter, the process of demystification will have begun, through the offering of models that are mutually empowering.

In order to learn, to grow and develop, it is necessary, it seems to us, to take calculated risks. The privilege of being involved in another's process of self-discovery is in itself a reward. Such benefits are now available: it is for services to put their house in order and to respond positively and appropriately to the demands of people who are daily learning about and acting upon their own status as citizens.

The main purpose of this chapter has been to demystify and open up the whole area of counselling and psychotherapy. We believe that there are areas that are best left to highly skilled and trained psychotherapists. However, without in any way denying or de-valuing their skill, we feel very strongly that there *are* new techniques and approaches now available that will enable staff at all levels readily to acquire skills that will not only enable and empower the people they work with, but will also serve to enrich their own working lives. By doing this, people with learning disabilities will be able to have greater access to the community participation and presence that was the basis of the original movement designed to liberate them.

Appendix

ANLP (Association for Neuro-Linguistic Programming)
ANLP Secretary
100B Carysfort Road
London N16 9AP
Tel.: 081 241 3664   (Book lists available)

UK training organisations
1   British Hypnosis Research
    8 Paston Place
    Brighton
    East Sussex BN2 1HA   Tel: 0273 693622

2   Integration
    25 Brading Road
    Brighton
    East Sussex BN2 3PE   Tel.: 0273 680523

3   International Teaching Seminars
    1 Mulgrave Road
    London NW10 1BS   Tel.: 081 450 0173

4   NLP Training Programme
    22 Upper Tooting Park
    London SW17 7SR   Tel.: 071 682 0733

5   Pace Ltd.
    86 South Hill Park
    London NW3 2SN   Tel.: 071 794 0960

6   Proudfoot School of Hypnosis and Psychotherapy
    9 Belvedere Place
    Scarborough
    North Yorks YO11 2QX   Tel.: 0723 363638

7   Sensory Systems
    28 Bellwood Street
    Shawlands
    Langside
    Glasgow G41 3ES   Tel.: 041 632 3179

8   John Seymour Associates
    17 Boyce Drive
    St Werburghs
    Bristol BS2 9XQ   Tel.: 0272 557827

References

Lee, W. Y. (1986) *Human Sexuality: A Staff Training Manual for Individuals with Special Needs*. Ontario, Canada: Sexuality Clinic, Surrey Place Centre.

Lomas, P. (1987) 'The misuse of therapeutic power', in his *The Limits of Interpretation*.

McGee, J. et al. (1987) *Gentle Teaching – A Non-aversive Approach to Helping Persons with Mental Retardation*. Human Sciences Press.

O'Brien, J. (1988) *Against Pain as a Tool in Professional Work with People with Severe Disabilities*. Atlanta, Georgia: Citizen Advocacy Assn.

O'Connor, J. and Seymour, J. (1989) *Introducing Neuro-Linguisting Programming. The New Psychology of Personal Excellence*. London: Crucible.

Rose, N. (1986) 'Psychiatry – the discipline of mental health', in P. Muller and N. Rose (eds), *The Power of Psychiatry*. Oxford: Polity Press.

Szivos, S. (1989) 'Self esteem among young adults with learning difficulties'. Unpublished doctoral dissertation, University of Exeter.

Williams, P. and Schoultz, B. (1981) *We Can Speak for Ourselves*. London: Souvenir Press.

Williams, P. (1986) 'Evaluating services from the consumer's point of view', in Beswick, Zadick and Felce (eds), *Evaluating the Quality of Care*. Kidderminster: British Institute of Mental Handicap.

Wolfensberger, W. (1972) *Normalisation*. Toronto: National Trust on Mental Retardation.

Notes on Contributors

Rosalind Bates is a Consultant in the Psychiatry of Mental Handicap and has worked in Bromley since 1982. She works in the Community Mental Handicap Teams giving a service to people living in a range of community based services and in their own homes. As a result of a team approach, 152 people have been moved from a large hospital to services in Bromley. She gives input to the management and day to day running of this service and has recently been appointed as Clinical Director of the services. Apart from treating people with mental illness and neuropsychiatric disorders, she is particularly interested in helping people with emotional problems.

Joanna Beazley-Richards works freelance as a psychologist, psychotherapist and consultant, specialising in teaching Transactional Analysis to people with learning difficulties, their families and to staff. She is currently, with her husband Steve, establishing a learning centre in East Sussex where people who have, or who do not have, learning difficulties, can learn self-empowerment. Joanna also trains transactional analysts, counsellors and supervisors.

Joan Bicknell was Professor of the Psychiatry of Mental Handicap at St George's Hospital Medical School from 1980 to 1990. A pioneer in the development of community-based services for people with learning disabilities, Professor Bicknell is also a prolific author in the field, especially in the areas of the psychodynamics of mental handicap and the organisation of services. Professor Bicknell is now retired and lives in Surrey.

Hilary Brown is Senior Lecturer in Mental Handicap at the Centre for the Applied Psychology of Social Care, University of Kent and works as a consultant in Health and Social Services. She has a particular interest in issues to do with sexuality, having worked with and written on, positive options for service users, parents and staff. She is currently conducting a three year research project with Dr. Vicky Turk into sexual abuse of adults with learning difficulties. She is the co-editor (with Ann Craft) of *Thinking the Unthinkable* – papers on sexual abuse and people with learning difficulties – and also of a trainers' manual *Working with the Unthinkable* published by the FPA. Hilary Brown is also co-editor (with Helen Smith) of *Normalisation: a reader for the 90's* published by Routledge.

Suzanne Conboy-Hill is Top Grade Clinical Psychologist with Brighton Health Authority. She also does work for the Lisa Sainsbury Foundation, facilitating workshops for nurses caring for dying, disabled or bereaved people. She is an Honorary Visiting Research Fellow at the University of Sussex.

Hedy Ditchfield is a Principal Clinical Psychologist with Plymouth Health Authority. She is particularly concerned with staff training and service planning. Her interest in parental adjustment to the birth of a child stems from her work with the National Childbirth Trust with whom she is an antenatal teacher.

Helen Fensome works for the Greenwich Health Authority, partly with adult out-patients and partly in the rehabilitation service. She is particularly interested in psychoanalytic theory, and in applying psychoanalytic principles to working with adults with mental health problems.

Eileen Griffiths holds a joint appointment as Head of Psychological Services at the RAF Headley Court Defence Services Medical Rehabilitation Unit and as Teaching Fellow at the Psychology Department, the University of Surrey. Her interests are the effects of traumatic disability on self concept and self presentation.

Sheila Hollins is Professor and Consultant in the Psychiatry of Learning Disability at St George's Hospital Medical School and Head of the Academic Division of the Psychiatry of Disability in the Department of Mental Health Sciences. She has clinical, teaching and research interests in psychotherapy, and has published and lectured widely. She co-edited a major textbook with Joan Bicknell: *Mental Handicap – a Multidisciplinary Approach* published by Bailliere Tyndall in 1985. She is a member of the steering group of the Mental Handicap Section of the Association for Psychoanalytic Psychotherapy.

François Reynolds practises in London offering individual and group personal development. He also facilitates Cutting Edge Workshops, in communication and education, which take into consideration the 'Life Force Factor'. In 1989 he co-founded 'New Dimensions in Education', a charitable foundation set up to bring the new ideas from Neuro-Linguistic Programming, Educational Kinesiology and Transactional Analysis etc. to teachers and the general public. He is Principal of St Christopher's School in Norwich and is a member of the Subud Association.

Valerie Sinason is a Principal Child Psychotherapist working in the Tavistock Clinic's Child and Family Department, Day Unit and Adult Department. She is psychotherapist convener of the Mental Handicap Workshop there. She convenes the Mental Handicap

Section of the APP (Association of Psychoanalytic Psychotherapy in the NHS), represents mental handicap on the BASPCAN Disability and Abuse Working Party and the ACCP Research Group on Abuse. Her book *The Sense in Stupidity: Psychotherapy and Mental Handicap* is in press with Free Association Books.

Jon Stokes is a psychoanalytic psychotherapist and Specialist Clinical Psychologist in Psychoanalytic Psychotherapy at the Tavistock Clinic, London where he is Chairman of the Adult Department. He has a particular interest in the psychodynamics of institutions and works as a consultant to both public service and commercial organisations. He is currently developing Group Relations Training for professionals with management responsibilities in inter-professional work settings.

Neville Symington is a Member of the British Psycho-Analytic Society. He is author of the book *The Analytic Experience*, and various articles. In 1980 he started at the Tavistock a Workshop on the Psychotherapy for Mentally Handicapped Patients. This Workshop presented a Symposium at the British Psychological Society Conference at York in 1981. In 1986 he migrated to Australia with his wife who is also an analyst. He is now in private practice in Sydney.

Susan Szivos holds a joint appointment with South East Thames Regional Health Authority and the Centre for the Applied Psychology of Social Care at the University of Kent at Canterbury as Lecturer/Training Adviser in Mental Handicap. She is interested in processes of self esteem formation among people with learning difficulties, service philosophy and staff training and research in community care.

Alexis Waitman is a freelance trainer and consultant in human resource development working in both public and private sectors. She retains an interest in and commitment to 'talking therapies' by practising counselling and therapy with a wide variety of clients, utilising a range of approaches. Trained as a social worker and social psychologist, she has spent some 20 years working in the public sector in the areas of mental health and mental handicap.

Robert Wilkins is Consultant Child and Adolescent Psychiatrist at Paxton Family and Young Persons Unit, Reading, where he heads a multidisciplinary team which uses family therapy in its assessment and treatment of a wide range of children's problems. Dr Wilkins has published several scholarly papers and more general articles on children and is the author of three books, including one on treating behavioural problems in children by orthodox and paradoxical methods.

Index